Tory Nation

Tory Nation

How one party took over

Samuel Earle

**SIMON &
SCHUSTER**

London · New York · Sydney · Toronto · New Delhi

First published in Great Britain by Simon & Schuster UK Ltd, 2023

Copyright © Samuel Earle, 2023

The right of Samuel Earle to be identified as the
author of this work has been asserted in accordance
with the Copyright, Designs and Patents Act, 1988.

1 3 5 7 9 10 8 6 4 2

Simon & Schuster UK Ltd
1st Floor
222 Gray's Inn Road
London WC1X 8HB

www.simonandschuster.co.uk
www.simonandschuster.com.au
www.simonandschuster.co.in

Simon & Schuster Australia, Sydney
Simon & Schuster India, New Delhi

The author and publishers have made all reasonable efforts to contact
copyright-holders for permission, and apologise for any omissions or errors
in the form of credits given. Corrections may be made to future printings.

A CIP catalogue record for this book is available from the British Library

Hardback ISBN: 978-1-3985-1851-3
eBook ISBN: 978-1-3985-1852-0

Typeset in Perpetua by Palimpsest Book Production Ltd, Falkirk, Stirlingshire

Printed and Bound in the UK using
100% Renewable Electricity at CPI Group (UK) Ltd

MIX
Paper | Supporting
responsible forestry
FSC® C171272
FSC
www.fsc.org

To my mothers

CONTENTS

'What follows in this [book] might appear to some to be a somewhat harsh critique. On the other hand, in the tradition of honouring one's adversaries, it could be read as an acknowledgement of the vision, flexibility, sophistication, and unwavering determination of those who have dedicated their lives to keeping the world safe for capitalism.'

Arundhati Roy, 2014

INTRODUCTION

On 13 December 2019, Britain's newly elected prime minister Boris Johnson welcomed 'a new dawn'. The Conservative Party had secured its largest parliamentary majority since 1987. Almost fifty new seats had swung the Conservatives' way, including many in the so-called 'red wall': working-class constituencies in North and Middle England traditionally considered Labour strongholds. Johnson and his fellow Tories were jubilant. 'Rejoice!' the front page of the *Daily Mail* sang.

Johnson simply did what most Conservative leaders do: win elections. Across its long, winding 200-year-odd history, nineteen different leaders have contested elections, and only four have failed to win at least one, with the party holding power for roughly two-thirds of the time – a record of victory that has earned the Conservatives the moniker of 'the most successful political party in the world'.[1] By many accounts, the Conservatives are also the *oldest* party in the world, with their roots stretching back beyond the 1830s, when the term Conservative became common, and lying in the emergence of the Tories as a political faction in the seventeenth century.

The party's main opposition, meanwhile, spends most of

1

its time as just that: the opposition. Since the official formation of the Labour Party in 1906 – a source of existential
anxiety for Conservatives at the time – only four of Labour's
nineteen leaders have ever won an election, and only three
with an outright majority. In the last seventy years, that
number falls to two; in the last forty years, to one: Tony Blair,
Labour's most successful leader and its most conservative.
'The best centre-right option there is', as the *Economist* quipped
in 2005, as Blair accomplished his third straight win. Take
away Blair's victories, and Labour has only been in power for
eighteen of the last 100 years. The Tories, either alone or in
coalition, have ruled for the rest.

Such single-party dominance might well alarm the citizenry
of a proud, liberal democracy – especially one where well-
funded public services and wealth redistribution, not
Conservative strong points, consistently poll as very popular
policies, and where the National Health Service is close to a
national religion.[2] At the very least, one might expect that
the Conservatives' ascendancy is the subject of endless debate
and dissection: how has the Conservative Party wielded so
much power, for so long, not only today but throughout
history? What does this say about the party, and what does
this say about us?

But the success of the Conservatives is remarkable not only
for its longevity but also for the strange incuriousness that
accompanies it. Each Conservative win is typically explained
away either by the contingencies of time and place – a strong
or weak economy, a particularly canny Conservative leader
or campaign, a weak Labour candidate – or by supposedly
'innate' Conservative Party qualities like 'competence',
'stability', 'pragmatism' or 'unity'. It is often said that the
Tories simply know how to win elections. The long arc of

Tory rule is lost from view. Any sense of democratic disquiet is dispelled.

Across the Conservatives' history, the word 'stability' recurs again and again: it is the Conservatives' abiding promise, that they will keep things recognisably the same, that tomorrow will look like today. They are the safe pair of hands, the purveyors of continuity, competence and sound finances, ensuring the smooth functioning of the state. 'I vote – if I have to vote – for the party which is likely to do least harm,' Conservative philosopher Michael Oakeshott once said. 'To that extent I am a Tory.' The Conservative Party's founding intent, laid down in Robert Peel's Tamworth Manifesto in 1834, was to stop Britain from becoming a 'perpetual vortex of agitation'. Around the same time, the leading Whig politician Thomas Macaulay described Conservatives as 'the ballast, without which there would be no safety in a tempest'.[3]

But in recent years the Conservatives have seemed more like the tempest itself, unmooring Britain from its foundations and trapping it in a ruinous cycle of economic dysfunction. Through austerity, Brexit, a devastatingly mishandled pandemic and five different leaders in seven years, the news has been unceasingly frenetic, often surreal, and the Conservatives have become the lords of our disorder, stoking divisions, attacking venerable institutions, flirting with the far right, overthrowing leaders overnight and pursuing their causes with no heed to national stability. The Conservatives' standing as the party that does the least harm no longer seems persuasive. Even their historic claim to patriotism and national greatness – so central to the Conservative brand – is in question: as the Conservative circus swirls, with an endless rotation of policy, personnel and gloomy economic forecasts, more and more Conservatives worry that their dear old party has turned their dear old country into a laughing stock. Many ask: what happened to the Conservative Party?

Most press coverage of the Conservatives' seeming descent into the rabbit hole focuses on the party's leaders. This framing comforts the Conservative Party in several ways. First, by painting each new leader as an aberration, the party rehabilitates the reputations of their predecessor. As Liz Truss's prime ministership unravelled, for example, Cameron, May and Johnson emerged as model politicians by comparison: beacons of competence and stability rather than co-conspirators in the unfolding catastrophe. Only in this way could Johnson have the licence even to propose replacing his replacement as Conservative prime minister, little more than a month after leaving office. Even when Rishi Sunak's appointment became obvious, the *Daily Telegraph* journalist Tim Stanley commented that 'many people will slowly come to see that Liz was one of our more human and likeable PMs'.[4] Second, by presenting each outgoing leader as an aberration, Conservatives avoid confronting the darker truth: that these leaders are not aberrations at all, but authentic expressions of the Conservative tradition. That tradition, as this book will show, has always been more radical, self-serving and disruptive than its mild-mannered, small-c 'conservative' reputation suggests.

The focus on this or that leader also distracts from the party's most destructive – and collective – legacy. The Conservatives' programme of austerity, launched by Cameron and perpetuated by every Conservative prime minister since, has starved and overstretched public services, created one of the stingiest and most punishing welfare states in the developed world and contributed to the longest period of wage stagnation – for many, wage regression – since the Napoleonic Wars.[5] Life expectancy is down, child poverty has soared and there are few signs of a reprieve on the horizon. Life under the Tories has become nastier, poorer, more brutish and shorter.[6] The fact that the Conservatives show little sign of changing course, and still attract support, allies and donations, tells us more about the nature of the Conservative Party than the character of any one leader.

Tory Nation takes a long and broad view of the Conservatives' history and record of victory, treating Conservatism as both a political and cultural force. While it is often said that political parties gain from having clear, consistent messaging and reliable reputations, the Conservatives have always thrived as much through their contradictions as their consistencies: they are the party of the people and of big business; populism and the establishment; anti-intellectualism and elite education; Little England and Global Britain; nationalism and globalisation; tradition and progress; Victorian values and greed. But over and above these tensions, one element of Conservatism usually remains constant: the Conservatives keep on winning. How?

The strange dissonance between the Conservative Party's ability to win elections and its destructive record in government stands as one of the defining riddles of British politics. Trying to solve this puzzle, or at least map its contours, is the purpose of this book. It's a puzzle with many pieces, relating not only to parliamentary politics or the personalities of particular leaders, what they stand for and who they represent (the twin focuses of most books on the Conservative Party), but also the nature of Britain's culture, history and democratic evolution, the role of the press in bolstering the Conservative cause, and Labour's seeming helplessness amid it all. The point isn't that Labour never win, but that, for various reasons, it is harder for Labour to win than for the Conservatives — that the bar for an 'electable' Labour leader is higher than for a Conservative one — and that, on the rare occasions when Labour succeeds, they usually govern on the Tories' terms.

The Conservatives' ability to hold on to power and bounce back from seemingly terminal defeats may well be its defining trait. The party has a knack for flourishing in conditions that should be threatening. Over two centuries, the Conservatives have become a formidable, shape-shifting, election-winning machine. In pursuit of victory, Conservatives have feared democracy and overseen the expansion of the suffrage; embraced the free market and sanctioned public ownership of national industries; championed liberty and suppressed civil liberties; taken Britain into the European Union and feverishly sought its exit; enforced homophobia and introduced gay marriage; stoked xenophobic prejudices and appointed one of the West's most ethnically diverse governments. The Conservatives have assembled an unlikely cast of leaders along the way: Benjamin Disraeli, the middle-class son of a Jewish literary figure, in the mid-nineteenth century; Arthur Balfour, the departing prime minister's nephew, at the start of the twentieth; the 14th Earl of Home, an antique member of the aristocracy, in the 1960s; Margaret Thatcher, a shopkeeper's daughter, in the late '70s; John Major, the working-class son of a circus performer, in the '90s; Cameron and Johnson, two Old Etonians with ancestral links to the royal family, in the twenty-first century; and most recently Rishi Sunak, Britain's first non-white prime minister.

Perhaps the Conservatives' greatest historical achievement has been securing consistent support from the working class. While the Conservatives' roots are deeply entwined with the nation's ruling class, the party's well-earned reputation as toffs has always belied a surprisingly broad appeal. Conservatives have worked hard to identify their interests with the values and aspirations of the nation at large, wrapping up privilege in an aura of deference, tradition and patriotism. As early as 1867, a leading Conservative strategist and politician, John Gorst, was exploring how to 'make Conservative principles effective among the masses'.[7] The success of this strategy has ensured that at least a third of working-class voters regularly support the Tories, and in the two elections after Brexit it has been closer to half.

The Conservatives' popular identity rests on three distinct, yet mutually reinforcing, pitches to voters: the party of patriotism (standing for national greatness and stability), the party of prosperity (for competence, liberty and economic progress), and the Nasty Party (promising protection from 'alien' threats, whether immigration, minorities or the left). Together, these three pitches allow Conservatives to mask their ruling-class roots and appeal to ordinary voters on multiple levels: economic and emotional, rational and moral, individual and collective, speaking to their fears, fantasies and conceptions of fairness. Conservatives might not deliver on their promises, but what matters is the extent to which they are associated with them. Overall, these pitches combine into a single battle cry that echoes throughout the party's history: vote Conservative for a stronger economy and a prouder, more stable society; put opposition parties in power at your peril.

In no other Western democracy does a party claim such a singular, long-lasting legitimacy over the country's character, customs and history, while casting opponents as outlandish intrusions. Tories and their friends have questioned Labour's right to rule from the moment it emerged as a credible political force.

'To read the capitalist press, whether Tory or Liberal,' Beatrice
Webb complained in 1923, 'the Labour Party barely exists: it is
a mere group of disorderly extremists without brains or money.'[8]
The Conservatives, inspired by the press, simply called them
'the Socialists'. Even Sir Keir Starmer, who does his best to
placate Tory Britain, is cast simultaneously as a weak leader and
a terrifying radical, ready to sabotage the nation. During her
successful (of sorts) leadership campaign, Liz Truss attacked
Starmer as a 'plastic patriot'. Only a Tory, it seems, can be a
real one.

The Conservatives' hold over Britain's history and identity
is unsettling, and is reinforced by the party's disproportionate
time in power. If the Tories govern for at least two-thirds of
the time, after all, then in a sense two-thirds of British history
is Tory history. 'Conservatives are deeply aware of the extent
to which their history is also the history of their country,'
Conservative leader Michael Howard explained in 2004.
Through this act of conflation, Britain's historical grandeur
becomes the Conservatives' grandeur: it was the Conservatives,
as much as Britain, that conquered a quarter of the world,
oversaw the first Industrial Revolution, won two world wars,
spread the English language across the globe, and so on.

This sweeping embrace of British history and identity also
veils fundamental tensions within the very idea of Great
Britain, which is often referred to interchangeably as a country,
a nation, a collection of four countries or nations, an island
and an archipelago. Under the banner of the Union and 'One
Nation' rhetoric, the Conservatives claim to stand for all of
its separate components: England, Scotland, Wales and
Northern Ireland. But insofar as Britain can be called a Tory
Nation, it is usually thanks to votes in England, especially in
the South. This is where the party's truest loyalties lie. In

1910, at the same time as the Conservatives billed themselves as the 'Unionist' Party, over three-quarters of their seats were south of Manchester.[9] But the fact that Wales, Scotland and Northern Ireland remain under Conservative rule even in the absence of Conservative support is itself championed as an expression of Conservative success, with the Union celebrated as proof of Britain's 'greatness' and standing as an essential pillar of the Tory Nation.

The Conservatives' claim over Britain goes ever further than this. Beyond fronting their own purported achievements while in power, they seek to absorb the achievements of their political opponents as well – even, or especially, where these were achieved against the Tories' opposition. The abolition of slavery, the enfranchisement of women and the working class, the dissolution of Empire, the welcoming of refugees from war zones (such as the Kindertransport during the Second World War) and the creation of the NHS – all these important chapters in the nation's past often happened in the face of fervent opposition from Tories somewhere along the way, but they are now celebrated by the Tories as proof of Britain's – and their – magnanimity and good sense.

This carnivorous approach to British history – whereby the Conservatives gobble up anything, past or present, that might popularise their cause while casting aside everything else as either false or foreign – is central to what this book calls the 'Tory Nation'. The Tory Nation isn't the same as 'the establishment', although many poles of institutional power in Britain – the bulk of Westminster, Fleet Street, the City, the monarchy, the military, etc. – are essential to its upkeep, assuring a degree of Conservative rule even when the party is out of power. The Tory Nation is much bigger than that: it's a vision of Britain, a culture, character and history – an entire nation – shaped and defined along Conservative lines, deeming who is 'electable' and what type of politics is 'possible'. In this telling, part fact and part fairy tale, Britain is marked out across the world by an essential and exceptional stability, a unique absence of historical upheaval, an unrivalled continuity of its institutions, an unusually wise and open-minded ruling class, and a sage and stoic people who instinctively prefer tradition and common sense to the abstract promises of the left.

Even as it shows signs of unravelling, many feel affection for this vision of Britain. Few other places in the world offer their citizens such a reassuringly timeless identity, the chance to cast oneself back to the dawn of time, confident that, as Vera Lynn once sang, 'There'll always be an England'. In the twenty-first century, our political life is still shaped by institutions with roots going back half a millennium or more. The House of Lords stretches back, in principle, over 700 years, and by some accounts even further. Eton, the elite boarding school that has taught a third of Britain's prime ministers, was founded in 1440; the University of Oxford, which housed half of them, dates its origins to 1096. The royal family claims a 'thousand-year history'. For citizen and tourist alike, it is hard not to feel charmingly small next to the stunning aged-ness and anachronism of it all.

This reverence for the past and tradition is also woven into our culture. In film and literature, most of the nation's favourite characters and storylines contain at least a seed of the Tory Nation: whether it's the Old Etonian James Bond, who breaks the rules with a gentleman's charm; the humble wizardry of Harry Potter, who risks it all to save his enchantingly regimented boarding school from evil outside forces; or the magic of Mary Poppins, the English nanny who only wants to keep the house in order. Original screenplays set in the present day are hard to come by. On the whole, major releases range from blue-blooded dramas – *The Queen*, *The King's Speech*, two *Downton Abbey* movies, and, more playfully, *The Favourite* – to wartime epics: *Darkest Hour*, *Dunkirk* and *1917*, stories that stage historic battles from which Britain emerges not so much victorious as eternally undefeated.

The popularity and mass proliferation of the Tory vision of Britain captures what the Italian Marxist Antonio Gramsci famously called 'hegemony': when a set of ideas and values become so dominant that they appear neutral and natural, removed from the political purposes they serve and to be accepted without question. Hegemony means, etymologically, 'dominance over', but the triumph of one worldview over another shouldn't be understood as a sinister plot or propaganda imposed from above. Gramsci firmly believed – and inspired a generation of thinkers to believe – that people are active participants in their culture, a culture that in turn shapes them. Politics is lived from below rather than enforced from above – a lot of the time, channelled through culture and everyday life, politics isn't even experienced as politics at all.

Gramsci saw political parties as the essential player in modern politics: they have the potential to bridge the gap between the state and its citizens, traversing 'politics' and 'culture', framing and uniting a constellation of interests through a 'conception of the world'. Gramsci once wondered what it would take to write the history of a political party. It would need to be more than just an account of its origins, he thought, or of its support base or leading characters. Even if every political party is initially created to serve the interests of a single class or set of people, Gramsci reasoned, in practice no such group exists in isolation: 'it has friends, allies, opponents and enemies'. Only by taking this 'complex picture' into consideration could the true story of a party ever be told. 'Hence it may be said,' Gramsci concluded, 'that to write the general history of a party means nothing less than to write the general history of a country.'[10]

This book follows on from Gramsci's lead. It is much more than just a tale of the Conservative Party, or of its friends, allies, opponents and enemies; it is a history of Britain, a history of how the Tories' efforts to rule over it have shaped the nation's evolution and identity, creating the conditions of the current moment. If we see cracks in the Tory Nation today, as Britain's essential and exceptional stability morphs into something else, it should remind us that the Tory Nation's vision of Britain has only ever been partially true: rival pasts, identities and narratives have always existed. The eruptions of recent times – the calculated cruelty of austerity, the cavalier misrule of Brexit, the brazenness of Johnson's lies and his fatal bungling of the pandemic, the delusions of Liz Truss's free-market fantasies, the cynicism of confected culture wars – have deep roots in both British and Conservative history.

The Tory Nation ultimately rests less on invention as on selective emphasis and erasure. Any account of the prudent moderation of Britain's past rulers, for example – rulers who, we're told, would never succumb to the vanity and carelessness of the current Conservative crop – conveniently ignores the realities of Empire and its dissolution: those who lived under the British Empire record the callous self-entitlement of its rulers only too well. Any tale of Britain's uniquely stable modern history, untroubled by revolution or civil war, similarly becomes less enchanting when we lift our gaze beyond England's borders. After the Second World War, for instance, no other advanced democracy subjected part of its territory to a quasi-military occupation that lasted thirty-seven years, as happened in Northern Ireland. Ireland has always been a place where the contradictions of the Tory Nation – between Britain's gentle, private people and its world-conquering imperialism – meet on the map. Perhaps it is inevitable that these contradictions are coming home: as Britain declines on the world stage, they have nowhere else to go.

The Tory Nation's blind spots are actively maintained, buried into British history to escape attention. Britain's dream-sleep as the polite and plucky underdog – always punching above its weight and never punching too hard – continues unbroken. But these rival pasts never disappear, and their legacies live on. As Britain plunges into a new age of uncertainty and economic hardship, while Conservatives declare the nation's 'independence' against a European 'Empire', this is all too clear. Rather than see the party's reckless turn as unprecedented, we could also see it as a reunion of sorts: the return of the repressed.

At the time of writing, some commentators are penning obituaries to the Conservative Party. These are born of the same short-sightedness that enables the Conservatives' enduring rule: an obsession with the last ten minutes of British politics, a reluctance to think about Conservative power beyond the Houses of Parliament.

Besides, especially during the 2019 election, the Conservative Party has reminded us of at least one secret behind its historic success: its ability to disassociate itself from the consequences of its own actions. Having overseen a decade of domestic turmoil and a stark coarsening of living conditions, the Conservative Party then presented itself as the panacea for the problems that it had created. Johnson promised to 'Get

Brexit Done', as per his election slogan, ending a four-year battle over European Union membership initiated by his party, and to reinvest in public services after ten years of Tory-imposed austerity. 'Our country has now embarked on a wonderful adventure,' Johnson declared upon victory. Three years later, the *Daily Mail* was celebrating another 'new dawn': Rishi Sunak was prime minister, now promising a return to austerity. 'Together we can achieve incredible things,' Sunak declared.

Rarely has a political party wielded so much power, for so long, with so little accountability. If elections in Britain tend to take one of two forms, 'kick them out' or 'let's keep going', the Conservative Party's perennial trick is to appear as the answer to both, as it suits: the brave challengers of the status quo and its defenders, always rescuing the nation from a Labour threat that never quite materialises.

This power of disassociation is at the heart of the Conservative Party's unrivalled record of victory. Britain's departure from the EU – finally 'done' on 1 January 2021 – proved a huge asset. Its 'Year Zero' effect, as Liz Truss once put it, allowed the party to pretend it had taken on a new incarnation, untarnished by the past; that it was a different beast from the party that has been in power for the best part of the last 200 years; a 'new dawn' is always rising. But this power of disassociation cannot be accomplished alone: it requires a compliant media, a believing public and an electoral opponent that cannot help but play along. The story of Conservative success is, to a remarkable extent, the story of Britain itself: a nation where, in Giuseppe Tomasi di Lampedusa's famous refrain, everything changes, so long as everything stays the same.

TORY HISTORY: SURVIVAL INSTINCTS

'There is one thing you can be sure of with the Conservative Party, before anything else – they have a grand sense of where the votes are.'

Enoch Powell, interviewed by
Robert McKenzie, 1981

'The Bottom Line is Winning Elections.'

The title of a seminar offered by
Conservative Central Office, 1994

'There are some things one can only achieve by a deliberate leap in the opposite direction.'

Franz Kafka, in conversation with
Gustav Janouch, 1920

In 2005, the mood among Conservatives was bleak. Labour had just won a third election on the trot, and the Tories – readying themselves for their third leader in four years – were in a rut. In *The Strange Death of Tory England*, published that year, the Tory journalist Geoffrey Wheatcroft mourned the passing of not just a party, but a nation. As Blair's 'modernising' mission swept the Tories aside, hereditary peers in the House of Lords were booted out en masse, national sovereignty was scorned in favour of European Union integration and 'conservatism' became a dirty word. 'New Labour' seemed to mark the end of 'Old England', and – not for the first time – its oldest surviving party appeared to be on the brink of extinction. 'Who needs the Tories?' Blair asked, mischievously, as he dominated the political landscape.

Conservatives were unused to such a long spell in opposition, but in a sense they were simply the victims of their own success. Blair's winning platform, after all, accepted many treasured Conservative aims and principles: celebrating the free market, privatising public services, clamping down on petty crime, schmoozing the press, stigmatising welfare, and so on. Writing in the *Spectator* in 2004, former Conservative MP Matthew Parris had told his fellow Tories to see these trends for what they were: victory. 'Anyone would think that the Right was not winning,' he wrote. 'But we are . . . We have won the argument. Britain is an incomparably more right-wing country now than when I was at university in the early 1970s.'¹ Wheatcroft was unconvinced: on the economy, maybe Parris was right, but in cultural terms the right faced a litany of loss. Wheatcroft rued that 'the very day' Parris wrote those words, Blair also banned fox-hunting – hammering yet another nail into the Tory Nation's coffin. (Blair would later say that the ban was 'one of the domestic legislative measures I most regret': 'The passions aroused by the issue were primeval.')

In any case, after Blair's third victory in 2005, the Tories could deny it no longer: the face of the future was Tony. The same year, in December, they thus found a Blair of their own to lead them: the 'modernising' David Cameron – an Old Etonian, married to the daughter of a baronet, who was young, lived in west London and was cosy with the press. Cameron explicitly dubbed himself the 'heir to Blair', and promised a kinder Conservative Party: more compassion, less Euroscepticism (stop 'banging on about Europe', he said), more environmentalism, more diversity, more contrition. 'This party has got to look and feel and talk and sound like a completely different organisation,' Cameron said.[2] 'It's got to be positive.'

While some Conservatives saw Cameron's modernising mission as a betrayal of the party's roots, he was in fact drawing on an ancient Tory tradition: surrender to survive. Way back in 1867, Lord Salisbury, one of the wealthiest and largest landowners in Britain who would later become the Conservatives' longest-serving prime minister, wrote an essay titled 'Conservative surrender'. In it, he called on Conservatives 'to accept a political defeat cordially, and to lend their best endeavours to secure the success, or to neutralise the evil, of the principles to which they have been forced to succumb'. Not all change could be resisted, Salisbury realised, and sometimes admitting defeat was the best form of defence, for it is better to be in government with compromised values than being in opposition with pure ones. 'A Conservative in Parliament is, of course, obliged to promote a great many things which he does not really approve,' Trollope observed in *The Prime Minister,* his satirical novel of 1876. 'But as the glorious institutions of the country are made to perish, it is better that they should receive the *coup de grâce* tenderly from loving hands than be roughly throttled by Radicals.'

In his first few years, Cameron followed this advice. The idea of compromise with New Labour was made easier by the fact that New Labour had already made so many compromises with the Conservatives. Blair's main twist on the Tories' platform was raising state spending on public services and measures to tackle poverty, without any attempt to popularise the welfare state. In September 2007, the Conservatives simply said they would copy Labour's formula: shadow chancellor George Osborne formally committed the Conservatives to matching Labour's public spending.[3]

That same month, however, the political landscape began to drastically change. An economic crisis, largely caused by irresponsible banks and lending habits, loomed on the horizon. The Great Recession was announced the following year, and the Conservatives were quick to capitalise. In a speech in October 2008, George Osborne now declared that 'the economic policies pursued by the government over [the past decade] are discredited beyond repair'. 'You presided over the biggest economic disaster in our lifetime,' Osborne said, addressing Prime Minister Gordon Brown and the Labour Party, 'and we will not let you forget it.'[4]

The Great Recession wasn't an obvious springboard for the Tories' renaissance: the realities the crisis exposed – the perils of free-market capitalism, the greed and recklessness of the financial sector, the need for government regulation – weren't ones that played easily into Conservative hands. But the Conservatives never let a good crisis go to waste and so, through a combination of ruthless messaging and loyal messengers in the media, they used the economic downturn to redirect a burgeoning sense of social injustice away from inequality and the economic system, and towards Labour and the European Union. The very same spending commitments that the Conservatives had recently committed to now became reckless and reflective of New Labour's profligacy. Multiculturalism, formerly celebrated, turned into a threat, another reason underpinning the Crash. In 2010, in coalition with the Liberal Democrats, the Conservatives returned to power. They heralded, in Cameron's words, 'a new age of austerity'.

Cameron didn't abandon his Blair impersonation completely. He declared his support for gay marriage in 2011, and made it a reality in 2013, against staunch opposition from within his party. He often spoke the language of social justice. But he rarely offered more than lip service. Overall, Cameron's overtures to the right far outnumbered those towards the liberal centre. He slashed state spending, ramped up attacks on immigration and multiculturalism, and in 2013 promised an in/out referendum on EU membership if the Tories won the next election in 2015.

While Cameron's opportunism often drew controversy and accusations of duplicity, he proved himself a fluent practitioner of the party's playbook. Across two centuries, Conservatives have performed a similar set of tricks: appropriating the arguments of opponents, changing shape to meet a changing world, keeping the far right on side and ruthlessly exploiting crises – all while keeping Conservatives somehow the same, and never far from power.

No other political party in the world has survived for so long. The only credible rival in terms of longevity is the US Democrats, founded in 1828, which has undergone far starker mutations over the years. But in fact the party's origins lie long before its baptism as the Conservatives in the 1830s, in the creation of the Tory Party in 1678, from where today's Conservatives take their nickname.

The word 'Tory' started as a seventeenth-century slur from the Gaelic 'toraeigh', meaning 'bogtrotter' or 'bandit'. It then became the nickname for Royalists in parliament whose allegiances lay above all with the Crown. They were up against the Whigs, whose name had similarly derogatory origins: in Scots, 'whiggamor' meant something like a country bumpkin. In the end, both Tories and Whigs reclaimed these insults as the titles of their tribes. By the mid-eighteenth century, they loosely represented two main coalitions. The Tories championed established authority – the landed aristocracy, the Anglican Church and the monarchy – while Whigs were more open to commercial interests, electoral reform and nonconformity religion.

The mutual hostility between Tories and Whigs hid the common ground on which they stood. Their political visions were really improvisations on the same themes, and they both ultimately represented the ruling class. As the philosopher David Hume summarised in 1742, in his essay 'Of the Parties of Great Britain', a Tory was 'a lover of monarchy, tho' without abandoning liberty' and a Whig was 'a lover of liberty, tho' without renouncing monarchy'. In the preface to his book *Political Essays*, published in 1819, the commentator William Hazlitt called the distinction between the two 'laughable': they 'remind one of Opposition coaches, that raise a great dust or spatter one another with mud, but both travel the same road and arrive at the same destination'.

Back then, Britain boasted one of the oldest parliaments in the world, but it was far from being a democracy. Only about one in every eight adult men could vote. The landed aristocracy dominated decision-making and most seats were uncontested. Then, across the nineteenth century, a sequence of suffrage reforms changed that. In 1832, the Whigs passed the first Great Reform Act, expanding the electorate to include some of the industrial middle class and encouraging (if not enforcing) elections as the route to parliament. Another reform followed in 1867, this time surprisingly engineered by Benjamin Disraeli and the Tory leadership (against the fears of most Tory MPs), which brought more working-class voters into the fray. From December 1884, after the most significant of the Great Reform Acts, about two-thirds of men could vote. While women were still completely excluded and in Ireland male suffrage was more limited, talk of 'democracy' at least became more meaningful: the working class made up a majority of the electorate for the first time.[5]

It was the first of these reforms, bitterly opposed by the Tories, that gave rise to the modern Conservative Party. Two years later, in 1834, Robert Peel gave his speech known as the Tamworth Manifesto – officially delivered to his constituents but with clear eyes on a national audience – that both reconciled the Tories to the new suffrage and announced its resistance to further change. His aim, as he later explained, was to build a party 'which should enable us to . . . say, with a voice of authority, to the restless spirit of revolutionary change, "Here are thy bounds, and here shall thy vibrations cease."' His speech never mentioned the word 'Conservative', but it is widely regarded as the decisive moment in the Tories' formal evolution into the Conservative Party. The term 'Tory' was increasingly deemed tired and reactionary. 'Conservative', by contrast, contained notions of a more noble quest: the conserver of a sacred order.

Not everyone was convinced by the name change. A sense of compromise – even of outright capitulation – to the Whigs seemed implicit in the new label. 'A Conservative is only a Tory who is ashamed of himself,' the diplomat John Hookham Frere, an Old Etonian, quipped. The aristocrat Charles Greville wrote that Robert Peel was trying 'to raise a party out of all the other parties'. Benjamin Disraeli, who became one of Peel's loudest critics and eventually his successor, suggested that a Conservative government simply meant 'Tory men and Whig measures'. This wariness surrounding the new name ensured that the Tory moniker survived, both as insult and badge of honour.

Despite his foundational role in the party, Robert Peel

stands as a controversial figure within the Conservatives' history. In 1846, during a second stint as prime minister, he abolished the Corn Laws, a set of taxes that suited landowners in Britain but raised costs on grain for poor people, a problem made worse by a famine in Ireland. Peel's decision to remove them – betraying the interests of the party's traditional base – followed a growing campaign by industrialists, who were also disadvantaged by the inflated price of grain. The extent to which Peel was moved by the plight of the poor or simply by expedience – in a changing electoral landscape, courting the landowning interest was not enough – remains a matter of debate, but either way, many Tories never forgave him. For the first and (so far) only time, there was a formal split among Conservatives. Two-thirds of Tory MPs voted against repealing the Corn Laws, and it only passed through parliament with the support of the Whigs. Ostracised, the 'Peelites' pulled away to form their own faction and eventually joined the Whigs. The Whigs dominated British politics for most of the next three decades, renaming themselves the Liberals in 1859.

But Peel nonetheless pioneered the Conservatives as a shape-shifting party. In Disraeli's quip, Peel 'caught the Whigs bathing, and walked away with their clothes'. Disraeli didn't mean it as a compliment, but it subsequently became the Tories' favourite strategy in times of crisis: stripping opponents bare, stealing their policies (often in cheapened form) and mimicking their strengths. It continued throughout the twentieth century and, via Cameron, into the twenty-first.

Besides adaptability, the other lesson Peel imparted on his party was arguably even more important. The Conservatives' formal split, combined with its long absence of power, etched itself into party folklore, instilling a warning that proved central to its subsequent success: the pursuit of power requires at least an outward display of unity when it matters most – election time – even as vicious disagreements swirl away on the inside. Since Peel, every Conservative leader has placed keeping the party together as one of their main priorities. Many of the Conservatives' contortions over Brexit – Cameron calling the in/out referendum to quell UKIP's rise in the first place, Johnson campaigning on the slogan 'Get Brexit Done' and even, paradoxically, expelling twenty-one of his own MPs to secure the support of Brexiteers – stemmed from the fear of being deserted by a core faction, and an awareness of the consequences. 'Don't do a Peel' remains a popular party refrain.

The Conservatives' instinct for discipline and loyalty can be overstated, not least because it sometimes coincides with raucous arguments and rivalries. Any such instinct stems not from a romantic ideal, nor an inherent regard for order and authority. The party's ultimate loyalty lies not with any one leader but with winning elections and holding on to office: to this end, all kinds of compromises can be made. But the moment a leader is regarded as a dud, their time is up, with no love lost. Boris Johnson and Liz Truss – whose fates were sealed, respectively, by the Tories' double defeat in the by-elections on 23 June 2022 and then a steep collapse in polling popularity – are only the most recent examples. 'It is not a principle of the Conservative Party to stab its leaders in the back,' Balfour joked in 1922, 'but I must admit that it often appears to be a practice.'

It might seem obvious that a political party would prioritise power: what other purpose could a party have? But in the Conservatives' case, defeat is uniquely terrifying. Because their aim is, in broad terms, to preserve the social order, the prospect of an enemy victory carries the potential of irreversible damage. By this logic, the Tories must win every time to keep things as they are. The enemy need win only once. In *The Foundation of the Conservative Party*, the historian Robert Stewart describes this as the 'peculiar difficulty' afflicting right-wing parties, particularly their radical fringes, in two-party systems. He explains:

> A radical wing can break away from a left-wing party in the reasonable belief that doing so attracts attention to its cause, protects it from adulteration, and enhances its future prospects. The radical can break up his party without sacrificing the world which he hopes to create. It remains to be created. The extreme Conservative has less scope. If he breaks up his party, he not only loses his immediate object, as happened with . . . the Corn Laws in 1846, but he also weakens the force of Conservatism, hands power to his opponents, and thereby assists radical triumphs which are almost certain to be permanent.[6]

Progressives, in other words, don't suffer from the same anxiety as Conservatives: they can take comfort in the conviction that their time will come eventually (although there is a case to be made that, since Stewart wrote those words, climate change has brought a new urgency to the left). This logic suggests at least one reason why, since Peel, the Tories' opponents have been generally more ready to split, leaving the Conservatives to reap the rewards. When the Liberals split over Irish Home Rule in the 1880s, for example, the Conservatives absorbed their rival's Unionist wing and held government for the better part of the next thirty years. This absorption proved particularly influential in shaping the Tories' future. The party expanded its coalition of support to become, effectively, two parties at once: a Conservative Party and a Liberal Party, standing for the shires and the city, the aristocracy and industrialists, Conservative tradition and liberal capitalism. It was, former Conservative minister Lord David Willetts told me, 'an extraordinary combination that on the Continent would have been two separate parties'.

The rise of the abour Party at the start of the twentieth century fuelled this fusion even further. Before then, Conservatism and liberalism could still define themselves by their differences: the Conservatives championed stability, national unity and inherited power and privilege; the Liberals represented individual liberty and equal opportunity. But when socialism emerged as a serious political threat, embodied by Labour, the Conservatives and Liberals found common cause around private property – esteemed bedrock of both liberty and order – which needed to be defended at all costs. Over the following decades, the line between Conservative and Liberal dissolved, until only the Conservative Party remained as a credible electoral force, representing both parties' platforms within a formidable, but forever fraught, coalition.

Since 1874, when the Tories ended almost three decades in opposition, the Conservatives have contested thirty-eight elections and suffered only seven significant defeats: three of those were at the hands of Tony Blair in 1997, 2001 and 2005; the remaining four were against William Gladstone in 1880 and Henry Campbell-Bannerman in 1906 (both for the Liberals), and Clement Attlee in 1945 and Harold Wilson in 1966 (both for Labour). On the nine further occasions when they failed to enter government, the Conservatives' absence from power didn't last long, because their opponent's victory was so slim – either with a single-digit majority or through a minority government – as to make meaningful non-Conservative rule effectively impossible; the opposition governments rarely lasted longer than two years. The Conservatives' election victories, by contrast, come with fewer caveats. Of the twenty-two times they formed a government, they won working majorities in sixteen of them, fourteen with double digits.

Even these figures don't do the Conservatives' dominance justice, however, because the party's victories usually happen in longer sequences than their opponents', meaning their legacies are often all the more substantial. The Conservatives have spent eight or more consecutive years in power on five occasions since 1874. Their opponents have done so only twice. The twentieth century is now referred to as 'the Conservative Century': the party was in power for a total of seventy years. In 1964, after three successive defeats, Labour campaigned on the slogan '13 wasted years' – and they've been able to recycle that slogan more frequently than they'd like.

Other political parties, in other countries, boast impressive winning records: in Japan, the Liberal Democratic Party has been in power almost continuously since 1955, when it fused together the nation's two conservative parties; in Sweden, the Social Democratic Party (founded in 1889) dominated government from 1932 to 1976, and again between 2014 and 2022. But what sets the dominance of the Conservative Party apart isn't just the longer time period it covers – spanning two centuries – but Britain's first-past-the-post (FPTP) voting system. Whereas countries like Japan and Sweden have proportional representation (PR), usually constraining their successful parties with the need to build coalitions, Britain's FPTP system is a winner-takes-all arrangement. It often turns small majorities in the vote into emphatic parliamentary control, granting the victor unrivalled control of the state.[7] This suits the Conservatives, making their electoral dominance both easier and more consequential. It also serves as a safety mechanism for Conservatives: because FPTP disadvantages smaller parties, which have little hope besides putting pressure on the two major parties, the Tories never fall below second place. A return to power is always within reach.

Many commentators on the left point to FPTP as the cause of the Conservatives' success. But it could just as easily be seen as a symptom. FPTP is one of many anachronistic, unreformed pillars of British politics that the Conservatives have excelled in maintaining. Tellingly, on one of the rare occasions when electoral reform looked likely, under a minority Labour leadership in 1929–31, the government fell before the legislation could pass. The Conservatives then took back control of parliament for the next fourteen years, and talk of electoral reform fell silent.

The Conservatives are helped by the fact that FPTP doesn't only suit them: it secures Labour's place as one of the two major parties as well, and occasionally allows them to reap the rewards of FPTP's democratic distortions. In 1997, for example, Blair won over 60 per cent of seats with 43 per cent of the vote. It also similarly ensures that Labour never falls below second place. No wonder that Labour politicians tend to be no more interested in electoral reform than the Tories, even in a context where they achieve power for only about a third of the time. In a more proportional system, smaller parties would chip away at Labour's vote share, jeopardising both its status as one of the two major parties and, as a result, much of its funding from trade unions – plausibly resulting in an even worse electoral situation for the Labour Party itself, if not the left in general. And so the FPTP game carries on.

It's therefore wrong to say that the Conservatives' dominance is the inevitable by-product of a rigged system, but FPTP does make their winning record both more achievable and more influential. FPTP gives winning parties the power to impose their vision on society uncowed by coalition politics: a parliamentary majority means almost total power over the state. Britain's lack of a codified, or formally written, constitution, as exists in most other democracies, also means there are few official checks and balances on the governing party. The historian Peter Hennessy has described Britain as having a 'good chap' theory of government, relying on elite restraint and respect for norms and customs. It is described by others in less merry terms: as an 'elective dictatorship'.[8] Conservatives are usually at the helm.

All this means that the Conservatives' winning record brings more power in Britain than it would in another democratic environment. Landslide wins can transform the country. The left has sought to take advantage where it can: after the 1906 election, the biggest leftward swing in British history, the Liberal government laid the foundations for the welfare state, introducing state pensions and health and unemployment insurance; after 1945, Labour expanded the welfare state even further, launching an unprecedented wave of reform that created the NHS. Conservatives were right to worry that some of these changes would be irreversible. But the power to transform Britain works both ways, and usually falls in the Conservatives' favour. During the global resurgence of free-market economics in the '70s and '80s, for example, Thatcher's hat-trick of parliamentary majorities reoriented the relationship between the state and the private sector to an extent that would have been unfathomable in most other countries. Only New Zealand suffered a swifter and starker widening of inequality in the developed world.[9]

As part of her political project, Thatcher had long dreamed of abolishing local government, seeing it as a potential breeding ground for socialist policies beyond national government control. After returning to power in 2010, through austerity, and under the guise of cleaning up Labour's mess, Cameron and Osborne sought to make that dream a reality, slashing councils' capacity to deliver and maintain basic services. The result is that, across the country, social housing, libraries, leisure centres, local museums, legal aid, bus services, parks and youth centres – among other things – have become luxuries that many communities cannot afford. The cumulative effect has been extreme. In May 1979, when Thatcher took power, a fifth of Britain's total area was publicly owned – a higher proportion than ever before. Today, only about a tenth is.[10] Along the way, Britain has become both the most centralised state in the Western world and more porous to private business interests than any other advanced democracy.[11]

How have the Conservatives' achieved such dominance? Conservatives don't like to dwell too much on their strategy. They prefer to say that their success springs from the conservative impulses of the British people, as if their record of victory was merely the authentic expression of national character. Conservatives often pretend that they aren't even interested in politics: that's the left's boring obsession. 'Conservatives do not believe that political struggle is the most important thing in life,' Quintin Hogg explained in *The Case for Conservatism* in 1948. 'In this they differ from Communists, Socialists, Nazis, Fascists, Social Creditors, and most members of the British Labour Party. The simplest among them prefer fox-hunting – the wisest, religion.' In 1990, Michael Oakeshott said in a similar vein: 'Leave talking about politics to the left. They have nothing better to do.'

The aristocratic posture of effortless superiority runs deep within the party: there is no greater victory than one achieved without trying, through natural talent, instinct and chance; Labour, meanwhile, then suffers the double indignity of not just failing the exam, but failing it after months of swotting. As Musa Okwonga reflected in his recent memoir, at Eton, the playground for many Conservative prime ministers, 'visible effort is mocked', 'the trick is to achieve without seeming to try'.[12] The historian John Robert Seeley captured this lofty disposition when, at the height of Britain's Empire in 1883, he remarked in *The Expansion of England*: 'We seem, as it were, to have conquered and peopled half the world in a fit of absence of mind.' Conservatives like to think that they have conquered British politics in the same way.

But this posture of supreme indifference, or indifferent supremacy, is a classic Conservative affectation. Just as the highest achievers at Eton simply hide how hard they work and how much inherited privilege and power they hold, and just as the Empire relied on an elaborate and bloody choreography, so too do the Conservatives perform disinterest in politics while plotting relentlessly behind the scenes. The party has proved remarkably adept both at relegating internal divisions and debates in pursuit of victory, and responding dynamically to defeats that threatened its extinction. Almost all ideals are secondary to winning. Belying its image as old and anachronistic, it has often pioneered techniques for mobilising voters and embraced new technologies. The rewards have confounded all expectations: the more democratic Britain has become, the more successful the Conservatives have been.

But at the same time, no matter how often the Conservatives win or bounce back, a certain fear and fragility, a sense of imminent extinction, haunts the Tories like a dark shadow. Ever since the expansions of the suffrage in the nineteenth century, the chances of a party intimately connected to the ruling class and the preservation of privilege seemed slim. The forces of democracy and progress were stacked against them; the votes just didn't add up. At the very least, the Tories had a fight on their hands, and they weren't used to fighting: most of their wealth and power was simply inherited, passed down from one generation to the next, in the natural order of things. 'It will be interesting to be the last of the Conservatives,' Lord Salisbury wrote glumly in 1882, as the age of mass suffrage loomed. 'I foresee that will be our fate.' (A year later, his chief secretary confirmed Salisbury's worst fears. 'The Radicals have the Trades Unions, the Dissenting Chapels and every society for the abolition of property and morality working for them,' he wrote. 'Our supporters only want to be left alone, to be allowed to enjoy what they have, and they think they are so secure that they will make no sacrifice of time or of pleasure to prepare against attack or to resist it.')

Such gloomy forecasts are familiar to any Conservative. In May 2019, the *Guardian* journalist Andy Beckett published an essay on the coming decline of the Conservative Party, headlined: '"A zombie party": the deepening crisis of conservatism'. Beckett argued that, after a decade in Downing Street, Conservatism might seem ascendant, but appearances were deceiving: really, the party was intellectually moribund and electorally flailing. 'The Conservatives last won a solid general election majority 32 years ago,' he wrote. The average Conservative voter was now a pensioner. The membership had plummeted so low that, in 2017, the party received more money from bequests from the dead than living members. What future could such a party have?

'There's a strong current of Tory pessimism which is defeatist,' Charles Moore, former editor of the *Spectator* and the *Daily Telegraph*, told me. 'The logic goes: if the voters really understood our way of life and what we stood for, then they would never vote for us.' While one side of the Conservative mind assumes permanent rule, on the other side, every thunderous defeat, however rare, feels fatal, plummeting the party into existential despair. Every return to Downing Street comes as an impossible surprise, a resurrection, even as history suggests that it is one of the most reliable trends in British politics.

But the Conservatives' anxiety about losing power has usually proved more energising than paralysing. Whereas their electoral opponents have often believed that history is on their side – whether the Whigs, the Liberals or Labour – the Tories' ambivalent embrace of modernity has carried no such consolation. If anything, they have tended to instinctively agree with their opponents: they are rowing against the tide and, unless they either paddle fast enough or build a better boat, they'll end up beached on the shores of modernity. This lack of faith in the future has turned its leaders and party officers into tireless operators. A famous left-wing slogan could just as easily belong to the Conservative Party: 'Don't Mourn, Organise!'

The party's election machinery evolved from Peel onwards, but especially in the second half of the nineteenth century. No other party in Europe proved more successful in generating a grassroots movement. Local associations and cross-party clubs proliferated across the country, all aiming to promote popular conservatism. Mixing politics with entertainment and social networking, these local clubs proved a big hit: the Primrose League, for example, founded in 1883, boasted a membership of 1.5 million by the early 1900s, becoming one of the largest political organisations in Britain ever. Its events featured, in one scholar's summary, 'a mixed bag of entertainers, including flying trapeze artists, clowns, minstrel shows, trick bicycle riders, jugglers, ventriloquists, marionettes, and brass bands'. By 1885, even Lord Salisbury saw reasons for optimism: the Primrose League was 'an organization with which no party in any country would be able to offer any comparison', he enthused. ('Of course it's vulgar,' Lady Salisbury reflected, 'but that's why we are so successful.')[13]

The Conservatives maintained that organisational flair throughout the twentieth century. Their response to Labour's resounding win in 1945 was illustrative, catalysing a dramatic wave of initiatives and reforms. 'As in the days of Peel,' Conservative MP Rab Butler declared, 'the Conservatives must be seen to have accommodated themselves to a social revolution.' He called for a new Tamworth Manifesto.[14] By 1952, membership had peaked at a mind-bending 2.8 million people – the largest ever paid membership for any voluntary organisation in Britain.[15] (The number has since nosedived in line with many other Western democracies, but even in the 1990s the Conservatives claimed a membership of 760,000 – triple Labour's tally at the time.) The Conservatives also embraced new technologies. The party sent MPs on radio training courses in the late 1940s and created their own television and radio training studio in 1951, seven years before Labour. They harnessed the potential of the polling and marketing industries, appointing an ad agency – Colman Prentis and Varley – in 1948. The resultant party propaganda was, for its time, unprecedented. A small series of election posters showed colourful pictures of aspirational domesticity – a family washing the car, or eating dinner together in front of the television – with the caption: 'Life's better with the Conservatives. Don't let Labour ruin it.' For Labour, by contrast, their main poster even in 1959 offered drab pictures of the party leader, Hugh Gaitskell, with the words: 'the Man with a Plan'.[16]

Later, in 1978, the Conservatives partnered with the advertising agency Saatchi and Saatchi and changed the game again. Saatchi and Saatchi effectively put the Conservatives on a permanent campaign footing, building a reputation for punchy and aggressive comms. Under their direction, the party mastered the art of acting like a renegade outsider even when comfortably residing in Downing Street. During the 1983 election, for example, Thatcher's advertising campaign focused almost exclusively on Labour's danger and incompetence rather than any positives from her first four years in power. 'Political campaigning is, above all, an adversarial activity,' Maurice Saatchi explained. 'A world of trial by combat in which you would hit, and be hit.' It was only after Saatchi and Saatchi's success that Labour resolved to hire their own full-time ad agency.[17]

Labour's comparative slowness can partly be put down to Tory guile, but it also reflects the intrinsic advantages of the ruling class: money and connections. As early as 1852, a book titled *Electoral Facts* argued that political influence no longer stemmed from personal character or charisma but from 'pecuniary resources'.[18] Amid Labour's rise and the Liberals' decline, the Conservatives became the main bulwark against the socialist threat – and received a huge boost in funding as a result. With the exception of 2005, when it was roughly even, the Conservatives have outspent Labour in every election, sometimes by twice the sum.[19] In 2020, only one member of the Sunday Times Rich List's top 50 donated money to Labour – and even they gave the Tories money as well.[20] The democratic era has clearly posed the Conservatives many challenges, but David versus Goliath this is not.

For all the time and money spent on comms and campaigning, it is still common to hear that Conservatives neglect the cultural and strategic side of politics by focusing too much on economics. This narrative of neglect is really another form of Conservative self-flattery: Conservatives, we're told, have been so focused on ensuring the nation's prosperity that they've forgotten to play the bigger political game. By contrast, the left are painted as cultural obsessives who infiltrate institutions and transform the nation out of the public eye.

This fiction both wildly inflates the left's success and deliberately forgets the lengths to which Conservatives go in pursuit of victory. Conservatives have long understood the importance of what Gramsci called a 'cultural front'. To this end, Conservatives have launched think-tanks, newspapers, book clubs, television networks, and more, while actively seeking to undermine supposed pillars of progressive politics: universities, local government, the BBC, Channel 4 – anything, in fact, that can be seen as cultivating non-Conservative viewpoints. Conservative MP Keith Joseph, a key figure in Thatcher's cabinet who requested Gramsci's *Prison Notebooks* for holiday reading in the 1980s, was particularly attuned to this project. He called for a 'battle of ideas to be fought in every school, university, publication, committee, TV studio'. Conservatives continue the fight today, with varying degrees of success.

Their readiness to mobilise their resources was also visible after the 2017 election, when young people overwhelmingly voted for Jeremy Corbyn's Labour Party against the Conservatives. The Conservatives immediately went to work on reversing this trend. They announced such youth-pleasing policies as freezing tuition fees at £9,250 and raising the upper threshold for a young person's railcard from twenty-five to thirty. Conservative MPs were advised to talk more about environmental issues –

resulting in many of them flocking to social media simultaneously to praise a David Attenborough documentary in December 2017 – and to increase their Instagram presence to look like 'real people'. According to *The Times*, there were also plans to offer party members discount cards for restaurants 'like Nando's' to incentivise young people to join, an idea that Nando's swiftly distanced itself from.

These overtures went along with a remarkable sprouting of Conservative-affiliated initiatives and organisations, all hoping to entice the young with the magic of free markets. Among them were: Activate (2017), Onward (2018), Freer (2018), New Generation (2018), Refresh (2018) and Young Conservatives (2018) – united by a common purpose, names that sounds like brands of toothpaste and close links to the Conservatives, the Tory Press and think-tanks like the Institute of Economic Affairs (IEA) and the Centre for Policy Studies (CPS). 'This generation are #Uber-riding #Airbnb-ing #Deliveroo-eating #freedomfighters,' Liz Truss declared on Twitter in May 2018, to widespread derision. Truss first made the rallying cry at the launch of Freer (launched by the IEA); the speech then became an article for Refresh (launched by the *Daily Telegraph*); Robert Colvile (director of the CPS, columnist at the *Sunday Times*, former editor of the *Telegraph*'s comment pages) later turned it into a T-shirt. The message hasn't proved successful so far – young people remain unconvinced by what the Conservatives can offer in a context of stalled wages and unaffordable housing – but it illustrated the expansiveness of the Tory machine, and how it can be marshalled towards specific purposes.

Throughout its history, then, the Conservatives' dominance has drawn on several factors: an ability to assimilate opponents and adapt, a tactical prowess and superior finances, and an unrepresentative voting system. One final reason needs mentioning before we move on: luck. 'All the political history of the last fifty years shows that the [Conservative] Unionists party cannot win a General Election without some special aid, such as Home Rule, or the South African War,' the influential Conservative politician Sir Michael Hicks-Beach wrote to Balfour in 1911, during the Liberals' second term in power. 'Without that we are in a minority.' Decades later, the Conservative PM Harold Macmillan was asked what the hardest part of being prime minister was. He supposedly replied 'events, dear boy, events'. The truth is that, more often than not, events have been kind to the Conservatives.

As the Great Recession in 2008 showed, events and upheavals can transform the political landscape far more than the personality of any politician. For a Conservative government, such moments may grant their reign a new lease of life, or if the party is out of office, they can pave the way for a return. There are countless examples. The First World War began in 1914 with the Conservatives in opposition, but then the war effort required their inclusion and they dominated the coalition, slowly overseeing the Liberals' dissolution. ('British Conservatives owe Kaiser Wilhelm II an immense debt,' the historian Ewen Green has written.[21]) The onset of the Great Depression in 1929, which occurred just as Labour secured the most seats in parliament for the first time, similarly set the stage for a Tory takeover by stealth, leading to Labour's removal from government in 1931.[22] In 1951, when the Conservatives returned to power after their humbling defeat in 1945, Labour actually won the most votes but the Conservatives secured twenty-six more seats. Meanwhile, Thatcher's eleven-year rule would hardly have lasted so long without either the discovery of North Sea oil

– which footed the bill for the rise in unemployment and fall in progressive taxes under her leadership – or the opportunity for a jingoistic war in the Falklands, which galvanised her flailing prime ministership.

These pieces of good fortune for the party – often experienced as great misfortunes for many others – don't necessarily present obvious opportunities to exploit. They require a certain daring, a readiness to take risks. This gambling tendency is widely recognised in more recent Conservative leaders like Cameron and Johnson, but it is far from a twenty-first-century phenomenon. In 1867, when Disraeli and Lord Derby sought to expand the suffrage, they dreamed of putting the party 'permanently in power' at the risk of destabilising the country, hoping that newly enfranchised workers could be brought on side.[23] Derby confessed that it was 'a leap in the dark', prompting harsh criticism from some of his contemporaries. As Homersham Cox, a reforming Whig, wrote at the time: 'Hitherto it has not been considered good statesmanship to commit the destinies of our empire unreservedly to fortune . . . The policy of political "leaps" remained to be invented by a government which calls itself Conservative.'[24] But Derby and Disraeli's gamble ultimately paid off and, since then, Conservatives have been happy to try their luck as well.

The sheer, unpredictable adaptability of the Conservatives in pursuit of power makes it easy to wonder whether they have any substance beyond a hunger for success. Conservatives appear ready to support any policy that fastens their grip on power, to leap through any hoop that leads to victory. But while Tories place great emphasis on winning elections, that isn't the sum of their ambitions. This misplaced view confuses the ends with the means: Conservatives want to win elections, but why? It surely isn't just the thrill of winning or the glee of being in government, though there is probably plenty of that, too. (Etonians in particular seem to love the buzz of being in Number 10.) Conservatives, like any other political tribe, are motivated by something more than mere power: they share a bundle of beliefs, a vision of society, a set of interests. The purpose of power is to impose those values and interests upon society – and to prevent political opponents from imposing theirs.

The Conservatives' adaptability, shown by almost every Conservative PM since Robert Peel, makes it difficult to discern what the party's consistent values and interests might be. 'There is virtually no policy that you couldn't find a Conservative case for,' Lord Willetts told me. 'Conservatism is almost like a Mary Poppins bag full of goodies and tricks.' In recent years, the Conservatives have foraged the depths of this bag even more than usual, transforming their appearance multiple times in the eyes of the electorate. They have positioned themselves as the bastions of the NHS, climate change action, and, through Brexit, the right to self-determination – while having spent most of the previous century opposing the welfare state (including the creation of the NHS), cosying up to the fossil fuel industry (and all the environmental damage it causes) and championing Empire (the antithesis of self-determination). More recently, they have shorn off those commitments again, pushing low taxes, attacking 'net zero' targets and suggesting that the NHS needs more privatisation.

Conservatives are especially hard to pin down because of their capacity for inverting the attack lines of their opponents. So, for example, while the Conservatives happily take donations-for-favours from foreign oligarchs, it is allegedly the left who are under the sway of foreign powers. While the Conservatives defend the interests of bosses, inherited wealth and property owners, Labour are the ones who are out of touch and driven by elite self-interest: they only pretend to care about poverty and equality, Conservatives often say, so that they can feel good about themselves. The Conservatives are the party of both the aristocracy and hard work, while the Labour Party is the home of grifters, shirkers and slackers: all those who want to free-ride on the labour of others (much like the idle rich who invariably vote Tory). Over the years, some Tories have even toyed with the idea of renaming themselves 'The Workers Party', making the takeover of Labour's turf complete. Edward Heath, Thatcher's predecessor, said of the Conservatives: 'We are the trade union of the nation as a whole.'[25]

In such a topsy-turvy context, defining the nature of Conservatism seems hopeless, perhaps even pointless, like trying to define the colour of a chameleon: its essence is in its adaptability, constantly changing in response to its environment and taking on the qualities of its surroundings, with the ultimate aim of self-preservation. But to define Conservatism through its adaptability repeats the same mistake as defining it through its desire to win elections. Why do Conservatives adapt? To win elections. Why do they want to win elections? That is the question that needs an answer. Adaptability is the strategy. Winning elections is the goal. What's it all for?

2

WHAT CONSERVATIVES BELIEVE

'Every true Conservative man or woman had something
of the diehard in his or her constitution.'
                    Anonymous local party chairman, 1922

'We must get back to basic Conservative principles – but
don't ask me what they are.'
                    Sir Denis Thatcher, in conversation, 1997

'I'm not a deeply ideological person. I'm a practical one.'
                    David Cameron, in an interview, 2005

In 1975, the Conservatives' newly elected leader Margaret
Thatcher was attending a policy seminar with senior Tories
when she famously pulled a book from her bag and declared:
'This, gentlemen, is what we believe.' The book was *The
Constitution of Liberty* by the Austrian economist and sociologist
Friedrich von Hayek, first published in 1960. It became a
blueprint for 'Thatcherism': the market faith that increased
deregulation, privatisation and competition were the solution
to all of society's problems. From this standpoint, the potential for the state to play any active role in improving society
was not just flawed, but fatal. One of Hayek's earlier books
was called *The Road to Serfdom*.

Given Thatcher's devotion to the free market, the source

of her inspiration might not seem surprising. But her fondness for Hayek sat awkwardly within the Conservative tradition for two reasons. First, aside from anything Hayek advocated, Conservatives usually prided themselves on *not* following the doctrines of intellectuals or economists, especially those of a continental variety. What 'true' Conservatives believe, rather, comes not from books or scholarship, libraries or universities, but experience and inheritance: a nation's customs, traditions and good old-fashioned common sense. As the party's semi-official historian, John Ramsden, once put it, the history of the Conservative Party 'does not owe much to the work of philosophers'.

Second, Hayek didn't seem like much of a Conservative, either. His intense faith in free markets actively sought to transform society, and he celebrated unfettered capitalism's unpredictable effects. Conservatism was supposed to be about, well, conserving: protecting the status quo, safeguarding traditions, revering the past. Hayek, however, had the feverish self-certainty of a revolutionary, claiming that if he could not convert enough people to his free-market cause, no less than 'the future of civilisation' was at stake. None of this was very Conservative. In fact, the final chapter of *The Constitution of Liberty* was explicitly titled: 'Why I'm Not a Conservative'.

All this fits neatly with the popular perception that, with Hayek's books by her side, Thatcher transformed not only the country but the Conservative Party. Under her leadership, in this telling, the Conservatives became newly fanatical and ideological – she was the first Conservative leader to have an 'ism' named after her, for example. The party abandoned all concern for steadiness and repositioned itself as a dynamic, transformative force in society. 'Economics is the method,'

Thatcher declared, 'the aim is to change people's souls.' She echoed Hayek's ambivalence about the 'Conservative' label. 'What's the real problem with the Conservative Party?' Thatcher said. 'The name of it. We are not a "conservative" party; we are a party of innovation, of imagination, of liberty, of striking out in new directions, of renewed national pride and a novel sense of leadership . . . That's not "conservative". The name is all wrong.'[1]

Innovation. Imagination. Striking out in new directions. These weren't the typical values that Conservatives sought to champion (even if they had often embraced them in their election strategies). Edmund Burke, the eighteenth-century statesman widely regarded as the founder of Conservatism, believed that 'the spirit of innovation' was at the root of most evil. The problem with revolutionaries, as he saw it, was that they had *too* much imagination – a complacent, and reckless, curiosity for striking out in new directions – so that they couldn't appreciate the miracles of the present and past. 'To be Conservative, then,' as Michael Oakeshott wrote in his influential 1956 essay 'On Being a Conservative', 'is to prefer the familiar to the unknown, to prefer the tried to the untried, fact to mystery, the actual to the possible, the limited to the unbounded, the near to the distant, the sufficient to the super-abundant, the convenient to the perfect, present laughter to utopian bliss.' Thatcher seemed to be on the wrong side of all these divides. Could she even be called a Conservative?

Many on both the left and right were shocked by Thatcher's radicalism. Ian Gilmour, a Tory baron and party veteran, was at a loss: her brand of politics 'is merely reactionary', he lamented, 'it is not Conservative'. The then-conservative philosopher John Gray decried a 'Maoism of the Right' and singled out Hayek's influence for blame. Another Conservative thinker, Roger Scruton, compared Thatcherism to Marxism, with its singular emphasis on economics. But Marxists weren't happy either. Gerry Cohen, a Marxist philosopher at Oxford, declared that Thatcher represented 'a betrayal' of Conservative values and published a paper on 'Rescuing conservatism from the Conservatives'.

Today, however, Margaret Thatcher stands as the epitome of British Conservatism. She is the party's most successful leader, winning three elections in a row, and, according to the polls, by far the party's favourite, well above Churchill or anyone else. Far from betraying the Conservative tradition, Thatcher is now its benchmark: the Conservative to whom all others must compare themselves and swear their allegiance — otherwise, they are likely to be the ones accused of betrayal. During the 2022 Conservative leadership campaign, the two main contenders Liz Truss and Rishi Sunak took increasingly elaborate steps to prove that they, not their opponent, were the true heir to Thatcher's legacy. A Conservative election campaign led by a Thatcher hologram is surely not far off.

Perhaps this reversal, from betrayal to divine embodiment, reflects the sheer force of Thatcher's personality: a leader who single-handedly remade Conservatism in her own image. But it might also suggest that the scale of her Tory transformation was always slightly overblown. Many tenets of 'Thatcherism', after all, predated the eponymous leader. The Conservatives increasingly claimed the mantle of 'liberty' over the course of the twentieth century. Churchill read Hayek and, in 1945, the Conservative Party's chairman Ralph Assheton, 1st Baron Clitheroe, dedicated much of the party's print ration to distributing 12,000 abridged copies of Hayek's *The Road to Serfdom* as election propaganda.[2] Thatcher cited Churchill's 1950 campaign and its slogan 'Set the People Free'

44

as her inspiration. Meanwhile, Conservatives like Keith Joseph and Enoch Powell, both important influences on Thatcher, presaged her free-market radicalism.

The truth is that Conservatism has always been an ideology that pulls in different directions and draws on different emotions. Pick any pressing topic – the free market, the welfare state, minority rights, membership of the European Union, nationalism, military interventionism – and you will find conflicting Conservative stances. There are One Nation Tories, High Tories, Free Market Conservatives, Compassionate Conservatives, Progressive Conservatives, Thatcherites, libertarians, wets, dries, and more. Some Conservatives are centrist and liberal, others are extremist and authoritarian, many are a mix: at once liberal and authoritarian, combining a commitment to economic freedoms with a punitive law and order agenda – a free market and a strong state.[3]

Conservatism is capacious, like all the most successful ideologies, and the balance of forces within the Conservative Party changes over time: the fringe becomes the mainstream, and vice versa. The challenge is to find what beliefs or motivations bind Conservatives together. A glance towards the party's past shows that many supposed Conservative commandments – prioritising stability, liberty, law and order – are held lightly and inconsistently. A search for continuities is likely to encounter only contradictions. Conservatism is an ideology of society that often denies both the value of ideology and, at times, the meaning of society. Conservatism is at once eminently sensible and moderate, and uniquely prone to reactionary turns. It avows liberty, but is ambivalent about democracy. It is suspicious of ideas and intellectuals, and led by alumni from some of the most expensive, exclusive schools and universities in the world. (Over three-quarters of

Conservative leaders attended Oxford or Cambridge. About half went to elite public schools like Eton and Harrow.) Above all, Conservatism is the historic creed of Britain's ruling class, and yet it claims to represent the values, interests and instincts of the entire nation.

Of all Conservatism's contradictions, however, perhaps none is more influential than the relationship between Conservatism and capitalism. 'Whatever else the Conservative Party stands for,' Enoch Powell once said, 'unless it is the party of free choice, free competition and free enterprise, unless – I am not afraid of the word – it is the party of capitalism, then it has no function in the contemporary world.'[4] Their affiliation is now so standard as to seem unremarkable. But their pairing remains fractious. Capitalism's mantras, after all, are 'move fast and break things' and 'creative destruction'. As an economic system, it is irreverent, paying no heed to national borders or traditions and constantly seeking to uproot society in pursuit of profit: 'the spirit of innovation' is essential. 'Markets preserve nothing, but ingest all aspects of an existing social landscape and excrete them, shorn of meaning and memory, as transactions,' as Alice observes in Sally Rooney's *Beautiful World, Where Are You*. 'What could be "conservative" about such a process?' In *Why Vote Conservative*, a pamphlet published by David Willetts in 1997, the Conservative MP recalled knocking on the door of a Conservative voter to be told they no longer recognised the party: it had become a 'demolition squad'.

However indivisible capitalism and conservatism may seem, these tensions are always simmering away beneath the surface. Debates within the party have tended to play out along consistent lines: about how 'free' the market should be, how much equality or inequality should be tolerated, the balance between liberty and law and order, between social harmony and competition, and between the nation and the individual. These ideological dilemmas intermingle with strategic ones: how best to hold on to power, and how to make a politics of privilege and inequality popular in the democratic age. This constellation of concerns defines Conservatism – but countering views within its boundaries are often held fiercely.

This is why, for a party that claims to follow no strict doctrine, accusations of betrayal are such standard fare. The Conservative credentials of almost every important Conservative leader have been questioned by some rival faction, either when they are still leader or later down the line. Robert Peel, Benjamin Disraeli, Stanley Baldwin, Winston Churchill, Margaret Thatcher, David Cameron and Boris Johnson all suffered this fate. Perhaps there is nothing *more* Conservative than being accused of betraying Conservatism. It is also telling that the one figure in the Conservative canon whose standing is not disputed is Edmund Burke, a thinker claimed by all Conservatives – but who was categorically not a Conservative. To understand the nature of the Conservative tradition, he is a useful place to start.

Edmund Burke is the closest thing the Conservatives have to a philosopher king. He stands as an avatar for Conservatism in its finest form. But Burke was not born a Conservative, nor did he die one – he became one only posthumously. The political label 'Conservative' wasn't popularised until the 1830s, decades after Burke's death in 1797. But by the start of the 1900s, Burke had become the unwitting 'founder' of the Conservative creed: the patron saint of prudent reform, stalwart supporter of the status quo, all too aware of the dangerous delusions of political tinkerers and radicals – the 'greatest hero' of the Conservatives, according to Michael Gove.[5]

Burke was born in Ireland in 1729 and moved to England as a young man. He became a Whig MP and forged his reputation in opposition to the French Revolution. Whereas many rejoiced at the storming of the Bastille and the fall of a broken regime, Burke was horrified: the revolution, fuelled by the violent fiction that you could create a new society from scratch, forged of abstract principles like 'égalité' and 'liberté', was 'the most horrid, atrocious and affecting spectacle, that perhaps ever was exhibited to the pity and indignation of mankind', he wrote in *Reflections on the Revolution in France* in 1790. As the revolution descended into the Reign of Terror, Burke's warnings were hailed as prophetic. His praise for the plodding, humble quietness of England's uncodified constitution – with its 'strong impression of the ignorance and fallibility of mankind' – received new plaudits. 'There is no Man who calls himself a Gentleman that must not think himself obliged to you,' King George III wrote to Burke, 'for you have supported the cause of the Gentleman.'

Even then, until the late nineteenth century, Burke was arguably remembered more for his eloquence (and occasional long-windedness) than any particular political philosophy. Yet in the 1880s, a combination of growing calls for Irish Home Rule and an expansion of the suffrage saw Conservatives rouse a more politicised Burke – defender of the nation, weary of restless reformers and their perilous promises – from the grave. The Conservatives needed a compelling political identity to fight elections with, a vision of society and good governance to champion. Despite being a Whig and authoring an ambivalent philosophy at best, Burke provided it. By 1912, Arthur A. Baumann, a businessman, author and former Conservative MP, could claim that 'the writings of Burke contain the most complete body of

Conservative doctrine, expressed in the most perfect language that has ever been given to the world'.[6]

The transformation of Burke into Conservatism's intellectual father assured his posthumous legacy, but it also flattened him out as a thinker. Burke was excised from his time and place, and then reduced to platitudes about careful reform and careless progressives. His maxims were repeated like incantations: 'good order is the foundation of all good things'; 'manners are of more importance than laws – upon them in a great measure the law depends'; 'a state without the means for some change is without the means of its conservation'. At times, Burke really did reflect a Conservative caricature. He eulogised an eternal England. 'Four hundred years have gone over us,' he wrote in *Reflections*, 'but I believe we are not materially changed since that period. Thanks to our sullen resistance to innovation, thanks to the cold sluggishness of our national character, we still bear the stamp of our forefathers' – and he meant it as praise. He also harboured the characteristic Conservative pessimism: by the time he died, he was so afraid of a revolution in England that, according to one historian, 'he gave orders for his remains to be secretly buried, lest triumphant democrats dig them up for desecration'.[7]

But overall Burke was a bolder and more complicated thinker – both more progressive and more reactionary – than Tories like to think. He attacked the East India Company and its imperial pillaging of India and elsewhere, mocking a 'geographical morality . . . as if when you have crossed the equatorial line all the virtues die'. He defended the right of American revolutionaries to take up arms against colonial rule. He rallied against the state-mandated oppression of his fellow Irishmen, supported Catholic emancipation and laid out an early (albeit prejudiced and piecemeal) plan for abolishing slavery.[8] But despite such causes, Burke was also energised by an intense hostility towards social and economic equality – 'that monstrous fiction', as he called it. For society to function, Burke believed, people needed to know their place.

Burke's paeans to the virtues of moderation therefore sat alongside a belief in the inevitability, and even the desirability, of extreme inequality: economic, social and political. Humans were fallible creatures, and that meant that any proposed reform – to lessen poverty, say, or weaken the aristocracy – was bound to backfire. Burke saw only two agents for acceptable social change: the Lord and the laws of commerce – and they were really the same thing. It was simply not 'within the competence of Government, taken as Government', Burke wrote, 'or even of the rich, as rich, to supply to the poor, those necessaries which it has pleased the Divine Providence for a while to with-hold from them'. For Burke, the 'laws of commerce' were 'the laws of nature, and consequently the laws of God'.

In short: all inequalities between rich and poor have their reasons, and it would be foolish to intervene – the magic of the market is the only help at hand. Surrounded by suffering, poverty and inherited privilege, Burke marvelled at 'the truth, the correctness, the celerity, the general equity, with which the balance of wants is settled' by the market.

Almost 200 years later, when Thatcher championed a similar message, some cast the fervency of her style as a betrayal of Burkean Conservatism. But in fact Burke's own faith in the free market – not to mention his 'contempt for the poor' – stood out even in his own day.[9] Burke was a great fan of his contemporary Adam Smith, the grandfather of laissez-faire economics, and he described *The Wealth of Nations* as 'perhaps the most important book ever written'. Both Smith and Burke saw the market as akin to a miracle, far more intelligent than any government or group of reformers could be. 'It is by far the best policy to leave things to their natural course,' Smith advised. Burke's economic writings would only be popularised later in the twentieth century, wielded by the school of Austrian economists. Hayek, leading the charge, hailed Burke as 'one of the greatest representatives of true individualism'.

It's easy to see why, then, despite – or perhaps because of – his ambivalent political philosophy, Burke offered a fitting origin story for modern Conservatism. All the major themes of modern Conservatism are there: a celebration of both tradition and capitalism, a distrust of state intervention, an interconnected emphasis on the fallibility of human minds and the free market, a defence of inequality on the grounds of social stability, and a preference for the here-and-now over 'the fairyland of philosophy'. The infinite malleability of Burke's own thought – with different 'progressive' or 'reactionary' Burkes often summoned against each other – only makes his founding status more apt, foreshadowing the elusive, conflicting nature of Conservatism.

Conservatism likes to present itself in much the same way that Burke praised the British constitution: as a loose, uncodified accumulation of wisdom, emerging organically out of its context, prioritising stability, precedent and tradition over innovation and abstract ideas. On the rare occasions when, in books or essays, Conservatives do codify their creed, they invariably emphasise its uncodifiability. Michael Oakeshott memorably described Conservatism as 'not a creed or a doctrine, but a disposition'. Ian Gilmour, the old Tory don, agreed. 'British Conservatism,' he wrote, 'is not an "-ism".

Still less is it a system of ideas. It cannot be formulated in a series of propositions, which can be aggregated into a creed. It is not an ideology or a doctrine.'

Conservatives actively cultivate the enigmatic nature of Conservative ideology. Since one of their founding principles is a suspicion of doctrines, it follows that Conservatism itself cannot be such a doctrine. If Conservatives lay claim to any 'ism', it is realism: they see and say it like it is. The left, by comparison, are naïve, living in their conceptual castles in the sky and mistakenly believing they can bring them back down to earth. Thatcher, while allying herself with Hayek and other ideologues, felt the need to insist that her policies were 'not the panaceas of political theorists. They are ideas that have worked.' 'The facts of life do invariably turn out to be Tory,' she said. Even Hayek wanted to stress that his intellectual tradition 'is as remote from perfectionism as it is from the hurry and impatience of the passionate reformer, whose indignation about particular evils so often blinds him to the harm and injustice that the realization of his plans is likely to produce'.

Of course, every ideology likes to lay claim to 'reality', chiding opponents for failing to see what's in front of them. But the Conservatives' realist posture is particularly important to their political identity: it is on this basis that their refusal to entertain the popular hopes and dreams of their day – their steadfast opposition to calls for greater justice and equality – is performed as a lofty maturity, more caring than cruel and not in the least self-serving. 'I must see with my own eyes, I must, in a manner, touch with my own hands, not only the fixed but the momentary circumstances, before I could venture to suggest any political project whatsoever,' Burke solemnly insisted. This sentiment – the emphasis on politics as it is, rather than politics as it could be – continues to rally Conservatives. It is the concrete, rather than the imagined, that concerns them. The fact that it is also often the 'concrete' that conveniences them is irrelevant to their thinking.

When Thatcher notoriously claimed that 'there is no such thing as society', this was the Tory tradition she was tapping into. The remarks caused so much controversy that Downing Street, in a rare foray into political philosophy, ultimately had to issue a clarifying statement: '[Thatcher] prefers to think of the acts of individuals and families as the real sinews of society rather than society as an abstract concept.' Conservatives take a similar view of terms like 'welfare' or 'public spending': what's really being described, they say, is individual people's money, acquired through taxation, and this needs to be emphasised again and again. In this vein, during her leadership campaign in 2022, Liz Truss tried to do her best Thatcher impression when she reprimanded Tom Newton Dunn, a former political editor at the *Sun*, for asking her about proposed 'handouts' to help families cope with soaring energy bills: 'they are not giveaways, Tom. This is people's money . . . You're framing it in a left-wing way, Tom. I'm afraid the whole media does this all the time. It drives me mad.'

This suspicion of abstractions also underlines the Tories' opposition to concepts like 'structural' or 'institutional' racism. These concepts broadly suggest that, after centuries of racist practice and thought, tackling racism requires more than just rewording the law to create formal equality: discrimination persists through other forms of behaviour, often invisible, such as unconscious bias and social prejudices. Conservatives frequently ridicule this notion, going so far as to question whether such a thing could ever exist. In May 2021, the Conservative government commissioned a report that concluded, in the government's summary, that 'the well-meaning "idealism" of many young people who claim the country is still institutionally racist is not borne out by the evidence'. (The snooty reference towards 'idealism', contrasted to 'the evidence', was telling.) During a viral appearance on *Question Time* that October, the influential Canadian conservative psychologist-cum-philosopher Jordan Peterson went even further. He claimed that there are only racist individuals, not really 'racism' as such, a term which he put in scare quotes with his hands. 'The question is: Who, when, what, exactly – because otherwise it degenerates into something like a discussion of structural racism and when it becomes abstracted up to that level . . . that actually doesn't address the issue.'

Conservatives prefer to be guided by 'common sense' rather than such left-wing theorising. Despite being profoundly abstract, the concept of 'common sense' features prominently in the Conservative playbook. The Conservative leader William Hague spoke of a 'Common Sense Revolution' in 2001. Ten years later, as the Tories pursued austerity, David Cameron declared: 'Let this be our message – common sense for the common good.' Johnson often invoked it, even declaring that 'common sense' was the 'single greatest weapon' against the coronavirus, as opposed to scientific models or social measures. In the summer of 2020, a group of Tory backbenchers launched the 'Common Sense Group', trumpeting a new 'exclusive' finding that '84% of the public agree with the statement: "We need to restore some common sense in this country"'. Truss was once declared their 'Common Sense Champion'. In 2021, Jordon Peterson was awarded the Common Sense Society's inaugural Sir Roger Scruton Prize. Rishi Sunak described his approach as 'common sense Thatcherism' – pressing all the Tories' buttons at once. No matter how Conservatives change, their commitment to 'common sense' remains the same.

The beauty of 'common sense' is that it can mean almost anything, at the same time as it rhetorically grounds Conservative thought in the everyday. This has particular appeal to a band of politicians who rarely have much 'common' about them, a phantom thread that ties the likes of Rishi Sunak, Boris Johnson and David Cameron to the 'common man'. The concept's faux-humility and anti-intellectualism – implying that Conservatives share the views of ordinary folk without elucidating what they are – stages an imaginary consensus, to which the Tories are uniquely attuned. When the aristocrat Arthur Balfour – like Cameron and Johnson, one of Britain's twenty Old Etonian prime ministers – was asked what his guiding political principles were, he replied modestly: 'I suppose the principles of common sense.'

The prizing of common sense reveals Conservatism's populist component, which elevates instinct over expertise. 'I am beginning to believe that there is nothing so dangerous as cleverness in an administrator,' Lord Hugh Cecil, Balfour's cousin and fellow Old Etonian, asserted. According to Macmillan, another Old Etonian prime minister who received a first from Oxford, 'clever people in a nation at any given moment are nearly always wrong. Distrust the clever man.'[10] So when Michael Gove declared during the Brexit referendum campaign that the British public were tired of experts, he was not betraying the Tory tradition but continuing it. 'No lesson seems to be so deeply inculcated by the experience of life as that you should never trust experts,' Lord Salisbury, Balfour's uncle, said in 1877. 'If you believe the doctors, nothing is wholesome. If you believe the theologians, nothing is innocent. If you believe the soldiers, nothing is safe. They all require to have their strong wine diluted by a large mixture of common sense.'

But it says something about Conservatism's slipperiness as an ideology that the source of its populism also contains the seed of its elitism. When instinct is elevated over expertise, the quality of governing becomes ineffable: the keys are not hard work, training or knowledge, but something more elusive. Hence one of the most controversial components of Conservatism: the idea that some people are born to rule. 'Conservatives regard ruling as a special kind of skill, possibly arcane and certainly not universally distributed among members of the human race,' the late Conservative philosopher and free-market advocate Kenneth Minogue wrote.[11] 'It is learned by practice and example and therefore is likely to be most highly developed among members of a long-established ruling class.' In 1929, the political scientist Karl Mannheim identified the same feature of Conservative thought: 'For the political leader it is not sufficient to possess merely the correct knowledge and the mastery of certain laws and norms. In addition to these he must possess that inborn instinct, shaped through long experience, which leads him to the right answer.'[12]

Few Conservatives would speak this way today. But their commitment to the preservation, and continued elevation, of a specific ruling class is a recurring feature of Conservatism, and even now the sense of entitlement still shines through. When David Cameron was asked why he wanted to be prime minister, his response was revealing: 'Because I think I'd be good at it.' It isn't hard to imagine what might have given Cameron – a third-generation (or sixth-generation, on his mother's side) Etonian, the great-great-grandson of slave owners, with relatives and family friends in both the Conservative Party and the royal palace – that impression.

For all the talk of common sense, Conservatives aren't famous for their faith in the common man and woman to rule over their own lives. As we've already seen through their ambivalence about democratic reforms, they have historically opposed the expansion of the suffrage, conceding to such reforms usually out of expedience as they pursue power rather than out of a belief in people's worth. The premise of one-person-one-vote – with the implied nationwide equality – was antithetical to everything Conservatives stood for. Burke captured the predominant Conservative disposition towards democracy when he argued that those with unprestigious jobs – he cited hairdressers as an example – 'ought not to suffer oppression from the state; but the state suffers oppression, if such as they, either individually or collectively, are permitted to rule'.

Throughout the nineteenth century, and in many cases long after, Conservatives maintained that 'a natural aristocracy' was best placed to rule over society: apart from anything else, their lives of leisure meant that they alone had the time to consider national affairs objectively. For most workers, by contrast, as Robert Peel's home secretary, Sir James Graham, once explained, 'the lot of eating, drinking, working and dying must ever be the sum of human life'.[13] Lord Salisbury similarly reasoned that the general public were 'ordinarily engrossed by the daily necessities of self-support', and so could only attend to public affairs 'partially and fitfully'. Giving them a say in how society was run apparently wouldn't be good either for them or for society.

The notion of democracy repelled Conservatives for two interconnected reasons: first, because it denied the inherent superiority and inherited wisdom of the traditional ruling class, to the detriment of the nation's governance; second, as described, because it relied on a misguided attachment to 'equality', where every person's opinion could hypothetically count the same as another's. Disraeli believed that there was nothing more harmful to the state than 'that pernicious doctrine of modern times – the natural equality of man, a principle which, were it possible, would deteriorate the great races and destroy all the genius of the world'. (Disraeli did not hide who he meant by 'the great races', as we'll see in Chapter 5). If democrats had their way, Salisbury reasoned similarly, 'the whole community shall be governed by an ignorant multitude, the creature of a vast and powerful organization, of which a few half-taught and cunning agitators are the head . . . it means, in short, that the rich shall pay all the taxes, and the poor shall make all the laws'.

This ambivalence about democracy endures. In *The Constitution of Liberty*, Thatcher's cherished text, Hayek similarly complains of the limited horizon of workers, whose lives are 'largely a matter of fitting into a given framework'. The right to vote had no integral value in Hayek's mind; dictatorships were fine so long as they didn't last for ever. 'It is possible for a dictator to govern in a liberal way,' Hayek explained. 'And it is also possible for a democracy to govern with a total lack of liberalism. Personally, I prefer a liberal dictator to democratic government lacking liberalism.'

Twice, in 1977 and 1981, Hayek visited Chile's violent dictator Augusto Pinochet, who rose to power through a US-backed coup in 1973 and led a murderous regime, and expressed no opposition when the country's new, authoritarian constitution was named after his book. (In 1962, he also sent a copy to António de Oliveira Salazar, Portugal's dictator between 1932 and 1968, saying it might 'assist' him.) Hayek even returned from one visit to Chile imploring Thatcher to follow Pinochet's lead on the economy. The British PM was friendly with the Chilean dictator as well and, in a letter responding to Hayek, Thatcher praised Pinochet's impact – a 'remarkable success', and 'a striking example of economic reforms from which we can learn lessons' – but demurred. 'I am sure you will agree that, in Britain with our democratic institutions and need for a higher degree of consent, some of the measures adopted in Chile are quite unacceptable,' she told Hayek. 'Our reform must be in line with our traditions and our Constitution.'

Thatcher found plenty of ways within 'our traditions' to play the authoritarian. She forced through the Poll Tax, reportedly knowing that it would push poorer, Labour voters from the voting register. (When Labour suffered their surprise defeat in 1992, Thatcher reportedly quipped that 'the Poll Tax worked after all'.[14]) Under a raft of legislation, the right to strike was curtailed, the police acquired greater licence to quash demonstrations, border controls harshened, and, under Section 28 of the Local Government Act, schools were prohibited from teaching anything that gave a positive portrayal of homosexuality. She only resisted bringing back capital punishment because of the political controversy it would cause.[15] The Conservatives' more recent forays into anti-democratic territory – proroguing parliament, trying to outlaw disruptive protest, attacking the courts and pushing through voter-ID under a fictitious threat of voter fraud, clamping down on strikes even harder – are of a piece. Ultimately, the Tories' mythic reverence for 'the British people' merely disguises a deeper dislike for democracy.

On 8 May 2018, an article in the *Daily Telegraph* asked: 'Could an Army coup remove Jeremy Corbyn – just as it almost toppled Harold Wilson?' The article reassuringly explains that 'first, things would need to get pretty bad'. But one could imagine the right-wing reception if such an outcome were to have evolved. As *The Times* wrote in 1973, justifying Pinochet's overthrow of Chile's democratically elected government: 'Whether or not the armed forces were right to do what they have done, the circumstances were such that a reasonable military man could in good faith have thought it his constitutional duty to intervene.'[16] The late Roger Scruton – described by Boris Johnson as 'the greatest modern conservative thinker' – was surely correct when he wrote that 'no conservative is likely to think democracy an essential axiom of his politics'.

Clearly, Conservatism represents much more than an aversion to change: it defends hierarchies, distrusts democracy, opposes calls for greater equality and believes that a ruling class is best for society. Curiously, however, when Thatcher's guru Hayek chose to distance himself from Conservatism in the final chapter of *The Constitution of Liberty*, 'Why I'm Not a Conservative', he chose the clichéd image of Conservatism to confront: Conservatives, Hayek declared, were united only in 'a fear of change', and were destined 'to be dragged along a path not of [their] own choosing', trying, if anything, to apply brakes.

The context of Hayek's Conservative critique warrants a brief historical diversion, as it highlights the adaptable nature of Conservatism. In the decades after the Second World War, the political centre ground was very different from today. The fallout of two world wars had empowered working-class consciousness and deepened egalitarian feeling within Britain, culminating in Labour's first parliamentary majority in 1945.

A rough economic consensus took hold, based on higher taxes, some nationalised services and a strong welfare state. (The fertility of Burke's thought meant that the economist most associated with this interventionist approach, John Maynard Keynes, was another fan of his work.) Conservatives spoke of a 'middle way', reconciling free enterprise with full employment, social harmony and higher taxation. The Conservatives' 'Industrial Charter', released in 1947, was regarded as a seminal moment. While it still stuck to many familiar themes, accusing Labour of 'doctrinaire political theory' and calling for a 'sense of realism' and 'free opportunity', it also committed Conservatives to protecting workers' rights and keeping a number of industries in public ownership.

Hayek was staunchly opposed to this leftward drift. Through his work, he wanted to wake Conservatives from their slumber, to stir them into action, to restore the courage of their convictions. As he tirelessly insisted, he wasn't calling for anything new, only a return to an earlier, more traditional and more sensible political practice. Hayek spoke of 're-teaching' and 're-stating' the economics of the free market. His most important disciple, Margaret Thatcher, campaigned in much the same way. She framed her economic approach as a way of restoring 'genuine Conservatism' and insisted that it was the compromises of the mixed economy – not her faith in the free market – which represented the Tory outlier. When she came to power in 1979, she wrote to Ralph Harris, the founder of the Institute of Economic Affairs, the libertarian think-tank: 'It was primarily your foundation work which enabled us to rebuild the philosophy upon which our Party succeeded in the past.' (Harris, who launched the IEA in 1955 with Hayek's help, was one of Thatcher's first appointees to the Lords.)[17] She later scorned a BBC interviewer for referring to 'market theory'. 'No, no, no,' she said. 'The market is not a theory . . . The market is one of the oldest systems of the village.'

Thatcher's project was therefore not a revolution but a restoration. This is lost in much of the debate about whether Thatcher, or indeed Hayek, can be considered Conservative. For both of them, post-war democracy – progressive taxation, public ownership, a strong welfare state, an emphasis on equality – was the aberration, an experiment that needed to be undone. It was time to return to what works: the market's 'natural' order.

Thatcher was far from the only Conservative to see the need for such a recovery. In 1974, Keith Joseph, later Thatcher's close ally, published a book revealingly titled *Reversing the Trend*. 'In my view,' a local Conservative chairman declared in 1976, upon Thatcher's election as leader, 'this last year will eventually be seen to be one in which the Conservative party was reborn to its traditional ideology.'[18] What marked Thatcher out – and what energised many of her Conservative critics – was the depth of her conviction and the fervour with which she pursued it. But this, too, she gave a traditional spin, tracing it back to the Bible. 'I am a conviction politician,' Thatcher said in 1979, during her first election-winning campaign. 'The Old Testament prophets didn't say, "Brothers, I want a consensus." They said, "This is my faith, this is what I passionately believe. If you believe it too, then come with me."'[19]

The restorative, even nostalgic, nature of Thatcher's quest is essential to understanding one of the more contested aspects of the Conservative tradition: its radicalism. Conservatism is often pitched as the opposite of radicalism, but radicalism is permitted – even encouraged – so long as it is in pursuit of restorative ends. As the Conservative MP John Hayes put it to me, the Conservative disposition can be captured in 'the words of what I hope will by my epitaph: fierce in defence of the gentle'. By 'the gentle', Hayes meant all Britain's ancient traditions, customs and institutions that quietly endure – the antithesis of noisy innovations, new social norms and state interventions. (Hayes is one of the party's noisiest culture warriors, and reportedly a trusted adviser to Home Secretary Suella Braverman.)

What is unforgivable, in Conservative eyes, isn't dogmatism per se, but dogmatism motivated by the hope that a new, untested and usually more equal social order can be built. Dogmatism to defend or restore an old social order is another matter entirely. Conservatives have no problem with people who show rage or fanaticism in pursuit of such ends – their ranks are filled with them.

Even Edmund Burke, the Conservatives' mascot of moderation, believed that, to fight radicals, you sometimes needed to act like one. 'To destroy that enemy,' he wrote, 'the force opposed to it should be made to bear some analogy and resemblance to the force and spirit which that system exerts.' One of Burke's contemporaries, the pioneering women's rights advocate Mary Wollstonecraft, saw in the intensity of his thought a revolutionary in gentleman's clothing: 'Reading your Reflections warily over,' she wrote, 'it has continually and forcibly struck me, that had you been a Frenchman, you would have been, in spite of your respect for rank and antiquity, a violent revolutionist.'[20] The myth that true Conservatism must mean level-headed moderation is just that: a myth.

This readiness to embrace radicalism in pursuit of restoration explains why Conservatives can seem so un-Conservative, however oxymoronic that sounds: their fondness for the familiar and tradition can legitimately lead them to upturn the present, so long as they believe that familiar, cherished traditions can be protected or brought back. Brexit offered a perfect illustration of this contradiction. Like with Thatcher's economic revolution, the Brexiteers saw their destructive project as a restoration, not a revolution, reversing forty-plus years of supranational integration. The European Union was attacked as a 'failed experiment' that needed to be undone. Their cause shared nothing with the 'utopian attempt', as Thatcher once described the French Revolution, 'to overthrow a traditional order . . . in the name of abstract ideas, formulated by vain intellectuals'. The Brexiteers saw themselves fighting *against* such a utopian attempt at overthrowing the traditional order, aiming to restore the old rulers to their rightful place instead. The age of deferring to Brussels' elites was over: the time had come for Britain's old elites – the Tories – to take back control.

This is what binds Thatcher to her Brexiteer acolytes, and why they are both decidedly Conservative, despite their crusading zeal and embrace of instability. Both movements saw their task as undoing the damage of previous Conservative governments. Thatcher was concerned with those Tory PMs like Harold Macmillan and Anthony Eden who she thought had overly appeased Labour's collectivism. The Brexiteers, meanwhile, were stirred by the Heath government's decision to take Britain into what was then the European Economic Community. They shared Enoch Powell's view that, through this surrender of Britain's sovereignty in favour of something utterly unprecedented, 'the Conservative Party ceased to be the Conservative Party . . . It became an incomprehensible stranger to me.'

The point isn't that 'true' Conservatism is pro-Brexit or Thatcherite, but that they belong just as much to the

Conservative tradition as more moderate expressions. The mistake of much political commentary is to pick one element of Conservatism and stamp it as 'true' Conservatism, and dismiss the others as unruly outsiders or aberrations. But any view of Conservatism that is singular – whether singularly sensible or singularly reactionary – can only ever be partial.

The great skill of the Conservative Party has been deciding which side to show and when, fuelled by the one piece of dogma that every Conservative shares: the conviction that Conservatives must hold on to as much power as they can. Sometimes, the task demands moderation; in other moments, it requires radicalism. This strategic dimension makes it difficult to distinguish sincere Conservative beliefs from cynical appropriations, earnest changes of heart from cunning sleights of hand, unshakeable principles from forced manoeuvres. Do Conservatives really loathe all political theories and idealism, for example, or is this merely a lofty tactic for discrediting particular political theories – specifically, those calling for a more equal society – and preventing them from becoming a reality? Are Conservatives really so convinced that society cannot be planned along fairer lines, or do they just not like the sound of a fairer society? Was post-war Conservatism anything more than a tactic to hold on to power? According to the former Tory chancellor Rab Butler, one of the key figures in establishing the so-called 'post-war consensus', the party's mission was 'to maintain the old order by appeasing and accommodating the progressive forces which threaten it'. Quintin Hogg, another of the Middle Way's architects, reasoned similarly: 'If you do not give the people social reform,' he warned, 'they are going to give you social revolution.'[21]

Even amid blatant displays of duplicity, however, there is no doubting that many Conservatives believe that their ideology is best for others, not only themselves. Salisbury sought to dispel, as he wrote privately, 'this absurd delusion that the dislike of democracy entertained by the Tory party means indifference to the welfare of the poor'. More recently, Lord Hannan has put the same point in a pithy joke: '"You Tories hate poor people!" Yup: we want to turn them all into rich people.'[22] Conservatives simply maintain that society is no saviour: only individual acts of generosity, along with the magic of the market, can offer reprieve. Writing during a famine in England, Burke insisted that private charity – 'a direct and obligatory duty upon all Christians' – was the only solution to people starving. Government, he said, 'can do very little positive good in this, or perhaps in anything else'.[23] This lack of faith in government to help remains at the heart of Conservatism. Only from this viewpoint could Conservative MP Jacob Rees-Mogg refer to the record-breaking number of new food banks in 2017 as 'rather uplifting': it was a sign that communities were clubbing together without relying on the state, and 'shows what a good, compassionate country we are'. Rees-Mogg didn't dwell on what the *need* for such food banks – which rose from 40,000 users in 2009–10 to more than 2.56 million by 2021[24] – said about the efficacy, or compassion, of Conservative economic policy.

And yet the Conservatives' faith in the free market to lift living standards remains all but total. They are adamant that the left's plans to redistribute wealth are not just misguided, but actively harmful, breeding dependency and bad habits, taking away the sense of personal responsibility and agency that makes life meaningful. Regardless of whether the Conservative approach is more or less effective in tackling poverty – given the dramatic spikes in child poverty and food bank use since 2010, the evidence suggests that it is far less so – it is clear that the rhetoric of personal responsibility resonates with people. The popular appeal of Conservatism, based largely on a mix of personal responsibility, patriotism and promises of prosperity, will be discussed later.

But if most Conservatives claim to be concerned by poverty, few if any would say the same about equality. This is perhaps the central pillar of Conservative ideology. Conservatives are not just unfazed by inequality, they are often active fans of it, arguing that inequality is the engine through which societies progress. 'This is the essence of the Conservative party's role – to formulate policy that conserves a hierarchy of wealth and power and to make this intelligible and reasonable to a democracy,' the social scientists Philip Norton and Arthur Aughey wrote in *Conservatives and Conservatism*, published in 1981. Resisting the redistribution of wealth is one of the few constants of the Conservative creed, the common thread that runs from Edmund Burke to Boris Johnson, and onwards to Liz Truss (who began – or perhaps ended – her prime ministership with a defence of bankers' bonuses) and Rishi Sunak. Even their acceptance of nationalised services, higher taxes and greater public spending after the war was motivated by the premise that anything less would put Labour in power, and therefore lead to *even more* nationalised services, *even more* taxes and *even more* public spending. Even when the Conservatives are redistributing wealth, they are resisting it.

This attachment to hierarchy, along with the insistence that inequality benefits those at the bottom, retains a strong grip on the Conservative psyche. 'The whole purpose' of the party, the veteran Tory journalist Peregrine Worsthorne once declared, is 'to translate the idea of aristocratic rule into terms which make sense in a democracy, which means organising mass support for what is basically an elitist or paternalist system of government'.[25] The notion of wealth redistribution is a rebuttal of this fundamental principle and is a source of constant panic and hyperbole. During the 1945 campaign, Churchill claimed that a Labour government would require a 'Gestapo' to implement its welfare policies. A year later, the supposedly more moderate Macmillan declared that 'the great dividing line is between those who believe in the prime socialist dogma, and those who see in such a development the grim nightmare of the totalitarian state'. In 2019, Boris Johnson was still attacking Labour along the same lines.[26] 'They pretend that their hatred is directed only at certain billionaires – and they point their fingers at individuals with a relish and a vindictiveness not seen since Stalin persecuted the kulaks.'

The Conservatives' foundational opposition to wealth redistribution supposedly stems from their conviction that grand plans for reform are doomed to disappoint. Old elites, interests and institutions are defended not so much on their own merits, but, rather, on the impossibility of improving upon them. Conservatives reserve a special ire for those who promise a fairer society, only to end up in guillotines and gulags, and can't resist placing every progressive policy suggestion in this frame: the road to serfdom is always one step to the left away. One might question the integrity of this ire: if any challenge to the elite's power and wealth is deemed too dangerous to entertain, it certainly aligns kindly with the interests of the powerful. But the difficulty of disentangling ideology from strategy is itself a defining aspect of Conservatism. Strategy and ideology stem from a single ambition that runs through the Conservatives' history: safeguarding the ascendancy, legitimacy and property of Britain's elites.

3

RULING BRITANNIA: AN ENDURING, EVOLVING ELITE

'The Tories in England long imagined that they were enthusiastic about monarchy, the church, and the beauties of the old English Constitution, until the day of danger wrung from them the confession that they are enthusiastic only about ground rent.'

Karl Marx, in *The Eighteenth Brumaire of Louis Bonaparte*, 1852

'The great Unionist Party should still control, whether in power or in opposition, the destinies of this great Empire.'

Arthur Balfour, Conservative PM, a speech, 1906

'If I have any more trouble from this fucking stupid, petit-bourgeois woman, I'm going to go.'

Lord Carrington, foreign secretary, on Margaret Thatcher, sometime between 1979 and 1982

In October 1963, as Prime Minister Harold Macmillan announced his resignation, a panel of ten Tory grandees met to decide his successor. They chose a leader in their image: an Old Etonian, like nine of the ten present, and an aristocrat, as antiquated as the selection process itself. Sir Alec Douglas-Home, or the 14th Earl of Home, seemed like a relic of the nineteenth century – and for many Tories that was the essence of his appeal. 'Lord Home is clearly a man who represents the old governing class at its best,' Macmillan informed the Queen, 'and those who take a reasonably impartial view of English history know how good that can be.'

Home, aged sixty, had a gilded lineage: twenty years in the Commons, a few years as foreign secretary and over a decade in the Lords, moving there in 1951 after inheriting his father's ancient title and castle, where his ancestors had resided over four centuries. The fact that such a figure still existed in the upper echelons of British society was itself remarkable: elsewhere, waves of democratic change, war and imperial invasion had displaced old elites and swept away aristocratic power and influence. But the fact that such a figure could still rise, unelected, to become British prime minister was absurd. Home's appointment seemed more befitting of a pope than a prime minister: a plume of white smoke may as well have risen into the air as the 14th Earl of Home, handpicked by ten people, was declared the leader of Britain's venerable democracy.

But for Conservatives this ritual was business as usual. Six of Home's seven predecessors as Conservative leader had similarly become prime minister without contesting either a leadership election or a general election. The Conservatives preferred to pass on the keys to Downing Street like a grandfather's watch or an old family farm, as if the prime ministership was the natural inheritance of any Conservative leader. The electorate could then grant their democratic approval later on, once the chosen one had already acquired the authority of office.

The Conservative Party has always been somewhat of a family affair: From Robert Peel to Sir Alec Douglas-Home,

1830 to 1965, nine out of the Conservatives' twelve leaders were either the son or son-in-law of a Conservative politician. In the 1930s, the Conservative Party was still nicknamed 'the cousinhood' because so many of its MPs were related. About a third of its 429 members of parliament could be placed on the same family tree, and two in every five belonged to the aristocracy.[1] Certain family names and titles recur with particular prominence: the Cecils (or Salisburys), Derbys and Devonshires. In 1960, no fewer than nineteen members of the Cecil family sat in parliament.[2] Family ties are traditionally worn like a badge of honour, proof that one belongs in the party. In 1902, Lord Robert Salisbury passed the prime ministership on to his nephew Arthur Balfour, who in cabinet meetings referred to his predecessor simply as 'uncle' (hence the expression 'Bob's your uncle'). Winston Churchill's father, Lord Randolph, was an influential Conservative politician and a one-time favourite to be party leader; his grandfather was the 7th Duke of Marlborough, another Conservative minister whose father and grandfather were Tory MPs, too. Churchill's successor, Anthony Eden, was married to Churchill's niece. Eden's replacement, Harold Macmillan, was son-in-law of the 9th Duke of Devonshire. Macmillan's government amiably included seven of the duke's relatives.

Even more than his predecessors, however, Home signalled a level of ruling-class continuity that set him apart. His lineage went way back. His great-grandfather had served in the Duke of Wellington's Tory cabinet, between 1828 and 1830, shortly before Peel launched the modern Conservative Party. 'All that I hope for,' the Duke of Wellington had declared at the time, 'is that the change in the position of the country may be gradual, that it may be effected without civil war, and may occasion as little sudden destruction of individual interests and property as possible.'[3] By putting the 14th Earl of Home in Number 10, the great-grandson of one of the duke's cabinet members, Conservatives could say that they had delivered Wellington's wish: the old guard was still in charge, their property and interests more or less intact. No doubt much had changed since Wellington's time: the expansion of democracy, the dissolution of Empire, the decline of Britain on the world stage, industrial and technological transformation, the rise of the working class. But with Home at the helm, Britain's past and present were tied together in a neat bow: the nation was the same as it ever was.

This fantasy of ruling-class permanence proved fleeting. In the 1964 general election, after only 363 days in office, Home suffered a narrow defeat to Labour. He became Britain's most short-lived prime minister since the eighteenth century, and only the second Conservative leader – after Arthur Balfour, at the start of the century – to contest a general election and not win at least once. When Home, in his parting act in early 1965, also introduced formal elections to appoint future party leaders, he also became the last Conservative leader not to be elected by his party, neither by MPs nor the membership. Many assumed that the Conservatives would never see the likes of Home again. In an age of television and mass suffrage, after all, what sensible party would elect an Old Etonian like Home to represent them? Home, far from embodying the English gentleman's eternal rule, now looked instead like the last gasp of the old governing class.

The next forty years appeared to confirm this hypothesis. Whereas Home's three predecessors all had ties to the landed gentry and public-school educations – Churchill, Eden and Macmillan, an Old Harrovian and two Old Etonians respectively – his three successors were from more modest backgrounds:

Ted Heath, Margaret Thatcher and John Major, none of whom was privately educated. In 1990, when Douglas Hurd ran for the leadership, he even complained that his Eton education and landed background now ruled him out, making him a pariah in his own party. 'This is inverted snobbery,' he declared during his leadership campaign, exasperated.[4] 'I thought I was running for leader of the Conservative Party, not some demented Marxist sect.' In the *Spectator*, the journalist Geoffrey Wheatcroft mourned 'The End of the Etonians'.[5]

In Tory Britain, however, time moves forward and back, and most obituaries are premature. Any influential institution, custom or class – especially one with ties to the Conservative Party – never really goes away. Even when the public school-boys were in retreat, they still held on to positions of influence. No fewer than sixty-one Old Etonians served as ministers in the Thatcher and Major governments, consistent with the tally in the 1950s and 1960s. Three of Thatcher's five foreign secretaries went to Eton. Her chief policy adviser between 1982 and 1983 was Ferdinand Mount, otherwise known as the 3rd Baronet Mount: his grandfather, great-grandfather and great-great-grandfather were all Old Etonian Tory politicians. The party was still in safe hands.

More recently, the old governing class has resumed the reins. Since 2005, two of the last four Conservative leaders have been Old Etonians – first David Cameron and then Boris Johnson. Both are distant relatives of the royal family. Cameron's extended family tree includes dukes, viscounts, and old Tory grandees – Ferdinand Mount is one of Cameron's cousins while another Cameron relative, Duff Cooper, was a minister in Churchill's government. In 2015, the Conservatives' winning election manifesto was overseen by six people – five of them Old Etonians. Even rivals for the Conservative leadership have tended to come from the same circles. Current chancellor Jeremy Hunt, who fought and lost against Johnson for the leadership in 2019, is another public schoolboy, the fifth cousin of Queen Elizabeth II and a descendant of Sir Streynsham Master, who played a pivotal role in colonising India in the seventeenth century.

The Conservative elite is more diverse than it once was. Etonians intermingle with state-schoolers; the landed gentry hold hands with bankers, the bourgeoisie and the nouveaux riches; the progeny of the Empire's rulers now sit side by side with the progeny of its liberated subjects. The number of Old Etonian MPs is down to eleven – less than a tenth of what it was a hundred years ago (although in the House of Lords, Britain's unelected second chamber, there are still more than eighty). But even as the Conservatives adopt new faces, accents and affectations, adapting to the realities of modern Britain, the party's old elitist roots endure, grounding its agenda, guiding its policy and ensuring a level of ruling class continuity for which Britain is rightly famous.

British conservatism may praise itself for an adaptable nature – a thought and practice rooted not in ideology but in pragmatism, tradition and 'common sense' – but beneath the veneer of amenable moderation, the Conservative Party's aims have been clear and constant: maintaining power, resisting the redistribution of wealth and safeguarding the legitimacy – the ascendancy – of the nation's elites. Unlike other countries, Britain has witnessed no revolution or serious political rupture in its modern history. Old elites are not overthrown but absorbed – above all, into the Conservative Party.

Perhaps nowhere else in the world have traditional elites endured and evolved with such stability. Whereas most other countries relaunched and refreshed their political systems after crises – wars, invasions, revolutions, civil war, independence – Britain's comparatively peaceful history has invited no such opportunity. Even the protracted English Revolution in the seventeenth century – which saw Kings Charles I beheaded, a military dictatorship and religious strife – was remarkable for the lack of lasting change it produced: the Crown returned to parliament, the one fortifying the other. It was, in the words of the historian Perry Anderson, 'the most tepid bourgeois revolution of any major European country': 'it left almost the entire social structure intact'.[6]

There have been great winds of change and tremors of upheaval since then – the Industrial Revolution, Ireland's secession in 1922, the advent of mass suffrage, the rise of the Labour Party, the end of Empire, entry into and exit from the European Union – but, usually under the direction of the Conservative Party, Britain's political system has survived them all. The result is that the ancient foundations of British politics – the monarchy, House of Lords, Established Church, uncodified constitution, public schools, the Conservative Party itself – still stand.

These foundations have, through their sheer staying power, woven themselves into the nation's identity. Brits are encouraged to take pride in the agedness of their institutions, to see themselves in the pomp and ceremony of the monarchy and the Lords. They are championed as endearing collective symbols, revealing a quiet, private (if also world-conquering) people, wisely cautious of extremes, adverse to drastic changes, avoiding the violence of revolution witnessed elsewhere. In this framing, Britain's historical evolution and the continuity of the ruling class takes on a democratic bent: it's what the British people wanted, regardless of whether they could vote.

The more plausible explanation behind Britain's historical trajectory is both cynical and impressive: the ruling classes' remarkable adeptness at preserving their interests and changing with the times. The French Revolution in 1789 was an illustrative moment. Whereas the old establishment's overthrow in France inspired many similarly spirited movements in neighbouring countries, in Britain the nation's leaders sought to ensure that upheaval abroad only reinforced the status quo at home. Whether Whig or Tory, aristocrat or merchant, duke or industrialist, Britain's expanding elite watched in horror at the events unfolding in France and then held hands out of fright: 'The sufferings of the Royal Family, the debasement of the nobles, the confiscation of the property of the rich, the persecution of the clergy, the national bankruptcy, and all the various evils which it produced,' as the diplomat Sir Samuel Romilly recounted in 1840, united 'almost every description of persons who have any influence on public opinion.'[7]

In *Conservative Parties and the Birth of Democracy*, the Harvard political scientist Daniel Ziblatt explores why a few countries like Britain avoided revolution in the modern era when so many other European countries succumbed. He settles on a surprising factor: a strong, capable and capacious Conservative Party, which Ziblatt defines as any party with traditional ruling class ties. 'Conservatives [especially, but not exclusively, in Britain] discovered the mobilizing power of modern political parties, which allowed them to protect their own interests,' he writes, 'in turn ironically smoothing the way for a more stable path of democratization.'

The theory seems, on one level, counterintuitive. We tend to see the threats to the status quo as coming from the left, those impassioned revolutionaries who want to overthrow the old order for a fairer, more equal society, unconcerned by

76

the damage they might cause. But armed with a vast array of evidence, Ziblatt shows that, on the contrary, the most de-stabilising forces in a society often come from the right. Unlike the left, the right usually includes the wealthiest players in a society, who have more weight to throw around when they don't get their way. When members of a privileged class sense that their ascendancy is threatened, they can act rashly, some-times mutinously, to take back or reinforce their control. A powerful Conservative Party assuages these fears, empowering the ruling classes to play the democratic game and paving the way for a peaceful democratic evolution.

For Ziblatt, no other party adapted to the modern era so well or enabled the continued rule of the old governing class so successfully. While British society and the world transformed across the nineteenth and twentieth centuries, the landowning classes continued to dominate the upper reaches of British society to an extent unseen anywhere else: in parliament, cabinet, the civil service, the army and the Established Church (nicknamed 'the Tory party at prayer'). Even as Britain expanded its imperial might across the world, enfranchised workers at home and revolutionised its economy, this stayed the same. By 1900, Britain was the largest importer and exporter of goods globally, boasting both the first industrialised economy and the largest empire in history. But somehow this globetrotting, industrial powerhouse was still embodied by the English gentleman, quietly residing in his country estate, watching the world go by – a buccaneering spirit offset by the aristocratic poise of effortless superiority; crude modernity, violent impe-rialism and unshakeable good manners, rolled into one.

The English gentleman still feared for his future. 'The mists of mere political theory are clearing away,' Salisbury wrote as the nineteenth century drew to a close, describing the

77

struggle for democracy as 'a struggle between those who have, to keep what they have got, and those who have not, to get it'. At times, various social movements of the marginalised represented perilous threats to the status quo, and were often pathbreaking in their scale and strategy: the Chartists in the 1830s and 1840s, fighting for universal suffrage; the rise of the trade union movement across the nineteenth century, battling for better pay and working conditions; and the suffragettes' militant campaign to enfranchise women at the start of the twentieth century. But the Conservatives ultimately outlived each threat, somehow conceding and consolidating their power simultaneously. They understood that no social order was permanent. The trick for Conservatives was to change society's shape – through guile and occasional good luck – while keeping the fundamental structures of wealth and power in place. 'We have not got democratic government today,' Anthony Eden, future Conservative prime minister, declared in 1928, as a Conservative-led reform granted all adult women the vote. 'We have never had it and I venture to suggest . . . that we shall never have it. What we have done in all progress of reform and evolution is to broaden the basis of oligarchy.'[8]

The continued advance and stability of the old ruling class in Britain is perhaps best captured by the persistence of three influential institutions: the monarchy, the House of Lords and public schools. Both the royal family and Britain's second chamber in particular go against the grain of modern democracy: they are twin symbols of hereditary rule and ancient hierarchy, commanding power, influence and prestige unelected, their origins obscured by the mists of time. They are also quintessentially British and represent an ideal of the Tory Nation:

at once entwined with ruling-class interests and claiming to rise above them, standing as treasured institutions that resist reform while other, more modern innovations rise and fall.

Loyalty to the monarchy lies at the very foundation of Conservatism. In the eighteenth century, the word 'Tory' referred to those who, during the English Civil War, defended the Duke of York's right to inherit the throne, while their opponents – later the 'Whigs' – maintained that the duke's Catholic faith ruled him out. A century later, when Edmund Burke agonised over the French Revolution, it was the execution of France's royal family – and in particular Marie Antoinette – that moved him more than anything else. 'The age of chivalry is gone,' Burke wrote after the Queen of France had met her end at the guillotine. 'The glory of Europe is extinguished forever. Never, never more, shall we behold that generous loyalty to rank and sex, that proud submission, that dignified obedience, that subordination of the heart, which kept alive, even in servitude itself, the spirit of an exalted freedom!'[9]

It's easy to see why a monarchy appeals to Conservative sentiments: a royal family provides a seductive illusion of permanence, lending the status quo a sacred glow. Both royals and Tories relish it. 'The existence of the Crown serves to disguise change and therefore to deprive it of the evil consequences of revolution,' Prince George observed in 1894, before he became king.[10] 'There is no doubt in my mind that . . . monarchy is the most reasonable form of government,' Roger Scruton wrote in *The Meaning of Conservatism*, over a hundred years later.

Over the course of modern British history, the royal family has done much more than merely embody a Tory ideal, however: it has also, on many occasions, actively worked to support the Conservative cause, whether in opposing the rise of democracy or resisting Irish Home Rule. In the 1880s, as the enfranchisement of the working class loomed, Queen Victoria declared that she 'cannot and will not be the Queen of a democratic monarchy', and was infamously frosty with the Liberal PM William Gladstone, who was driving the suffrage reform.[11] Later, in the 1910s, when a Liberal government was trying to push through Irish Home Rule and George V had succeeded Queen Victoria, the Palace corresponded with the Conservatives about ways to obstruct the Liberals. As the Oxford historian Iain McLean notes drily: 'The constitutional implications of a letter from the King's secretary to the leader of the Opposition, advising him how best to resist His Majesty's Government, are interesting.'[12]

These aren't isolated incidents. Members of the Palace have frequently sought to intervene in favour of the Conservatives. In the 1960s, a planned coup d'état against the Labour prime minister Harold Wilson involved at least one royal, Prince Philip's uncle Lord Mountbatten, along with members of the secret services, the army and the media – another three pillars of the establishment that, like the royal family, lean Tory. Mountbatten dreamed of bringing Empire's rule back home.[13] The former intelligence officer Brian Crozier admitted to lobbying the army against Wilson, stating that they 'seriously considered the possibility of a military takeover'. 'This was the British Watergate, a conspiracy designed to pervert the democratic choice of the people,' the journalist Jonathan Freedland wrote in 2006.[14] But further details are scant, and save for an episode in the hit Netflix series *The Crown*, which only served to reinforce the monarchy's standing as democracy's great defender, the scandal is largely forgotten.

One final example, less scandalous but perhaps the most

emblematic of them all: on 15 June 1988, the Palace made a call to Conservative Central Office to tell them that a young man who was interviewing for a job there had their backing. 'I understand that you are to see David Cameron,' the anonymous caller from the Palace said. 'I've tried everything I can to dissuade him from wasting his time on politics, but I have failed. You are about to meet a truly remarkable young man.' The identity of the caller remains unknown, complicated by the sheer number of possible candidates, such are Cameron's connections to the Palace. One of Cameron's referees for the job was family friend Sir Brian McGrath, then private secretary to Prince Philip. Another friend was Captain Sir Alastair Aird, then comptroller to the Queen, whose wife is Cameron's godmother. (Both denied making the call.)[15]

In any case, the call came, and the Conservatives heeded the advice. Cameron went on to lead the party and the country. There's little doubt he thought that he delivered on the Palace's faith in him, especially by safeguarding the Union from Scotland's independence movement during the 2014 referendum. 'The definition of relief is being prime minister of the United Kingdom and ringing the Queen saying: "It's alright, it's OK,"' Cameron boasted to another world leader, unaware he was being filmed, after Scotland narrowly voted to remain part of the Union. 'She purred down the line.'[16]

The House of Lords has arguably played an even more important role than the monarchy in ensuring the steady evolution of Britain's ruling classes. The Tories have enjoyed a default majority in the Lords for most of Britain's modern history, helping to soothe fears about democracy – they could be safe in the knowledge that, even in defeat, at least one of the two chambers remained theirs. The Conservative leader Arthur

Balfour had this in mind when, as the Liberals swept to victory in 1906, he notoriously declared: 'The great [Conservative] Unionist Party should still control, whether in power or in opposition, the destinies of this great Empire.'

The Conservatives controlled the Lords for almost the entire nineteenth and twentieth centuries, along with a majority of the twenty-first. Even in the absence of a popular mandate, they haven't been afraid to wield their power. After the Liberal landslide of 1906, the Lords became the old governing class's last line of defence: whereas in the democratically elected Commons the Liberals had more than double the Tories' number of seats, in the unelected Lords the Tories boasted almost five times as many.[17] The Lords sought to obstruct the government in ways that were previously unthinkable, rebuffing one Liberal bill after another, breaking centuries of precedent and supposedly sacrosanct custom, causing political disarray. In 1912, as Conservatives became increasingly agitated by plans for Irish Home Rule, the *Economist* noted the party's growing revolutionary spirit: 'We cannot escape from the one outstanding and extraordinary fact – that the leader of the Conservative party has definitely and repeatedly encouraged the outbreak of civil war.'

A series of reforms followed the Conservatives' attempts to impede the Liberals' popular mandate, limiting the Lords' powers, monitoring the appointment of new peers, introducing life peerages alongside hereditary ones and allowing women to sit in the chamber. But it remained a pillar of Conservative power. During the Labour government of 1974–9, for example, the House of Lords voted down Labour legislation more than 300 times. Under Thatcher, by contrast, it inflicted 156 defeats in eleven years – half the tally in twice the time.[18]

In 2006, Tony Blair became the first prime minister in over 200 years to prise the Lords from the Tories' grip. It required the largest reform to the second chamber in its history. Labour's election-winning manifesto in 1997 had promised to replace hereditary peers with life peers. Within ten years, Blair had transformed its make-up to reflect Labour's majority in the Commons – but it didn't last long. After resuming power in 2010, the Conservatives worked quickly to correct this historical anomaly. They created over a hundred new peers, regaining their majority in 2015. With almost 800 members in total, and no cap on its size, the Lords is now the second largest legislative chamber in the world, behind only China's National People's Congress, and more than seven times the size of the US Senate (while representing about a fifth of the population). The Lords also still affords automatic seats in parliament to religious clerics, making Britain the only country to do so besides the Islamic Republic of Iran. It remains entirely unelected.

Blair didn't even succeed in banishing all the hereditary peers. His plan faced one familiar force in the Tory Nation: the Salisbury family. The Conservative peers, led by Viscount Cranborne (great-great-grandson of Prime Minister Lord Salisbury), threatened Blair's team with constitutional mayhem if he removed all the hereditaries. 'My whole tactic was to make their flesh creep,' Cranborne recalled in 2021. 'I threatened them with the Somme and Passchendaele. I didn't mean it – it would have been a constitutional outrage. But I said it.'[19] In the end, thanks to Cranborne's work, the House of Lords Act of 1999 permitted almost a hundred hereditary peers to remain in the Lords on 'a temporary basis'. (The 15th Earl of Home, who became chairman of Coutts & Co. and the Queen's banker, was among them.) Eighty-five are

83

still there now, in the heart of Britain's democracy, owning a collective 170,000 acres between them; thirty-nine of them are Old Etonians.[20]

The Lords stands within British politics as an enduring monument to the resilience of the old governing class. Even now, the way in which powerful people are given peerages – as if wealth and influence alone entitled someone to rule the country, no need for an election – ensures that the spirit of the aristocracy survives. The introduction of appointments-for-life simply facilitated an old habit of Britain's elite: absorbing influential outsiders into the fray. Unlike in many other countries, Britain's aristocracy was never just a matter of inheritance and marriage: any worthy outsider could be ennobled, letting them play the part of the aristocrat. 'We say to any man of any rank, get enormously rich, make immense fees as a lawyer, or great speeches, or distinguish yourself and win battles – and you, even you, shall come into the privileged class, and your children shall reign naturally over ours,' the satirist William Makepeace Thackeray wrote in *The Book of Snobs*, published in 1848.

In this way, the Lords allowed the Conservatives' power not just to endure, but to evolve, broadening the make-up of the party's ruling class base to move with the times. As the forms of wealth and influence transformed, peerages were handed out to pacify potential usurpers. Whereas elsewhere in Europe the rising bourgeoisie often sought to displace the aristocracy, in Britain they dreamed only of joining in. 'There is this difference between the revolutions of England and the revolutions of the Continent,' Disraeli declared in *The Spirit of Whiggism*, published in 1836. 'The European revolution is a struggle against privilege; an English revolution is a struggle for it.' By the end of the nineteenth century, the historian David Edgerton writes, 'there was hardly a major businessman who was not ennobled'.[21]

Together, the old and new elites formed a mish-mash family, united by ties of blood, love, education, money and self-interest: the ancient peers and the parvenus, the aristocrats and the arrivistes, the dukes and the industrialists, the Marquesses of Salisbury and, 'Maggie' (later Baroness) Thatcher. Often channelled through the Conservatives, they fortified the status quo with their support, and received all its trappings in return: estates, peerages, class deference. In a famous passage from *The Lion and the Unicorn*, George Orwell pithily summarised this fusion:

> After 1832 the old land-owning aristocracy steadily lost power, but instead of disappearing or becoming a fossil they simply intermarried with the merchants, manufacturers and financiers who had replaced them, and soon turned them into accurate copies of themselves. The wealthy ship-owner or cotton-miller set up for himself an alibi as a country gentleman, while his sons learned the right mannerisms at public schools which had been designed for just that purpose.

Like the Lords, as Orwell writes, Britain's public schools provided another setting for old and new elites to intermingle, binding them around a common set of values and beliefs and cultivating a shared sense of superiority. So as Britain's ruling class diversified, the classrooms of elite boarding schools did, too, welcoming in the 'sons of the gentry and upper bourgeoisie alike'.[22]

Eton in particular has persisted almost like an aristocracy

in itself: reforming to preserve, broadening its elite criteria but remaining fundamentally elitist. Like the monarchy and the Lords, Eton stages the fantasy of an eternal England. The grounds and uniforms hark back to a bygone era. The tailcoats, waistcoats and stiff collars, set against a backdrop of spires, cricket fields and chapels, collectively suggest that, in some fundamental sense, the old English gentleman is still alive and well. This is partly why, in Conservative circles, the internal politics of Eton – its headmaster, curriculum, student body, plans for expansion and the like – is still closely monitored: the future of the Tory Nation remains, symbolically at least, in the school's hands.

Only the University of Oxford can boast a more illustrious alumni, but of its thirty prime ministers since 1721 (more than half the total sum), a public school education is the common denominator for two-thirds of them. 'The Tory public schoolboys arrived at Oxford almost fully formed,' the journalist Simon Kuper writes in *Chums: How a Tiny Caste of Oxford Tories Took Over the UK*. 'School had given them the confidence, articulacy and know-how to bestride the university . . . They didn't spend university trying on new accents and personas; they already knew what they wanted to be when they grew up. They were climbing the greasy pole before most students had even located it.'[23]

The public school system's dominance over Britain has suffered setbacks. Like the Conservative Party, it is no longer such a family affair. In 1960, three students out of every five at Eton were the sons of alumni. Even in 1980, it was two out of every five. Now, it is about a fifth.[24] The presence of the public schools in parliament has also diminished markedly. In 1997, for the first time in modern British history, Harrow didn't count a single former pupil in the Commons. Eton endured its own humbling a decade later: in 2007, Gordon Brown put together the first and, to date, only British government not to count a single Old Etonian among its ranks.

But more recently, in the highest echelons of British politics, Etonians have been everywhere again – not only in Number 10 (first with Cameron and then Johnson), but beyond: the school's alumni include Kwasi Kwarteng; Jacob Rees-Mogg; the Conservative Party's chief fundraiser, Ben Elliot (the Duchess of Cornwall's nephew); former chief of the general staff, General Sir Mark Carleton-Smith; the Archbishop of Canterbury, Justin Welby; and Britain's future king, Prince William. A study in 2020 of *Who's Who*, the guide to Britain's political and cultural elite, found Eton had more alumni listed among the 5,238 names than the next four schools combined: Winchester College, Harrow School, Westminster School and Marlborough College.[25] The 'End of the Etonians', as declared by Geoffrey Wheatcroft two decades ago, seems some way off.

In a way, Britain really is still trapped in the fourteenth century: some 700 years later, it remains a place with sirs and dames, hereditary peers, earls and countesses, barons and baronesses, marquesses and marchionesses, dukes and duchesses, and even a royal family; its citizens are still, officially, subjects; the monarch is still, officially, sovereign. These anachronisms are more than just theatre. About half the land in England is owned by less than 1 per cent of the population, with a small set of old aristocratic families accounting for a third of it – often the same names that held the land several centuries ago.[26]

The untroubled advance of the Devonshires is illustrative. One of the oldest, wealthiest and most influential families in British history, they have, from the fourteenth century onwards, rarely strayed too far from the corridors of power. Even in 2022, the 12th Duke of Devonshire, Peregrine Cavendish, who attended Eton and resides in a 300-room mansion, featured on the *Sunday Times Rich List* with a net worth of £900 million. (Most family histories begin with Sir John Cavendish, a politician who met his end in 1381 during the Peasants' Revolt, a violent uprising by farmhands against serfdom and rising taxes. Sir John Cavendish's house and wine cellar were ransacked. He was dragged through the market square by a mob and then beheaded. Surely no one could have imagined back then – neither Cavendish nor his killers – that his relatives would still be wielding such wealth and influence more than half a millennia later.)

The antiquated conventions and institutions of British politics – at once amenable to newcomers and impervious to them – bear the same imprint, and almost seem designed to charm radical ambition into submission, serving as a constant reminder of how very old and precious Britain is. The UK has been unchanged for centuries, the Houses of Parliament seem to say, so why would you think that you can change it? The sheer longevity of Britain's political and social order becomes self-reinforcing, both weakening the ambitions of outsiders and emboldening its defenders, framing the fight for the Tory Nation as a fight for tradition.

Even now, parliament remains a peculiar portal into aristocratic life, where every politician, regardless of their background, is referred to as 'the honourable member' in the chamber, to 'maintain the dignity of the house', in the argot of the Commons; the tenor of debate is governed by strict rules of politeness and etiquette and transgressions are rigorously punished. (In July 2022, Labour MP Dawn Butler was expelled from the chamber for simply stating that Johnson 'lied to the

House and the country over and over again'.) The vast staff
dotted around the chambers, organised into obscure hierarchies, are adorned in the elaborate uniform of butlers and
palace officials. Those in charge of security and ceremony are
called 'doorkeepers', the origins of which stretch back to the
1300s, with a dress code of black tailcoats, white bow ties and
an intricate golden 'waist badge'. A mace sits at the centre of
the Commons: a symbol of royal authority at the heart of
Britain's democracy. Who could not be seduced by such a
spectacle? So well-ordered, so well-mannered, so eternal. The
fact that every prime minister also receives the keys to
Chequers, their own country manor, further ensures that every
British PM immediately acquires an aristocratic way of life.

The rise of Margaret Thatcher – a grammar school girl,
born above her father's corner shop in Grantham, Middle
England – was supposed to change all this. She seemed to
represent a fatal blow to the old governing class, marking an
irreversible shift in British society: the eclipse of the aristocracy by the forces of meritocracy. She was only the second
Conservative leader elected by the party, and the first woman
to lead the country. 'I believe in merit,' Thatcher declared.
'I don't care two hoots what your background is. What I'm
concerned with is whatever your background, you have a
chance to climb to the top.'

Thatcher's un-aristocratic origins weren't always obvious.
She painfully learned the patois and plummy vowels of the
upper classes: her acquired 'RP', or received pronunciation,
was the accent of only about 2 per cent of Brits, and suggested
power and a public school education. She married upwards:
'Major [Denis] Thatcher, who has a flat in London (age about
36, plenty of money) . . .', was how she first introduced her
future husband to her sister in a letter. 'As one would expect

he is a perfect gentleman. Not a very attractive creature – very reserved but quite nice.'[27]

In the end, Thatcher's adopted persona gave a greater clue to her politics than her humble roots. Under her leadership, Britain did not witness a new era of equality or meritocracy, but, rather, a reinvigorated ruling class and a revitalised defence of inherited privilege. A full 91 per cent of her cabinet were privately educated. As she slashed taxes on the rich, inequality soared. Corporate tax fell from 52 to 34 per cent by 1990. She halved the top rate of income tax from 83 to 40 per cent. By 1997, the post-tax income of Britain's wealthiest top 10 per cent was ten times as much as that of the bottom 10 per cent – in 1979, when Thatcher had taken over, it was five times as high.[28] Some spoke of an economic miracle but, while national GDP rose, the miracle wasn't felt by everyone. In 1982, unemployment reached record levels, while the tax burden on most people went up. As Ian Gilmour put it: 'The sacrifice imposed on the poor produced nothing miraculous except for the rich.'[29]

Rather than overthrow Britain's old ruling class, Thatcher oversaw another phase of its expansion. New elites thrived and foreign banks flooded in. Before Thatcher, less than a tenth of the UK stock market had been owned by foreign capital. By the end of the century, it controlled over a third. London became the financial capital of the world, and a leading tax haven. The wealthiest clique in Britain became less aristocratic, and less British. When the Sunday Times Rich List launched in 1989 as a flagship survey of Britain's wealthiest residents – itself a sign of changing attitudes to wealth – ten of the top twenty were aristocrats. By 2018, only two were, and the sum of money required to qualify for the top 200 was also twenty-three times higher.[30]

But it wasn't just new elites who flourished under Thatcher. Beneath her rhetoric of meritocracy, she breathed new life into the aristocracy. Her laissez-faire economic programme was a boon for anyone with assets and, as the owners of vast estates and generations of accumulated wealth, the aristocracy had assets in abundance. The average wealth of an aristocratic family had fallen from £23 million before the war to £4.9 million in 1967, adjusted for inflation. From the 1980s, it started to rise again, and now stands at about £16.9 million. The popular image of the poor British aristocrat, living out their days in faded grandeur, is a fiction that serves their purposes just fine. When the 12th Duke of Devonshire declared in 2011 that 'the aristocracy is not dying – it's dead!', he had a recorded net worth of £500 million.[31]

All in all, Thatcher's 'peasant revolt' was a revelation for the ruling class: the rich got richer, and old elites recovered their self-belief – they finally had someone who would stand up for them again. In his official biography, Charles Moore recounts an episode where a member of Thatcher's staff responded to a letter from the Duke of Rutland with 'Dear Mr. Rutland', and the prime minister going apoplectic: these titles meant a lot to her.[32] It was only fitting that, at the end of Thatcher's reign, the Conservative PM secured a baronetcy for her husband, Denis – the only leader to do so in the past sixty years. The mascot of Britain's meritocracy could now see out her life as Baroness Thatcher, residing in her £30 million mansion in Belgravia. Her absorption into Britain's peculiar aristocracy was complete.[33]

Caught between her common roots and aristocratic affectations, Thatcher's relationship with the old ruling class was contradictory. On the one hand, her mere presence seemed to refute the founding creed of the Conservative Party by challenging notions of inherited wealth and privilege. But, on the other hand, Thatcher seemed to be fonder of the old governing class and its worth than many of her contemporaries and predecessors. Like so many newcomers to Britain's elite, Thatcher only wanted to join in. Sir Alec Douglas-Home remained her vision of an ideal Conservative leader. 'Alec would still be there if he had learnt how to communicate his message,' Thatcher said in the 1990s. 'He was a marvellous man.'

Some aristocrats found an unlikely solution to this tension: they convinced themselves that Thatcher was one of their own after all. A popular conspiracy theory – one that was 'widely believed in grand Tory circles', according to Moore – held that Thatcher's mother was the illegitimate child of the aristocrat Harry Cust, after her grandmother allegedly had an affair with him as a housemaid on the family's estate. Thatcher had Cust's blue eyes, they said, and an undeniably aristocratic air. Conservative MP Julian Amery, Baron Amery of Lustleigh, worked closely with Thatcher for years and concluded: 'There's blue blood there, no doubt about it.'

In this telling, while Thatcher may not have known it, her lineage in fact stretched back into the seventeenth century, with a grandfather, great-grandfather and great-great-grandfather who all went to Eton. She represented not a break with the old governing class, but yet another example of its stunning continuity. The natural order of Tory Britain endured. In his biography of Thatcher, Charles Moore ultimately dismisses the theory. 'Its details don't add up,' he concludes. But as an old-fashioned Tory and Old Etonian himself, he understands the fantasy's allure.

One afternoon in March 2022, during an interview at the House of Lords, Moore explained what the conspiracy theory said about the desire for continuity among Conservatives and Britain's ruling classes. 'A lot of people of a Conservative cast of mind would tend to see the relevant qualities of leadership as being inherited in a genetic way,' he told me:

The upper classes would compare it with animal breeding, like racehorses or hounds. The studbook of thoroughbred horses goes back to the eighteenth century – they all descend from the Darley Arabian in the early 1700s, I think – and you can trace every single horse all the way back there, otherwise they are not thoroughbred. In their mind there would be something like that for the people in which the right qualities, both by nature and nurture, are encouraged. Instinctively, although they would laugh about it, it's also in their heads that they're trying to legitimise Thatcher. Even now, they think about it more than you might imagine. In some ways it's reinforced by modern science because of what we've learnt about genes, so there's something there, and there's something in the way of thinking of Conservative people.

Moore's unsettling reference to genetics and 'modern science' might not speak for all Tories, but he knows the Conservative cast of mind well. Born in 1956, his education took him from Eton to Oxford before going on to edit the *Spectator* (1984–90), the *Sunday Telegraph* (1992–5) and the *Daily Telegraph* (1995–2003). He employed Boris Johnson as a journalist and, courtesy of his star columnist's ascent to prime minister, received a peerage in 2020. Moore is both a throwback figure – an Old Etonian who loves fox-hunting and pheasant shooting – and perfectly in tune with the times, championing Brexit and railing against out-of-touch

Remainers from the House of Lords as Baron Moore of Etchingham.

In Moore's view, 'the cousinhood' seems to represent not a nickname for an overly intimate elite, but an ideal: the closed circles in which the ruling classes operate nurtures an ability to lead, passed on from one generation to the next, which it is in everyone's interests to respect and obey. However undemocratic this vision of society is, he is right to see it at the Conservatives' hearts. The idea that the already privileged are best placed to lead the country – with the corollary that they are privileged for a reason, even when it is randomly assigned at birth – is in many ways the founding tenet of the Conservative Party: the main object that needs to be conserved. Across the party's history, some Conservatives have wanted to strengthen the monarchy, 'some the state, some businessmen', as the economist Nigel Harris has observed. 'But all prescriptions [have] tended to circle the same basic concern: the survival of a ruling class.'[34]

The challenge for the Conservatives has been how to make this purpose popular: how to persuade enough people, especially those outside the elite minority, that inequality is in their interests. Ever since the expansion of the suffrage in the late nineteenth century, when the working class became a majority of the electorate, the Conservatives have had to cater to more than just the ruling class to hold on to power. They have needed to mobilise support across classes, making the case that the party's programme, whatever its ruling-class roots, serves the nation as a whole because, as David Cameron once put it, we're all in it together.

4

A CONSERVATIVE COUNTRY?

'The English, of all ranks and class, are at bottom, in all their feelings, aristocrats.'
John Stuart Mill, in a letter to Giuseppe Mazzini, 1858

'Being Conservative is only another way of being British.'
Quintin Hogg, *Toryism and Tomorrow*, 1967

'I never got on with the English in general. People who believe that an elderly British matron is the Empress of the Indies and Queen of all Africa are dangerously removed from reality.'
James Baldwin, interviewed by Paul Gilroy, 1985

On Sunday 8 November 2015, more than 11 million people in the UK tuned in to watch the series finale of *Downton Abbey*, ITV's hit drama about the eponymous estate, its upper-class inhabitants and their small army of servants. The story is set in the early 1900s, at a time of aristocratic decline and social instability. But amid all the change and uncertainty, *Downton Abbey* evokes a utopian, quintessentially English idyll: a world where people are polite, the rich recognise their responsibilities and the poor gratefully accept their lot in life. In one scene from *Downton Abbey: The Movie* (2019), the eldest of the Countess' daughters, Lady Mary Crawley, ponders whether the time has come for the family to downsize. 'What am I doing [here]?' she wonders aloud. Her housemaid is unimpressed. 'I'll tell you what you're doing m'lady, you're making a centre for the people who work here, for this village, for the county. Downton Abbey is the beating heart of this community and you're keeping it beating.'

This 'one nation' vision of Britain – proud, happy and harmonious despite vast inequalities – could almost be a pastiche of Conservative propaganda. But the show's mass appeal reveals how a defence of the ruling class can resonate beyond a privileged few. A strictly ordered society, steeped in tradition and grandeur, can endear even those it seems to exclude, partly because it promises to provide everyone with a purpose. 'I think, in difficult and rude mannered times, it is comforting for people to see a story about a period of British history when everybody had a station in life, whether it was as a footman or an earl,' Julian Fellowes, the programme's creator, said in 2011.[1] 'I'm not saying that's necessarily right, but everybody has a role to play in keeping this huge operation going, upstairs and downstairs, and for the most part they got along.'

Fellowes is a lifelong Tory who used to write speeches for former Conservative leader Iain Duncan Smith. In 2011, his sympathetic treatments of the old governing class were aptly rewarded with a peerage from David Cameron. Lord Fellowes of West Stafford now inhabits his own *Downton Abbey* fantasy: he is married to the great-grandniece of the first Lord Kitchener of Khartoum, boasts a sprawling seventeenth-century country estate and has a son named Peregrine Charles Morant Kitchener-Fellowes. But while Fellowes is a fan of some British anachronisms, he is outspoken on others. At the same time as he endeavours to restore his property to its 1850 boundaries, buying up all the surrounding acres he can, he also campaigns against the 'absurd and outdated' rules that stop women inheriting hereditary peerages and his wife from inheriting Lord Kitchener's title. 'Of course she is expected to take on the duties of the name,' he complained in 2015.[2] 'But the name she may not have because she is female.'

Fellowes clearly isn't the only one drawn to this arcane world of titles and estates. Stately homes are a cornerstone of Britain's tourism industry, frequented by citizens and tourists alike, and represent the dream location for most couples planning a wedding. Besides *Downton Abbey*, which at its peak was watched by over a seventh of the total population, the nation's other favourite television shows typically offer pleasing escapes into quaint hierarchies: *The Crown*, *Poldark*, *Bridgerton*, the endless adaptations of Charles Dickens and Jane Austen, and so on. In 2019 alone, there were more than thirty new series of period dramas, either produced or set in the UK.[3] This vision of Britain is also one of our finest exports. *Downton Abbey* gained an audience of 120 million worldwide, making it the most successful British television show of all time.[4]

But even *Downton Abbey*'s success pales next to the popularity of Britain's most beloved period drama, one that is confoundingly contemporary: the British monarchy. In 2011, over a third of the British population – about 24 million people – tuned in to watch the marriage of Britain's future King and Queen, Prince William and Kate Middleton. As with *Downton Abbey*, support for the royal family – described by pollsters in 2011 as 'probably the most stable trend we have ever measured'[5] – offers another clue to how the Conservative cause can be at once elitist yet populist, quaint yet disarmingly modern.

The royal family live in unfathomable luxury, but they also have a peculiarly equalising effect: the status of 'royal subject' transcends wealth and class, so that the master and the maid must bow down before His or Her Royal Highness just the same. The spirit of togetherness inspired by Queen Elizabeth II's funeral in September 2022 showed how a monarch erases social inequalities at the same time as legitimising them. The magic of 'The Queue' – where many people waited for more than twenty-four hours, winding through the centre of London, to glimpse the Queen's coffin and pay their respects – was that everyone was expected, regardless of social status, to line up just the same. Celebrities were praised for following the procedure like everybody else, while others who used connections to skip it became objects of outrage. Next to the Queen, after all, we are all 'ordinary', whatever the difference in zeros that define our net worth. She was a symbol of harmony and permanence.

This unifying aspect of monarchy is the main theme of *Downton Abbey: The Movie*. When the Queen announces her intention to visit the estate, everyone – upstairs and down-stairs, the earl and his footman, the countess and the cooks – is united in nervous anticipation. On the eve of the royal visit, in preparation for their arrival, Lady Crawley even helps her servant Anna put out chairs in the garden in the pouring rain. 'You're a good friend to me, Anna,' Lady Crawley says, as they finish. 'I hope we're good friends to each other, m'lady,' Anna replies. The maze of hierarchies is also a source of comedy: obviously an earl must bow to the Queen, but should Downton's servants defer towards the royal family's servants? As it happens, the abbey's staff stage a quasi-coup against the Queen's entourage, so desperate are they to serve her royal majesty in 'our house' – it's a very British uprising.

During the nineteenth century, when other countries succumbed to revolutionary storms, some explained Britain's comparative stability not just through the mastery of its ruling class, but through the tranquil, deferential character of its people. Something in the British soul seemed to hanker for hierarchies, taking pleasure in looking up as much as in looking down – much to the frustration of anyone harbouring revolutionary hopes. 'We are a servile, aristocracy-loving, lord-ridden people,' the radical campaigner Richard Cobden despaired in the 1840s. 'It is not just that the most humiliating formalities of the feudal era have been retained,' Friedrich Engels lamented around the same time.[6] 'The worst of it is that all these formalities really are the expression of public opinion, which regards a Lord as a being of a superior kind.' Almost a century later, in the 1930s, the French-born writer Hilaire Belloc put it well: 'in Britain,' he wrote, 'aristocracy comes from below'.[7]

Britain's deferential streak helps to explain a favourite pop culture cliché: the British, or at least English, butler. 'It is sometimes said that butlers only truly exist in England,' Stevens, a butler himself, observes in Kazuo Ishiguro's novel *The Remains of the Day*. 'I tend to believe this is true. Continentals are unable to be butlers because they are as a breed incapable of the emotional restraint which only the English race are capable of.' A catalogue of films, television shows and novels attest to Stevens' grand claim. From *Batman* to *The Fresh Prince of Bel-Air*, it seems that a butler must almost always be English, offering an iteration of the same stereotype: a well-mannered servant who, per the Tory ideal, takes pride in their profession and feels no resentment to their superiors;

he is just happy – honoured, even – to work for such pleasant people.

The extent to which this really is an 'English' trait is difficult to say, and the extent to which it is a 'British' one may be even more dubious. On close inspection, any purported national characteristic is liable to descend into crude cliché. But clichés often contain at least a grain of truth, and, at least for a while, many political scientists and sociologists explained working-class support for the Conservatives through this very tendency: class deference. Rather than feel excluded by or suspicious of the upper-class origins of Tory politicians, voters were believed to be impressed and reassured by them. The plummy accents, elite boarding school educations and gilded lineages, all these were taken as signs that posh people really were the best placed to govern Britain. One famous study, *Working Class Tories*, published in 1967 by the American sociologist Eric Nordlinger, found working-class Conservatives preferred the idea of an Old Etonian as a political leader to someone from an eminent grammar school by a ratio of more than two to one. 'Politics is in their blood so it comes more naturally,' one explained. 'He has been brought up in the proper atmosphere,' said another. Among working-class Labour voters, the feeling was reversed: about two to one favoured a man from a grammar school as leader. (The prospect of a *woman* political leader, either public or grammar school educated, wasn't even put to voters.)

There is other anecdotal evidence to draw upon as well, suggesting a particular kind of subservience within the British character. During a general strike in 1926, tens of thousands of Brits voluntarily sought to perform the vacated jobs, framing a sense of duty to the country against any expression of solidarity with fellow workers. Even the strikers had commenced their direct action with a friendly football match with the police. The spectacle, as the historian Susan Pedersen recounts, 'was taken not only by almost the whole of the press but even by [Beatrice] Webb as evidence of "what a sane people the British are"'.[8] More recently, Britain has earned the title of being the 'unpaid capital of Europe', because of its workers' willingness to do unpaid overtime, averaging an additional 6.3 hours a week according to one study, with a fifth of workers reporting ten additional hours a week. That latter figure is the equivalent of someone's pay stopping on 16 October and them working for the rest of the year.[9]

But as explanations for Conservative success go, the concept of deference isn't entirely convincing. It effectively reduces Tory Britain to a nation of lords and butlers, all united in the belief that a small elite is entitled to govern the country. This conception certainly seems less plausible since the rise of Thatcher. With a grammar school girl in charge, as opposed to the standard Old Etonian, the Conservatives proved even more successful. While she took on all the mannerisms of an upper-class lady, the Conservatives also made a feature of her humble roots. One election ad in 1979, published in a women's weekly magazine, took the form of a quiz: 'Do this quiz to find out if you're Labour or Conservative.' The final question was: 'Which of these people is more likely to know what it's like to do the family shopping? A. James Callaghan B. Your Husband. C. Mrs Thatcher.'[10] She also famously drew parallels between managing a nation's finances and balancing a household budget: the same motherly qualities of caution, responsibility and cutting costs were required.

And yet, amid countless claims about 'the decline' or 'death' of deference, the concept remains relevant to understanding the Conservatives' mass popularity. Those who dismiss the

Tories as toffs forget that the English are actually quite fond of them. Orwell called it 'snob-appeal', adding that 'English people are extremely fond of the titled ass'.[11] The nation's most popular prime minister is revealing: Churchill, the hero of Britain's 'finest hour', who persists in the national imagination as a kind of ur-statesman, wedding an upper-class aesthetic to the plucky stoicism of the everyman. This stoicism finds embodiment in the gutsy refrain 'Keep Calm and Carry On', which has become something close to a national motto. It breeds acceptance of the status quo, and fosters a sort of enlightened cynicism regarding politics: Brits know better than to believe we can have nice things – and, besides, we'll get along just fine.

Such national characteristics, clichéd or not, align themselves with the Conservative cause, allowing Conservatives to claim that they are the authentic expression of national identity. The anthropologist Kate Fox makes no mention of party politics or ideology in her bestseller, *Watching the English: The Hidden Rules of English Behaviour*. But the way in which she describes English character is strikingly in line with one political party above all. 'We are not keen on dramatic change, revolutions, sudden uprisings and upheavals,' Fox writes. 'A truly English protest march would see us all chanting: "What do we want? GRADUAL CHANGE! When do we want it? IN DUE COURSE!"' (It is apparently not possible for a protest calling for, say, better wages, political reform or indeed revolution to be 'truly English').[12] It also seems telling that, despite boasting the most prestigious universities in the world, the only philosophical tradition Britain can lay claim to is empiricism, defined by its anti-theory, anti-abstraction and anti-dogma stance, reinforcing the idea that Brits don't care for abstract ideas or ideals.

This notion that the English are a plain-speaking people goes back a long way. 'We belong,' the *Economist* observed in April 1848, 'to a race which, if it cannot boast the flowing fancy of one of its neighbours [the Irish] nor the brilliant *esprit* of the other [the French], has an ample compensation in the solid, slow, reflective, phlegmatic temperament which has saved us from so many errors, spared us so many experiments and purchased for us so many real, though uncomplete and unsystematic blessings.'[13] Some 150 years later, George Steiner, the renowned German-Jewish literary critic who lived in Cambridge, could still describe Britain as a 'land blessed with a powerful mediocrity of mind. It has saved you from communism and it has saved you from fascism. In the end you don't care enough about ideas to suffer their consequences.'[14]

Common sense is the nation's compass; hard work will see us through. As *Downton Abbey*'s cook reprimands her assistant, who is mouthing off about the royal family from Downton's dark kitchen-basement: 'Less philosophy, more elbow grease.' Echoed by the Tories, this command sees Britain through every crisis.

The central place of both period dramas and the monarchy in British culture point to a nation that has evolved along Conservative lines. Britain's placid advance through history, free from radical rupture, has meant that many national traits are Tory traits: a reverence towards the past, an affection for the aristocracy, a culture that prizes continuity and a scepticism towards political idealism and philosophy. Many Brits don't seem to mind living in a dysfunctional democracy so long as it maintains an aura of timeless stability and splendour, what the late Scottish historian Tom Nairn called 'the glamour of backwardness'.[15] Through their sheer staying power, antique poles of ruling-class power – the monarchy, House of Lords, public schools, Oxbridge and the uncodified constitution – stand as objects of popular endearment, synonymous with the nation as a whole. Attacks on these elitist institutions then become attacks on Britain itself.

But the Conservative nature of British identity is not the organic phenomenon that Conservatives like to claim. Over successive generations, the Conservatives have also worked hard to fuse the party with national identity, casting Conservatism as Britain embodied and vice versa, and their opponents as foreign and/or factional. This has been the case from the dawn of democracy: anxieties about the expanding suffrage have always sat alongside a resolute assertion that, as Conservative MP John Gorst noted in the late nineteenth century, 'the Conservatives are the natural leaders of the people'. 'The only textbook of Conservatism is the history of the British people, their institutions, their accumulated wisdom and their character,' the Conservative Party's Research Department declared boldly in 1947. 'We shall not have to convert people to our principles,' Thatcher said in 1975. 'They will simply rally to those which truly are their own.'

In many ways, it was Benjamin Disraeli who pioneered this confident conception of British Conservatism. If Burke is the figure who first articulated the Conservatives' purpose, then Disraeli is the one who, a century later, put it in terms that would rally the masses. As party leader between 1868 and 1881, Disraeli sought to establish the Conservatives as Britain's true 'national' party: where their opponents were sectarian, Conservatives represented the spirit of the entire nation, standing as the gatekeepers of Britain's power, prestige and prosperity. According to Disraeli, every British citizen was a

Conservative at heart – especially workers. 'None are so interested in maintaining the institutions of the country as the working classes,' he insisted. 'The rich and powerful will not find much difficulty under any circumstances in maintaining their rights, but the privileges of the people can only be defended and secured by popular institutions.'[16]

Born in 1804, Disraeli's rise to the top of the party defied the conventions of his day. He was the son of a prominent Jewish literary critic, with no public school education, no landed estate and no Tory ancestry. Nonetheless, he seemed almost tailor-made to the political age. His was a time when, partly through the expansion of the suffrage (which he helped to commandeer) and partly through the rise of the popular press (which he revelled in), British politics was becoming a national spectacle. Disraeli, who was the author of several state-of-the-nation novels of varying quality, wove a captivating story of a Tory Party and a Tory Nation, together as one. 'By the Conservative cause,' Disraeli declared, 'I mean the splendour of the Crown, the lustre of the Peerage, the privileges of the Commons, the rights of the poor. I mean that harmonious union, that magnificent concord of all interests, of all classes, on which our national greatness depends.'

The Conservatives aren't alone among right-wing movements in associating themselves with patriotism, tradition and reverence for the past. It isn't all disingenuous – many Conservatives feel a love for their country deeply and naturally – but there is no doubt that they find such patriotism a useful campaigning device as well: trumpeting national pride puts Conservatives on the side of 'the people', rather than an elite, and it cuts across class lines. What's more, by pointing towards a privilege that everyone can enjoy – the privilege of living in a great country – patriotism also fortifies the Conservative quest to protect the status quo. If the nation wasn't 'great', after all, then the Conservatives' positioning as the party of continuity would hardly be a popular one. 'The Conservative Party's main appeal to the great mass of voters is its close association with national greatness,' Peregrine Worsthorne wrote perceptively in 1959.[17] 'The right is acutely aware that the kind of Britain it wishes to preserve very largely depends on Britain remaining a great power.'

For most of the Conservative Party's early history, Britain's great power status was never in doubt. Throughout much of the nineteenth century and into the twentieth, Britain could credibly claim to be most powerful country in the world. Not only did it boast the most feared military force and the largest empire globally, but the world seemed to revolve around it: the British pound was the global reserve currency, and the time was (and still is) set according to a master clock at the Royal Observatory, Greenwich. All the Conservatives needed to do was make the nation's imposing stature felt among the masses. Disraeli believed that popularising the monarchy, turning it into a national spectacle, would do the trick, embodying the grandeur of Britain's achievements and reputation in a single symbol. He proclaimed the Queen Empress of India in 1877, tying monarchy and empire together for the first time, while her royal regalia was adorned with precious Indian stones. Her crown became 'the emblem of the British race, to encourage its expansion over the face of the globe', as one contemporary commentator observed.[18] As the historian David Cannadine has shown, it was in this period that the monarchy in its modern, recognisable sense – 'splendid, public and popular', 'a unifying symbol of permanence and national community' – was 'invented'.[19] (It was only later, during the

First World War, when Britain was at war with Germany, that the Windsors changed their name from the German Saxe-Coburg-Gotha.)

Empire encouraged a new kind of patriotism, too. Even Britons who were at the bottom of the hierarchy at home were encouraged to look down on all others abroad. 'Without a shirt on their backs they find consolation in seeing a scrap of bunting in the wind – a Union Jack,' the French journalist Jules Vallès wrote of the London poor in 1884, 'shoeless, they are happy to see the British lion with the globe beneath its paw'.[20]

The Conservatives have generally been in favour of keeping as much of the globe beneath Britain's paw as it can: opposing Ireland's partial – and total – independence, resisting and mourning the dissolution of Empire, fighting to keep faraway islands like the Falklands, facing down Scottish nationalism and resisting calls for further devolution. Conservatives do so in the name of unity, portraying their electoral opponents as divisive forces that want to tear the precious Union apart. Given that the Conservatives' votes are usually confined to England, some wonder what purpose the Union serves. 'In pure political terms – if Scotland left the Union – the Conservative Party would benefit enormously,' John Major commented in 2014, as Conservatives campaigned against Scottish independence during the referendum. 'Why [then] do I – an English Conservative – care about Scotland remaining in the Union?' The main answer is that the Union is what makes Britain 'Great', a nation like no other.

After the Second World War and the dissolution of Empire, however, it became clear that Britain's greatness was, in every sense, shrinking. But Conservatives continued to peddle the same fading fantasy, ultimately becoming more concerned with preserving the reassuring myths of a golden past than securing present or future success. The result is a constant anxiety around how the nation remembers its history: the reputations of national heroes and their statues must be defended at all costs, while anyone who seeks to complicate Britain's immaculate self-conception – a beacon of liberal democracy and railways across the world – is condemned by Conservatives as 'hating' Britain or trying to 'rewrite the past'. Repeated Conservative calls to reintroduce imperial measurements or relaunch the Royal Yacht so that Britain can sail the seven seas again spring from this same impulse. Even when Conservatives concede that Britain is no longer what it once was, they only do so to insist that they can bring the old Britain back. 'Make Britain Great Again, vote Conservative' ran a popular campaign poster in the late 1950s – a refrain which Thatcher repeatedly quoted, and all her successors have echoed in spirit.

The Falklands War in 1982 was a perfect example of Britain's contrived 'greatness' since the Second World War. By rallying Britain to defend a small set of islands off the coast of Argentina, a vestige of a once vast Empire, Thatcher saw an ideal opportunity for national rejuvenation. 'There is no such thing as a little war for a great nation,' Thatcher insisted, quoting the Duke of Wellington. The Iron Lady could finally show from what metal she was made. When Argentina surrendered after seventy-four days, she hailed it as a historic victory. 'When we started out, there were the waverers and the faint hearts,' Thatcher declared in her victory speech:

The people who thought that Britain . . . was no longer the nation that had built an Empire and ruled a quarter of the world. Well they were wrong. The lesson of the Falklands is that Britain has not changed and that this nation still has those sterling qualities which shine through our history. This generation can match their fathers and grandfathers in ability, in courage, and in resolution. We have not changed. When the demands of war and the dangers to our own people call us to arms – then we British are as we have always been: competent, courageous and resolute.

This pantomime of national greatness and permanence – 'we have not changed' – now lies at the core of the Conservative Party. To keep the show on the road, the Conservatives must attach themselves to whatever myths and memories they can find to sustain the fantasy, if not the reality, of Britain's greatness.

Britain's departure from the European Union in 2016, after decades of Tory pressure, proved that the pantomime still has an audience. Brexit was motivated by many things, but, much like with the Falklands, its advantage to the Conservative Party – and its appeal to many voters – was that it allowed Britain to *speak* and *feel* like a great country again: strong, brave and independent; sovereign, victorious and unconquerable. 'We have become infantilised, incapable of imagining an independent future,' Boris Johnson declared. 'We used to run the biggest empire the world has ever seen, and with a much smaller domestic population and a relatively tiny civil service. Are we really unable to do trade deals?' 'This is Magna Carta, it's the Burgesses coming at Parliament, it's the great reform bill, it's the bill of rights, it's Waterloo, it's Agincourt, it's Crécy,' Conservative MP Jacob Rees-Mogg intoned in 2017. 'We win all of these things.'[21]

It is this vision of Britain – as a humble island with an epic history, eternally undefeated – that the Conservatives are committed to keeping alive. They 'believe in Britain'; other parties want to 'do Britain down'. It is compulsory for any aspiring Conservative leader to repeat these banalities. 'There are too many people in this country who are ashamed of our history, who talk our country down, who say the best days are behind us,' Liz Truss declared in her campaign hustings in August 2022, as a cost of living crisis unfolded across the country with worsening forecasts on the horizons. 'They are completely wrong.' This rhetoric does nothing to address the problems facing Britain – as Truss's prime ministership showed, it can often make them worse – but it serves to reinforce the Conservatives' position as Britain's party of patriotism, standing for national greatness and unity against decline and division.

But there is more to the Conservatives' popular appeal than this, of course. The Conservatives could never just play the aristocrat and hope for working-class deference, nor could they simply parrot national clichés and glide to victory. Since the start of the democratic era, Conservatives have had to prove that, for all the party's ruling-class roots, for all the elitism Conservatives condone, their programme serves everyone's interests – that, however unequal Britain might be, we're all in this together.

The Conservatives' affinity with the aristocracy, its defence of extreme wealth and its posh politicians lead many on the left to dismiss them as 'the party of privilege'. They are then perplexed by their opponent's mass popularity. 'How is it that so large a proportion of the electorate, many of whom are neither wealthy nor privileged, have been recruited for a cause

which is not their own?' Labour politician Peter Shore
wondered in 1952.[22] But this puzzlement not only misunderstands how many Brits feel about the extremely wealthy and
privileged – it also misunderstands how Brits might feel about
their own lives.

For Conservatives, wealth and privilege aren't shameful
causes to champion, and they don't need to be elitist either.
Wealth is framed in terms of ambition – who doesn't want
to be rich? – while privilege can similarly be understood along
more expansive lines. Privilege isn't necessarily the preserve
of a tiny elite; it is dispersed throughout society, existing
wherever there are hierarchies: within families (between
parent and child, husband and wife), workplaces (between
bosses, employees, temporary staff and all the ranks in
between), neighbourhoods (homeowners, landlords and
renters), and across lines of race, gender, age and sexuality.
Privilege can also be enjoyed across national borders. A
Conservative would say that to live in a peaceful and prosperous nation, undisturbed by revolution, invasion or civil
war, is surely the greatest privilege of all. 'To be born English,'
ran a popular saying at the height of Empire, 'is to have won
first prize in the lottery of life.'

Conservatives tend to champion pre-existing systems of
privilege, defending – at different points and to various
degrees throughout its history – the rights of parents over
children, married couples over unmarried couples, husbands
over wives, men over women, married women over unmarried women, bosses over employees, the employed over the
unemployed, homeowners over renters, white Brits over
ethnic minorities, and, perhaps most performatively, 'British
interests' over the interests of any other country or nationality. Insofar as we all inhabit overlapping identities – not

just in terms of our gender, age, race and sexuality, but also at work and at home, in neighbourhoods and among nations – the Conservative standpoint can rally a diverse demographic: the first-generation immigrant who is also a business owner, the working-class woman who owns her own house, and indeed anyone who finds meaning, security or a sense of standing in the status quo.

So while the left likes to say that oppression is intersectional, a Conservative might reply that privilege is, too, and they prefer to focus on the positives. 'We have been told that the working man cannot be conservative, because he has nothing to conserve – he has neither land nor capital; as if there were not other things in the world as precious as land and capital!' Benjamin Disraeli declared in 1874. Today, in a more confrontational vein, Jordan Peterson tells his readers to stop feeling sorry for themselves and appreciate what they have. 'Perhaps you are overvaluing what you don't have and undervaluing what you do,' he writes in *12 Rules for Life*. Roger Scruton spoke similarly. 'Whatever our religion and our private convictions, we are the collective inheritors of things both excellent and rare, and political life, for us, ought to have one overriding goal, which is to hold fast to those things, in order to pass them on to our children,' he wrote in *How to Be a Conservative*. The Conservatives seek to align themselves with this ethos, promising to shore up all the ways people benefit from the status quo while framing the left's programme for change as an existential threat.

A similar framing can be seen in the Conservatives' reputation as 'the party of property'. The label is true: Conservatives are overwhelmingly committed to the protection of private property. But over time, they have broadened their understanding of what property is worth defending: not just the estates of the landed gentry, but the interests of everyone who owns, or wants to own, a home. 'The chief object of government, in England at least, is the protection of property – the special object and care of the Conservative Party,' Salisbury declared.[23] An opposition to inheritance tax, renters' rights and taxes on, say, owning a second property is therefore common among Conservatives: they impede the rights of property owners.

Today, the correlation between homeownership and a Conservative disposition is much discussed: whether or not one owns a home ranks among the most significant determinants of voting behaviour, while around a third of Tory MPs are landlords. In 2019, six out of every seven seats that the Conservatives won had higher than average homeownership, whereas for Labour it was only one in four. Whereas only a fifth of owner-occupiers and a third of mortgage-holders backed Labour, the Conservatives claimed 57 per cent and 43 per cent respectively.[24] But the underlying idea, that the mere act of owning property cultivates a Conservative worldview – making owners more risk-averse, protective and invested in the status quo – has long been assumed. As the social reformer Francis Place declared in 1831, with the whiff of a workers' revolution in the air: 'Every man who has property to lose is bound to do all he can to avert it.'

This notion provided the intellectual motivation for Margaret Thatcher's infamous 'right to buy' scheme, wherein council houses – built in their hundreds of thousands after the Second World War – were sold off to tenants at bargain prices, with the hope of creating a new class of homeowning Tory voters. It was part of Thatcher's plan for 'popular capitalism': 'a crusade to enfranchise the many in the economic life of the nation'. But it was also about shifting power from the public sector to the private sector. In 1988, Thatcher also abolished rent controls. Today's housing crisis – extortionate rents, unaffordable homes and a chronic shortage of social housing, where landlords have all the rights and rewards and renters are almost powerless – is the result, along with local government's chronic absence of funding: like Cameron's programme of austerity, right to buy cut off councils from one of their main sources of income.

Right-wing politicians and movements around the world are loyal to private property and homeownership. But in Britain, the Conservatives' defence of private property takes on a particularly patriotic hue: owning a home is seen as a peculiarly national obsession, a symptom of a very British need for privacy. As early as 1851, the census was remarking that 'the possession of an entire house is strongly desired by every Englishman, for it throws a sharp, well-defined circle round his family and hearth – the shrine of his sorrows, joy and meditations'. This remains part of British folklore. 'The English all want to live in their own private little box with their own private little green bit,' Kate Fox writes in *Watching the English*. She quotes an Edwardian rhyme: 'The Germans live in Germany/The Romans live in Rome/The Turkeys live in Turkey/But the English live at home.'

Britain's emphasis on homeownership is sometimes understood as yet another product of its relatively peaceful evolution.[25] In fact, homeownership levels in Britain aren't particularly high relative to other countries – a trend that Conservatives have inadvertently compounded over the past fifty years through their part in the housing crisis. But so long as homeownership is still *seen* to be quintessentially British, or English – embodied in the old saying, 'an Englishman's home is his castle' – then the Conservatives can continue to frame their defence of private property as the authentic expression of national feeling and character, rather than an ideologically motivated defence of elite interests. By contrast, the left's call for expanded social housing and better renting rights can be condemned as defeatist or worse: un-British.

This is what makes the Conservatives' grip over national politics so formidable. By positioning itself as the party of patriotism and the party of prosperity, with each platform defined in mutually reinforcing ways, there is little room for Labour to build its own narrative: the weight of British history, culture and identity seems to be loaded against the left. Even though the Conservatives' election wins usually rest on fine margins, their winning record fuels the Conservatives' claim to be the natural party of government, further entwining the Tories with British history.

This is a triumph of storytelling and resources over reality, enacted over two centuries: if the facts of life turn out to be Tory, it is because Tories usually get to define what the facts of life, or at least of British politics, are. (It was fitting, on this front, that during an election debate in 2019, the Conservative Party changed its name on Twitter to 'Factchecker UK', trying to pose as a neutral purveyor of the truth.) The Conservatives' reputation as the most trustworthy custodians of the economy, for example, lies not in the party's economic achievements, but in the extent to which they have persuaded people, falsely, that a Conservative government means a healthy economy. A recent analysis comparing the Conservatives' and Labour's overall economic records in government shows that GDP actually tends to grow more under Labour than the Tories.[26] But the Conservatives consistently poll better than Labour on who is most trusted with the economy – an ascendancy which is then reflected in election results. Even in May 2022, after a dozen years of Tory rule had produced no rise in wages, soaring costs, pervasive uncertainty and a looming recession, the Conservatives were still ahead of Labour on 'most trusted to grow the economy', according to Ipsos.

The Conservatives' dominance of the economic narrative, coupled with their election success, offers another harsh reminder to the left that politics cannot be reduced to narrow class interests. That isn't to say that economics don't play a huge part in how people vote – it's more that people interpret their economic needs in different ways: as individuals and groups, in terms of self-interest and in terms of what feels fair. The Conservatives' economic pitch is about much more than the party's economic record in power. It also represents a moral vision about how an individual can, or should, build a better life for themselves, and about what kind of country Britain is. Whereas the left focus on welfare, social security and equality – ensuring that everyone can enjoy at least a minimum standard of life, because wealth and privilege are so randomly distributed that a collective safety net is fair – the Conservatives stress the place of personal ambition, hard work and taking responsibility for your own situation. A famous study published in 1968, *Angels in Marble: Working Class Conservatives in Urban England 1958–60* by Robert McKenzie and Allan Silver, asked members of the working class across the political divide whether they should stick together or go it alone to advance their interests. 'All the working-class Conservatives who were interviewed indicated a preference for individual over collective action for personal betterment,' they found.[27]

This draws on both an intuitive ethic of fairness – no reward without hard work – and an empowering message of autonomy and responsibility: your fate is in your hands. 'We are the party of strivers,' David Cameron declared in the wake of the 2008 recession. It's worth pointing out that such faith in the individual and emphasis on hard work wasn't always part of the Conservative lexicon. Only towards the end of the nineteenth century, when the party absorbed the Liberal Unionists and the aristocracy fused with the capitalists, did the old governing class learn to champion an up-by-your-bootstraps optimism. Before then, the Conservatives' message was more Downton Abbey than American Dream: accept your place, fulfil your purpose and appreciate what you have. After swallowing liberalism, however, Conservatives discovered that 'personal responsibility' provided a powerful foundation on which to campaign – one that dovetailed neatly with the notion of Brits as a private people. Stanley Baldwin, one of the Conservative Party's most accomplished ventriloquists of Englishness, liked to say that wanting help from the government 'was never the Englishman's way': independence and initiative were 'burnt into the bones of Englishmen' – 'he always asked to be left alone'.[28]

Advocating the value of 'personal responsibility' thus allows Conservatives to 'respect tradition' and resist wealth redistribution at the same time, claiming to 'trust the British people to look after themselves', unlike the patronising, unpatriotic left. This rallying message – hard work can get you anywhere – suits Conservatives all the better for being false: the traditional social order remains the same, and yet people blame either themselves for their misfortune or others like them for cheating the system, even when the odds are stacked against them.

This points to how the Conservatives' opposition to a strong welfare state and better-funded public services – two things which, on the surface, might seem like straightforwardly popular causes in a democracy – can resonate even among those who would benefit most from them. By promising that everyone can live a certain standard of life regardless of their work (or lack thereof), a welfare state can be framed as a means of making people's personal effort irrelevant: while some are rewarded for their indolence, others are punished for their hard work, since the taxes on their income are then used to fund the unemployment of others. The Conservatives are then able to oppose a safety net on moral grounds. 'Where is the fairness, we ask, for the shift worker, leaving home in the dark hours of the early morning, who looks up at the closed blinds of their next-door neighbour sleeping off a life on benefits?' George Osborne asked in a speech at the 2012 Conservative Party conference. 'When we say we're all in this together, we speak for that worker. We speak for all those who want to work hard and get on.'

Despite the fact that most people on benefits now work, Conservatives persist with this binary framing: benefits vs hard work, dependence vs independence, free riders vs no-pain-no-gain. This brings us to the final aspect of the Conservatives' economic pitch. Buried within Osborne's ode to 'that worker' lies a more insidious moral precept: the valorisation of not just hard *work* but hard*ship*. Once again, this part of the Conservative pitch finds a purported national character trait to draw upon: British stoicism, or what Stevens in Ishiguro's *The Remains of the Day* called 'emotional restraint'. According to Osborne's logic, the 'fairness' for the shift worker lies not in better working hours, a permanent contract or better pay, but in the faith that other people are suffering the same fate. The social theorist Mark Fisher characterised this Conservative sentiment as 'negative solidarity':

The reason that it's so easy to whip up loathing for 'benefit scroungers' is that – in the reactionary fantasy – they have escaped the suffering to which those in work have to submit. This fantasy tells its own story: the hatred for benefits claimants is really about how much people hate their own work. *Others should suffer as we do*: the slogan of a negative solidarity that cannot imagine any escape from the immiseration of work.[29]

'Negative solidarity' is central to the Conservatives' economic programme. The party's promise of a better life shouldn't ever be confused with the promise that life will be easy: for Conservatives, life is never easy, nor should it be. Striving through adversity is regarded as the highest achievement in life. Just as Burke believed that 'the great virtues turn principally on dangers, punishments and troubles', Jordan Peterson now declares that 'the purpose of life is finding the largest burden you can bear and bearing it'. Once again, the message of Conservatives is self-reinforcing: if striving through adversity if a virtue, then the more Conservatives roll back the state and tear at society's fabric, coarsening the conditions in which most people live, the more the Conservatives' message of self-help and valorisation of hardship can resonate. Conservatives therefore thrive in the adverse conditions they create.

In Britain, the proud myth of the 'stiff upper lip' means this is especially true. The most potent national myth is Dunkirk: that the Brits are at their best when their backs are against the wall. 'The Englishman is made for a time of crisis and for a time of emergency,' Conservative prime minister Stanley Baldwin once declared. 'It is in staying power that he is supreme . . . [His] way of facing misfortune with a cheerful face.' In recent years, it's as if the Conservatives have taken this as a mandate to inflict on the nation as much pain and misery as they can – slashing welfare, rolling back social services and refusing pay rises in line with inflation even as a bruising cost of living crisis unfolds – all the better to test, and then celebrate, the British people's mettle and resolve.

The social theorist Stuart Hall saw something similar at play during Thatcher's reign. Besides her promise of prosperity, 'she speaks to something else, deep in the English psyche: its masochism'.[30] Hall saw in the resonance of Thatcher's strict rhetoric 'the need which the English seem to have to be ticked off by Nanny and sent to bed without a pudding. The calculus by which every good summer has to be paid for by twenty bad winters. The Dunkirk Spirit – the worse off we are, the better we behave.' This has been a persistent theme of Conservatism since 2010, from Cameron's age of austerity to the framing of both Brexit and the pandemic as tests of grit and determination. Punishing economic policies and a coarsening social landscape are wrapped up in patriotic tributes to the plucky, indomitable spirit of the British people: less philosophy, more elbow grease.

The pitches for patriotism and prosperity are the central two pillars of the Conservatives' positive platform. They are almost impossible to disentangle. Conservatives define national greatness in part through a powerful economy, and they reinforce their economic agenda with national clichés and myths, boosting people's work ethic and their tolerance of hardship, defining the national character in terms that suit it. The result is that the Conservatives emerge as a quintessentially British entity: as grand as Big Ben and Buckingham Palace, as old and immovable as the White Cliffs of Dover, a symbol of the nation itself.

The Conservatives' long-standing commitment to casting their opponents as unpatriotic, foreign and divisive, in cahoots with enemies abroad and at home, is an inevitable side product of their claim to exclusively embody British interests. Whereas Conservatives represent the country, their opponents are an alien intrusion on the Tory Nation. Even to contemplate voting for them and against the Conservatives becomes, in this framing, something close to treachery, equivalent to siding with an enemy during a war.[31]

The Conservatives are determined that voters should understand their opponents in this way. Disraeli called the Whigs 'anti-national' and denounced the Liberals' 'continental' inclinations. Even the Liberals' long-standing leader, Gladstone, an Old Etonian aristocrat, was attacked for being 'un-English'. During the Boer War, between 1899 and 1902, the Conservatives accused their opponents of 'taking the enemy's side' and fought a winning 'khaki' election campaign on a warmongering platform. 'The lack of patriotism is as evident now as it has always been in the Radical party', a Conservative election leaflet declared in 1901, referring to the Liberals amid the Boer War.[32] The warnings only became more hysterical amid the rise of Labour.

This is the dark side of the Conservative Party's popular platform. In order to define itself as Britain embodied, the Conservatives brutally police who is and isn't a legitimate part of public life. In order to stand for national unity, the Conservatives constantly stoke phantom fears about scapegoats dividing society – immigrants, welfare claims, leftists, minorities of every kind – and insist that Labour, like the Liberals before them, will let these threats loose. And in order to stand for continuity, the Conservatives must drum up the threat of 'change' that these malign agents pose, blaming them for all

121

Britain's ills and playing to people's worst prejudices: only the Conservatives can keep Britain the same. Therefore, while both the party of prosperity and the party of patriotism have positive messages to convey, another platform of the party deals almost exclusively in fear. This is the 'Nasty Party', where the danger changes, but the message stays the same: *they must be kept out.*

5

THE NASTY PARTY: FLIRTING
WITH THE FAR RIGHT

'The Radicals ... are evidently glad to see all foreigners
who are criminals; who suffer from loathsome diseases;
who are turned out in disgrace by their fellow coun-
trymen; who are paupers; who fill our streets with
profligacy and disorder. *The Radical Welcomes Them All!*
The [Conservative] Unionist Government wants to keep
these creatures out of Great Britain.'
Conservative Party leaflet, 1904

'The life of nations no less than that of men is lived
largely in the imagination.'
Enoch Powell, speech at Trinity College, Dublin, 1964

'We Tories look at him – with his pint and cigar and sense
of humour – and we instinctively recognise someone who
is fundamentally indistinguishable from us.'
Boris Johnson, on Nigel Farage, in 2013

In the history of the Nasty Party, one moment stands out
above all: a racist speech delivered by then Conservative
shadow minister Enoch Powell in May 1968, in which he
warned about rising levels of immigration in Britain. 'As I
look ahead, I am filled with foreboding; like the Roman,

I seem to see "the River Tiber foaming with much blood",' Powell said, alluding to a line in Virgil's *Aeneid*. In Powell's violent prophecy, a race war loomed and it would not be enough simply to close Britain's borders: some of the immigrants already settled in the country would need to be sent 'home'. If not, he declared, claiming to quote one of his constituents, 'in this country, in 15 or 20 years' time, the black man will have the whip hand over the white man'.

Powell's 'Rivers of Blood' speech put the Conservative Party in a difficult position. It wasn't just that, in the eyes of many politicians, his rhetoric went too far. The bigger problem for Conservatives lay elsewhere: the speech's incendiary popularity. While most politicians and newspapers condemned its incendiary language, a Gallup poll found that 74 per cent of the British population shared Powell's fears. Reports of racist abuse soared. The change in atmosphere for people of colour was so stark that members of the West Midland Caribbean Association began to refer to 'BE' and 'AE' – 'Before Enoch' and 'After Enoch'. Although Tory leader Ted Heath expelled Powell from the shadow cabinet (but not the party), this only served to make him more of a martyr. He reportedly received more than 100,000 letters of support to his parliamentary office. Thousands of workers – often traditional Labour supporters – went on strike in solidarity with him. Almost overnight, Powell became the Conservatives' most popular politician, but one who had no place on the party's front bench.

Before his notorious 'Rivers of Blood' speech, Powell was better known for his extremist views on free-market capitalism than on immigration. He played a key role in spreading the free-market gospel of the Institute of Economic Affairs. The neoliberal economist Milton Friedman – like Hayek, a crucial intellectual in overturning the decades of social democracy after the Second World War globally – praised Powell as 'brilliant' and called for Britain to adopt an economic programme 'which only Enoch Powell seems to appreciate'. Ahead of Thatcher, who became his disciple, Powell was arguing that society did not exist, that it had no meaning beyond the market – 'the terms "free economy" and "free society" are to me interchangeable', he wrote in 1960 – and that, following on from Burke and Smith, the wisdom of capitalism should be understood in religious terms. 'Often when I am kneeling down in church, I think to myself how much we should thank God, the Holy Ghost for the gift of capitalism,' Powell said. But as he discovered, fears about minorities could prove much more popular than fantasies about free markets, appealing to a far greater cross-section of the public.

Despite the intensity of his anti-immigration diatribes, Powell's fearmongering was at least partly strategic. His violent warnings arrived at a time when Britain's place in the world was changing. As the nation clung to its heroic memories of the Second World War, it stuttered each time it tried to assert its fading superpower status. In 1956, Britain was humiliated when it tried to invade Egypt and seize control of the Suez Canal, only to withdraw after America voiced disapproval. Its economy was beset by crises and stagnation, earning it the nickname 'the sick man of Europe'. In the 1960s, when Britain tried to join the European Union (then known as the European Economic Community), France vetoed its membership twice. This dealt a special kind of blow to the nation's mythology: Europe was supposed to need Britain, not the other way around.

As the Empire unravelled, what it meant to be British was also being recast. According to Powell, the nation's burgeoning international aid budget (which doubled between 1957 and 1961) and growing anti-discrimination legislation (which outlawed denying jobs, services or housing to someone based on their skin colour or ethnicity) sprang from Britain's refusal to leave the guilt and/or greatness of Empire behind. The political class had forgotten its foremost duty to the (white) British, or English, Powell thought. 'The Tory Party has to find its patriotism again,' he said, 'and to find it, as of old, in "This England."' What the nation needed was a 'clean break with the imperial past' and the people that went with it. If the colonial subjects could not be ruled, Powell reasoned, they were not welcome.[1]

Powell's position on Empire was peculiar. He was among the last to let it go – even calling for a re-invasion of India in 1950 – but when he finally did, he did so resoundingly. 'The Tory party must be cured of the British Empire, of the pitiful yearning to cling to relics of a bygone system,' he declared in a speech in 1957. Like a thwarted lover, no longer able to stand the sight of his obsession, he railed against Britain's 'imperial neurosis'. As far as Powell's new patriotism went, the Empire – and the 'gigantic farce' of the Commonwealth, which sought to maintain ties with former colonies – was an unambiguous story of decline. It showed Britain 'at the heart of a vanished empire, amid the fragments of demolished glory'.

Far more important to Powell's worldview than Empire was the Second World War, in which he served as a soldier. For Powell, it was when the British were at war that they truly knew themselves: with the stiff upper lip and the spirit of sacrifice, the embrace of austerity and the Churchillian refrain: 'very well, then, alone.' War was a time when the British people were ready to die for what they believed in – and that, Powell thought, was the essence of patriotism, the soul of nations.

'Patriotism,' he said, 'is to have a nation to die for, and to be glad to die for it – all the days of one's life.'

For Powell, the sovereign nation was 'not conceivable' without war. But with old enemies now partners – namely Germany and France – in a new European peace project, a new enemy was needed. In Powell's imagination, immigrants and their 'allies' became the mortal threat that Britain needed to survive. 'It is like watching a nation busily engaged in heaping up its own funeral pyre,' Powell said of Britain's immigration policy in the 'Rivers of Blood' speech. Memories of war were essential to this tale of life and death. He compared journalists who defended anti-discrimination legislation to those in 'the 1930s [who] tried to blind this country to the rising peril which confronted it'. The legacy of the Second World War became for him an unending story of Britain under attack, one 'invasion' following another.

Powell wasn't alone in seeing the potential of a 'war on immigration' to cure Britain of its faltering self-belief. In an essay in 1965, the influential Conservative MP John Biffen – who later served in Thatcher's cabinet – made a similar case in even plainer terms, writing: 'It is possible that Tory attitudes on immigration will strike a working-class response and replace the old-style imperialism that traditionally attracted, say, the Lancashire working-class to the idea of Tory democracy.'[2] In the absence of Empire, in other words, xenophobia could offer a replacement source of pride, enabling even those at the bottom of British society to have someone to look down upon abroad. Much like the party's jingoistic forays after the Second World War, from Falklands to Brexit, anti-immigration fearmongering could sustain the fantasy of national greatness. The act of excluding others implied collective ownership over something great, over something worth protecting – otherwise why else would people want to come to Britain? The more people who wanted to come, the greater Britain was – fear and pride became two sides of the same coin, and immigration anxiety became a form of national self-flattery, a compliment that must be refused because there just wasn't enough of Britain's greatness to go around. 'There are literally millions of people in other countries who want to come and live here,' Michael Howard declared during his notoriously xenophobic, and ultimately unsuccessful, 2005 election campaign. 'Britain cannot take them all.'

In this reconfiguration of post-imperial Britain, the world was no longer beneath Britain's paw, but was instead queuing at the gates, desperate to be let in. This narrative was similarly empowering, and even more useful: it offered Conservatives not only a way of appealing across classes, but a simple alibi for Britain's ailing state. If Britain was no longer great, it was because it was too generous, spreading its greatness so thinly than the nation's 'native' citizens suffered for it. Even now, there is no social problem – low wages, poor economic growth, rising child poverty, underfunded public services, rising crime – that cannot be blamed on an overly lax or generous immigration system, malign minorities or boats trying to cross the Channel. Nevermind that Britain's immigration system is not generous by European standards, neither in terms of what it offers nor the numbers it lets in – fueled by such fictions, the excuse is always at hand.

While Powell's prophecies of doom never materialised, he proved prescient in a different sense: as a figure who foreshadowed the anxieties that would shape the Conservatives' future, blurring the lines between genuine racism and political expedience to the point that the distinction is pointless. He also, through his dismissal from Heath's shadow cabinet and lasting influence, captured a foundational paradox for the Conservative Party, one that is crucial to its success: how to harness the most reactionary forces of society while also keeping the party's moderate reputation untarnished by them. The Conservatives understand both the danger of being outflanked on their right and the popular potential of pandering to prejudice, placing the Conservatives on the side of 'normal people' against complacent elites. But it is also essential that Conservatives aren't seen as extremists: politeness, level-headedness and respectability are essential to the party's identity and longevity. The far left and the far right are the ones that get carried away with irrational passions; the Conservatives are there to calm them down. These tensions are at the heart of the Nasty Party's history, whether expressed through racism, anti-Semitism, homophobia, Islamophobia, transphobia or whatever other type of stigma leads the day. These tensions predate Powell, just as they have outlived him, but perhaps more than any other Conservative politician he brought them to the fore.

Conservatives have long understood the way prejudice and fearmongering can unite a coalition of voters who might otherwise be opposed. Through xenophobia, the rulers and ruled, rich and poor, bosses and workers can end up on the same side, so long as they aren't part of the demonised group. Karl Marx saw this at play in England in the mid-nineteenth century. Back then, Irish workers were the scapegoat of the day. 'Every industrial and commercial centre in England now possesses a working class divided into two hostile camps, English proletarians and Irish proletarians,' he wrote in 1870. 'The ordinary English worker hates the Irish worker as a competitor who lowers his standard of life.' Next to the Irish worker, Marx reflected, the English worker feels himself 'a member of the ruling nation . . . and so turns himself into a tool of the aristocrats and capitalists of his country against Ireland, thus strengthening their domination over himself'.[3] Like with patriotism, scapegoating someone as 'other' elevates everyone who does belong in the chosen national narrative.

Across the Tories' history, all kinds of minorities and groups have played this nefarious part in the national pantomime: Irish people, Catholics, Jews, Muslims, black people, students, teachers, unions, left-wing activists, environmentalists, LGBT people, and more. The party's method for fomenting panic has remained largely the same: exaggerate their threat and insist that opposing political parties are on their side. An adversarial Conservative pamphlet in 1904, for example, captures the typical Conservative characterisation of a Liberal or Labour immigration policy: 'Let 'Em All Come'. 'The whole scum of Europe may come to this country by merely concocting stories about being political or religious "refugees," however obviously improbable their stories may be,' a similar party pamphlet in 1906 read.[4] The trigger for its anxiety was a Liberal policy advising immigration officers to give refugees fleeing from religious or political persecution 'the benefit of the doubt, where any doubt exists'. The Tories took the seed of their opponent's stance and pushed it to the extreme: Let 'Em All Come. It remains a favourite formula. 'Look at their record over the last week,' David Cameron said of the Labour leadership in 2016, during the refugee crisis. 'They met with a bunch of migrants in Calais, they said they could all come to Britain. The only people they never stand up for are the British people and hardworking taxpayers.'

Examples of the Tories weaponising such prejudices are littered throughout the party's history. In 1924, Baldwin's

Conservatives fought an election campaign almost entirely dedicated to 'aliens' — with the term 'used as a code for "Jews",' according to the historian Martin Pugh.[5] 'In these days no alien should be substituted for one of our own people when we have not enough work at home to go around,' Baldwin declared, showing how a wealthy steel magnate by background could, through xenophobia, put himself on the side of the 'English worker'.[6] In 1955, transport workers in West Bromwich went on strike after the local transport authority hired its first Indian immigrant as a conductor. 'I believe,' Powell said, giving the workers his backing, 'the strikers . . . have apprehended the dangers for this country of any appreciable coloured population domiciled here.' That same year, convinced that immigration from the Caribbean was 'the most important subject facing this country', Churchill wanted to fight an election campaign on the slogan 'Keep England White', only to be ousted as party leader before he had the chance.[7] In 1964, a Conservative politician campaigned in Smethwick, West Midlands, on arguably the most notorious, and nakedly racist, slogan in the party's history: 'If you want a nigger for a neighbour, vote Labour'.[8] The problem of immigration is often presented as one of cohesion and harmony, and Powell did likewise in his 'Rivers of Blood' speech. But what the Tories' pattern of prejudice shows is that, for many, the fear isn't that immigrants won't integrate: the fear is that they will.

Thatcher took direct inspiration from Powell: she studied his speeches, praised his 'second to none' intellect and, in 1978, made her own Powellite prophecy. She revealed, in doing so, the cynicism that underlies the Nasty Party — the deliberate attempt to exploit prejudices, regardless of what the politician themselves thinks. 'People are really rather afraid that this country might be rather swamped by people with a different culture,' Thatcher said in an interview on the BBC, as she trailed behind Labour in the polls. 'And, you know, the British character has done so much for democracy, for law and done so much throughout the world that if there is any fear that it might be swamped, people are going to react and be rather hostile to those coming in.' Thatcher even promised to 'hold out the clear prospect of an end to immigration'. Delivering on this impossible prospect was never the point. The aim of Thatcher's intervention on immigration was to push Labour on to uncomfortable terrain, taking attention away from economic questions where the Conservatives' stance wasn't popular. All those targeted and demeaned by Thatcher's remarks were simply collateral damage in the Tories' pursuit of power. 'She felt hemmed in on incomes policy, so she thought she would take a free hit on immigration,' Richard Ryder, her political secretary, later explained.[9] Extensive in-house party polling showed that this 'free hit' would give her a boost. The Tory Press duly obliged. After Thatcher's 'swamping' remarks, the *Daily Mail* began a series of articles entitled 'Immigration – The Great Debate' that provided a platform for certain members of the public to air their fears of an immigration invasion. 'They've taken over my home town . . .' ran the headline of one characteristic contribution.

Not everyone in Thatcher's team agreed with the strategy. 'Just imagine if she'd said we were being swamped by Jewish people,' Chris Patten, at the Conservative Research Department, protested. But once in power Thatcher continued on the same track. One minister complained that cabinet meetings were consigned to three themes: 'Parliamentary affairs; home affairs; and xenophobia.'[10]

In such cases, the Conservatives' appeal to prejudice appears transparently calculated. But the party's history of bigotry can't just be reduced to trying to win votes: many Conservatives indulge such views all too sincerely as well. As an intellectual tradition, Conservatism is much more prone to racism, sexism, homophobia and other forms of stigmatisation than either liberalism or socialism. Prejudice of all kinds appears more frequently in the private writings, public statements and actions of Tory politicians than with Labour politicians, who generally have a far prouder – if far from flawless – record of supporting equal rights, whether in terms of gender, race or sexuality.

Benjamin Disraeli is often celebrated as Britain's first, and only, Jewish PM. But aside from the fact that he was baptised into the Church of England as a child, and that, had he not been, his leadership would have been extremely unlikely, he was hardly a paragon of tolerance and diversity himself. Disraeli's tirades against the Irish, for example, were vicious even by the standards of his day. 'They hate our free and fertile isle,' he wrote in 1836. 'They hate our order, our civilisation, our enterprising industry, our sustained courage, our decorous liberty, our pure religion. This wild, reckless, indolent, uncertain and superstitious race have no sympathy with the English character.'

Meanwhile, Britain's world-conquering imperialism – affirming the supremacy of 'the race that sways the world', as Disraeli put it – posited all foreigners as inferior, and so served as a lightning rod for racist beliefs. How else could the violence of Empire – the brutalities of conquest and containment – be justified? The idea of equality regardless of skin colour needed to be opposed at all costs. 'What would be the consequence on the great Anglo-Saxon republic, for example, were its citizens to . . . mingle with their negro and coloured populations?' Disraeli wondered. 'In the course of time they would become so deteriorated that their states would probably be reconquered and regained by the aborigines whom they have expelled, and who would then be their superiors.'[11] Disraeli was essentially presaging Powell's prophecy: that if immigration was permitted in Britain, the whip would no longer be in the hand of the white man.

Winston Churchill carried the baton of Britain's racial superiority with particular gusto: first as a journalist and a soldier, watching Britain's imperial wars unfold up-close, and then as a politician. 'I do not admit, for instance, that a great wrong has been done to the Red Indians of America, or the black people of Australia,' Churchill said in 1937. 'I do not admit that a wrong has been done to those people by the fact that a stronger race, a higher grade race, or, at any rate, a more worldly-wise race, to put it that way, has come in and taken their place.'[12] This prejudice cannot be passed off as a product of its time: the contrarian phrasing – 'I do not admit that . . .' – is proof enough that opposing opinions were common. It didn't take a radical progressive to see Churchill's bigotry for what it was, either. Arch-imperialist and Conservative politician Leo Amery believed that, on matters of race, Churchill was 'not quite sane', suggesting that here there was little difference 'between his outlook and Hitler's'.[13]

Such a claim – from a Conservative politician – seems unthinkable based on our popular understanding of Churchill and the Second World War. Churchill and Hitler are meant to be opposites, and their battle is portrayed as a dramatic clash of values: democracy against fascism, tolerance against anti-Semitism, peace against war. The reality is less romantic. Like other Tories, Churchill was stirred into action not by Hitler's anti-Semitism or his fascism, but by 'the threatening continental expansionism that it inspired in Germany', as the historian Priya Satia has explained, which jeopardised Britain's borders and its Empire. 'There were many, perhaps even a majority, on the Tory right more interested in preserving the peace and the British Empire than in opposing Hitler.'

Indeed, however much Tories point to Disraeli's Jewish heritage, Conservatives have a rich history of anti-Semitism themselves. Churchill is a prominent figure within it. That he helped to defeat Hitler doesn't change the fact that he was anti-Semitic, too. In 1920, Churchill suggested that 'international Jews' were leading a 'world-wide conspiracy for the overthrow of civilisation'. He warned Lloyd George that a government 'must not have too many of them [Jews]' in it.[14] He had good company in the Conservative Party. One of the closest allies of Conservative PM Stanley Baldwin was William Joynson-Hicks, described by the *Jewish Chronicle* as 'the most avowed and determined anti-Semite in the House'. In 1924, Baldwin promoted him to home secretary, where his prejudice was given free rein: his Special Restriction Order 1925 was an early example of immigration control, aiming to stop England being 'flooded', in his words, 'with the whole of the alien refuse from every country in the world'.[15] Later, as anti-Semitism soared in Europe, the Conservative PM Neville Chamberlain (who led the country between 1937 and 1940) could summon only half-hearted sympathy for persecuted Jews. In November 1938, responding to Kristallnacht ('the Night of Broken Glass') where Jewish homes and shops throughout Germany and recently occupied territories were ransacked and synagogues were destroyed by Nazi paramilitary troops, he remarked: 'No doubt the Jews aren't a lovable people; I don't care about them myself; but that is not sufficient to explain the Pogrom.'[16]

Many Conservatives went even further. They actively embraced fascism. Stanley Baldwin himself saw cause for common ground, albeit ground that he advised resisting. 'The policy of Fascism is what you may call an Ultramontane [absolutist] Conservatism,' he said. 'It takes many of the tenets of our own party and pushes them to a conclusion which, if given effect to, would . . . be disastrous to our country.'[17] But not all Conservatives shared Baldwin's reservations. For some, fascism was 'true Conservatism'. Overall, dozens of Conservative MPs, peers and officials were either members, funders or founders of fascist groups, including: the British Union of Fascists, also known as 'the Blackshirts', the January Club (a gentlemanly front for the BUF), the Anglo-German Fellowship, the English Mistery and its successor the English Array, the Right Club, the National Citizens Union, the Link, the Liberators and more.[18] One Conservative MP stated that there were 'no fundamental differences of outlook between Blackshirts and their parents, the Conservatives'.[19] A Conservative-owned newspaper called *Truth* pandered to anti-Semitic tropes, denouncing Fleet Street at large as a 'Jew-infested sink', and defended several Conservatives who were fellow travellers with the fascist cause during the Second World War. *Truth* was particularly outspoken in defending Admiral Sir Barry Domville, an ex-director of naval intelligence and an ex-chairman of the Link (a pro-Nazi organisation), after he was interned between 1940 and 1943 for being a Nazi sympathiser.[20] In 1940, a group of Conservative MPs wrote to the PM requesting that Jewish refugees not be naturalised as this would 'result in a permanent increase of our already over-large Jewish population'.[21] At the time, the Jewish community made up less than 0.8 per cent of the population. (Meanwhile, future Labour PM Clement Attlee, who served as Winston Churchill's deputy during the war, sponsored a Jewish family to come to Britain in 1939, and housed one of the sons for several months.)

This was not the full Conservative story during the war. In 1938, Lord Baldwin made a stirring call on the British public to aid refugees from 'an explosion of man's inhumanity to man'. Chamberlain expanded asylum provision after Kristallnacht. But hostility towards Jewish people riddled Britain's response to the war. Even the Kindertransport, where some 9,000 Jews below the age of seventeen were evacuated from the Continent on trains between March 1938 and September 1939, saving them from almost certain death, has a less positive side. Celebrated as a quintessential moment of British hospitality and tolerance, it is easy to forget that, firstly, the entire scheme was privately organised – the government agreed only on the condition that it would provide no funds and play no part in housing the refugees – and, secondly, the children's parents were granted no such safety. Perhaps the cruellest aspect of this historical amnesia is the way that Conservatives so frequently invoke it to justify denying refugees asylum in the present day. 'The myth was born that Britain did all it could for the Jews between 1933 and 1945,' the historian Louise London notes.

> We remember the touching photographs and newsreel footage of unaccompanied Jewish children arriving on the Kindertransports. There are no such photographs of the Jewish parents left behind in Nazi Europe, and their fate has made a minimal impact. The Jews excluded from entry to the United Kingdom are not part of the British experience, because Britain never saw them.[22]

Fascism is often associated with thugs, but in Britain, as elsewhere, it was often an upper-class affair. As the investigative journalist Tim Tate explored in *Hitler's British Traitors*, of the groups working in Britain to help the Nazis, 'the leaders – and much of the membership — of these groups belonged to the country's traditional ruling classes: Parliament, the aristocracy and the military.'[23] In Hitler, parts of the old governing class saw an ally against the threat of Communism and Bolshevism. Lord Rothermere, for example, the proprietor of the *Daily Mail* and among Britain's wealthiest individuals, published a notorious front page declaring 'Hurrah for the Blackshirts!'. While he disliked the word fascist, he happily cosied up to Hitler and Mussolini to the point of sycophancy. 'The Blackshirts Have What the Conservatives Need' another *Mail* article declared, at the same time as the paper provoked panic and fear of 'German Jews Pouring Into This Country', in the words of one *Daily Mail* headline in 1938. Hitler recognised an ally when he saw one. He described Rothermere as 'the only man who sees clearly the magnitude of the Bolshevist danger. His paper is doing an immense amount of good. I have the greatest admiration for him.'

For all the allegations of anti-Semitism made against the left in recent years, Labour boasts no similar history within its ranks. Indeed, at least until the Second World War, many Conservatives often accused the left, with varying degrees of explicitness, of being part of a nefarious Jewish network. Churchill wasn't alone in seeing the Jewish heritage of many revolutionary left-wing thinkers as more than a coincidence, whether Marx, Trotsky, Rosa Luxemburg or Emma Goldman. It spoke to 'inherent inclinations rooted in Jewish character and religion', Churchill said. (It is the misfortune of Judaism, the scapegoat par excellence, to be seen as the conspiracist force at the heart of both capitalism and Communism.)

Whether the pervasiveness of such prejudice speaks to 'inherent inclinations' rooted in the Conservative character and the party's religion is a matter of debate, but it certainly speaks to a side of Conservative history that the party would rather forget. The Conservatives do their best to cultivate amnesia, wrapping up Churchill's bigotry in a protective shell of patriotic myth, so that to tarnish his name means to tarnish Britain itself. In classic Conservative fashion, later generations of Tory have sought to reframe Nazism as a threat from the far left, drawing attention to its full name – 'National Socialism' – with deliberate historical illiteracy. Thatcher, for example, said that the National Front, Britain's main fascist movement in 1970s, was a 'socialist front', a line that many future Tories have continued. Never mind that the National Front and Thatcher shared a favourite politician – Enoch Powell – and that, during her tenure, one of her own MPs was revealed to have made a Nazi salute outside the Reichstag on a trip to Berlin in 1983.

After the Second World War, as the evils of fascism and Britain's brave opposition to the Nazis entered national folklore, the Conservatives became less blasé about far-right extremists in their ranks. Flirtations with fascism and everyday anti-Semitism were no longer accepted as ordinary, understandable prejudices or eccentricities. The results of the 1945 election – the dramatic landslide win for Labour – only accelerated the Conservatives' reckoning with its image. The Conservatives needed to do more than just reconcile the party to more interventionist economic policies and an expanding welfare state. The party had to look and feel and talk and sound like a completely different organisation, as Cameron would later put it. Conservatives needed to affirm that the dangerous beliefs and allegiances that some of its politicians had indulged – beliefs and allegiances that placed Conservatives on the wrong side of history – were either rogue outliers in the party's long-standing devotion to Britain and its people, or never happened at all.

The Conservatives committed to modernising their image. In early 1953, a young Jewish baronet named Keith Joseph approached the party about becoming an MP. Married to the daughter of a wealthy US banking family, he thought his connections might be useful to the party; he urged Conservative vice-chairman for candidates, John Hare, to meet his wife. 'I see his point in so doing, because she seemed to me to be a very charming young American, who I am sure would be an electoral asset,' Hare wrote to a colleague. But Hare also saw another reason to have Joseph on side. 'There is a good deal of talk about anti-Semitic prejudice within the Party and his adoption, therefore, by some constituency would be helpful also for this reason,' he advised.[24]

It's a neat illustration of the Conservative paradox in action – tapping into prejudices one moment, working to disassociate the party from them the next – and reveals one of their main tools for doing so: the politics of representation. Conservatives like to accuse their opponents of playing the game of identity politics, exaggerating what separates us on the surface – skin colour, gender, sexuality, class background etc. – over what unites us. As one Conservative poster declared in 1983, featuring a photograph of a black man, 'Labour say he's black, we say he's British'. But as the comments about Keith Joseph reveal – and many more recent examples abound – Conservatives are fluent in identity politics as well: a prominent politician from a particular identity softens any allegations of prejudice, and can be wielded as proof of a progressive mindset, despite what's happening elsewhere.

The Conservatives undertook an even more radical process of modernising its image in the wake of New Labour's dominance between 1997 and 2010, as Tony Blair positioned himself as the ambassador for a new, multicultural Britain and defeated the Conservatives three times in a row. The Conservatives had tried and failed to play the Nasty Party card: in the lead-up to the 2001 election, Conservative leader William Hague warned that Blair would turn Britain into a 'foreign land' if re-elected; then his successor Michael Howard, the son of Jewish refugees, made immigration the centre of his election campaign, deploying forty-eight-sheet billboard ads that declared: 'It's not racist to impose limits on immigration'.

By the time of Howard's campaign, a then relatively unknown Conservative MP, Theresa May, had already cautioned Tories who 'make political capital by demonising minorities instead of showing confidence in all the citizens of our country'. She said it was backfiring. 'Our base is too narrow, and so, occasionally, are our sympathies. You know what some people call us – the nasty party.' She pointed to a lack of diversity among new Tory MPs, in terms of ethnicity and gender. When Cameron took control of the party in 2005, he made escaping this image a priority. He pledged to 'change the face of the Conservative Party by changing the faces of the Conservative Party,' and denounced 'the appalling lack of diversity of candidates and MPs'.

Cameron later recalled 'forceful' opposition to his plans within the party. But the results were impressive. During the 2010 election, the Conservatives not only returned to power, they also came close to quadrupling their number of women politicians. The number of MPs from ethnic minorities also rose, but the steepest climb was yet to come. By the time the 2015 election was over, the number of Conservative MPs from ethnic minorities had risen sixfold, future leader Rishi Sunak among them. By 2022, the Conservatives could boast twenty-two MPs from ethnic minorities (twenty-two more than they had in 2001), after running seventy-six black and minority ethnic candidates in 2019, a 72 per cent increase since 2017. The growing diversity of Conservative MPs ran alongside an even more radical transformation of the Tories' top team. Since 2010, the Conservatives have claimed a number of milestones in British politics: the first Muslim cabinet member, in Sayeeda Warsi; the first home secretary and the first chancellor from an ethnic minority, in Sajid Javid; the first female home secretary from an ethnic minority, in Priti Patel; the first black foreign secretary, in James Cleverly. Come the election campaign to replace Boris Johnson in the summer of 2022, six of the eleven initial candidates weren't white – a remarkable display of diversity that no other major party in the Western world, on either the right or the left, could match. Liz Truss ultimately won the leadership election, but when her prime ministership quickly collapsed, runner-up Rishi Sunak, a practising Hindu and second-generation immigrant, replaced her. The Conservatives had delivered Britain's first non-white PM.

Such diversity in the Conservatives' upper ranks is a dramatic departure from the past. When John Taylor, a black barrister from the Midlands, was selected as a Conservative candidate in 1990, Labour had four non-white MPs and the Conservatives had none. Taylor hoped to change that, but he was swiftly attacked as 'a bloody nigger' by a party member who declared: 'We are here to repel the invader.'[25] Taylor lost the election, and partly blamed his party. 'The party must learn that holding three or four receptions for Asian million-aires every year does not amount to a race relations policy,' he said. (He was soon appointed to the Lords as a life peer.) Labour still have far more non-white MPs and non-white voters than the Tories, but their share is shrinking. Labour claim 63 per cent of the former and 64 per cent of the latter, down from over 80 per cent in 1997. Meanwhile, the Conservatives delight in pointing out Labour's enduring failure to front either a woman or a person of colour as leader: the Conservatives have now done so a collective four times.

The Conservatives are clearly proud of the tolerant image of the party that their front bench projects, but it hasn't led to any softening of the party's anti-immigration stance. If anything, the Conservatives seem to take it as a licence to push an ever-harder line, while shielding the party from allegations of nastiness and xenophobia. The rise in the number of MPs from ethnic minorities has thus coincided with a rise in policies designed to drum up the threat posed by immigration and ethnic minorities. These range from Theresa May's 'hostile environment' and 'Go Home' vans targeted at illegal immigrants to the recent post-Brexit policy of trying to send asylum seekers to Rwanda for detention. 'It gives the Conservatives a degree of cover for things that Conservatives would find difficult to say if it wasn't said by people of colour,' Sayeeda Warsi, a critic of these measures, told me when we spoke in November 2022, while making clear that this wasn't the only reason for the Conservatives' increasingly diverse front bench. 'To an extent, colour gives cover.'

In a campaign video during the 2022 leadership contest, Rishi Sunak devoted almost five minutes to the need to toughen Britain's 'broken' borders and claimed that immigration was 'completely out of control'. 'I will make the Rwanda policy work,' he said. 'It is essential that anyone considering trying to sneak into Britain knows that their journey will end in Kigali not King's Cross.' Towards the end, he invoked his own background. 'Britain is a generous, ambitious and compassionate country. Not only have we welcomed successive waves of immigrants to this land, people like my family, but we continue to do so . . . But basic human decency must be accompanied by hard-headed common sense.' It's a rhetorical device that other recent home secretaries like Sajid Javid, Priti Patel and Suella Braverman know well: invoking an immigrant identity while advocating an ever-harsher immigration policy. 'The British people deserve to know which party is serious about stopping the invasion on our southern coast and which party is not,' Braverman said on 31 October 2022, as the Tories tried to conjure up another 'migrant crisis'. 'The system is broken. Illegal migration is out of control and too many people are interested in playing political parlour games, covering up the truth, than solving the problem.'

Braverman had people from Albania in mind, but the targets of Conservative prejudice are constantly changing. Perhaps the Nasty Party's most consistent victim since 2010 has been Muslims, who are frequently cast as the 'enemy within'. A poll in 2019 found that almost half of Conservative members wouldn't want a Muslim as PM.[26] Conservative politicians often seem to share these prejudices. In 2013 Conservative politicians and several newspapers conspired to turn the notorious 'Trojan Horse' letter – widely agreed to be a hoax – into a crisis of Muslims not integrating within British society.[27] They have collectively subjected Muslims to an environment of constant suspicion and surveillance, asserting an intrinsic link between Islam and terrorism. Publications like *The Times* and the *Spectator* have published pieces with headlines like 'Islamophobia is a fiction to shut down debate' and 'There is not nearly enough Islamophobia within the Tory Party'. 'It's disturbing that we have people in positions of power who can tell these lies and be so ideological to go out and harm sections of our society,'

Sayeeda Warsi said. 'I always say: what's the end game? This is a community of four and a half million and it's growing. Shall we just write them off as second-class citizens?'

But as Warsi points out, even aside from the diversity of the Conservatives' front bench, the party's record of xenophobia and stigmatisation doesn't mean it is contradictory for ethnic minorities and other stigmatised groups to vote for the Nasty Party, just as it isn't contradictory for a working-class person to vote for a party of the ruling class. Such assumptions bely a one-dimensional understanding of identity. 'Basic Conservative principles – keeping more of what you earn, a state that doesn't interfere in your individual life, a state that supports entrepreneurship, the idea that if you're given the opportunity, you can change the course of your life – appeal across cultures and identities,' Warsi said. Prejudices can, too. 'People of colour are not necessarily advocates of all people of colour.'[28]

The problem for Conservatives, as they seek to broaden their popularity among ethnic minorities, is how to do so without forsaking the minority constituency on which their success consistently relies: the far right. Put differently, the task facing the Tories is how to gain the support of people with racist beliefs while being a non-racist party. This awkward balancing act explains Ted Heath's uneasy response to Enoch Powell after his 'Rivers of Blood' speech of 1968: simultaneously firing him from the shadow cabinet, letting him stay on as a Conservative MP and toughening the party's stance on immigration. Even if Heath privately saw Powell as a fascist, he also knew that Powell brought the party votes. As Samuel Brittan wrote in the *Spectator* a year later: 'Powell has undoubtedly attracted to his banner the anti-blacks, hangers, floggers, censors and the martinets, who support him' – he 'acted as a catalyst for unpleasant feelings which might otherwise have found a more dangerous outlet'. The Conservatives could stand as the party of Powell in some eyes, and the party to whom Powell was beyond the pale in others.

It's a balancing act that the party still struggles to sustain: from Thatcher dismissing the National Front as a 'socialist front' at the same time as it accused her of stealing its policies and supporters, to David Cameron mocking Nigel Farage's UK Independence Party (UKIP) as 'fruitcakes, loonies and closet racists' and then surrendering to their main demand in order to get their votes: an in/out referendum on EU membership. However much they might not like it, Conservatives know that their winning coalition usually requires having those 'fruit-cakes, loonies and closet racists' on side.[29]

Nigel Farage, who cites Enoch Powell as his 'political hero' and unsuccessfully courted his support in 1994, is the most powerful figure on the far right today. A former City trader from a London public school, he has transformed himself into Britain's anti-immigration impresario, hauling British politics to the right, arguably standing as the most influential British politician since Thatcher. Over the past decade, the Tories have been dancing to his drum: first through UKIP, as he convinced Cameron to call a referendum; then through Vote Leave, as he helped to sway the referendum his way; and then through the Brexit Party. In May 2019, he effectively caused the resignation of Theresa May: a month after launching, the Brexit Party won the European elections, sinking the Tories into a humiliating fifth place; May's resignation followed the next day. Soon Boris Johnson, boasting Farage's support, had replaced her, advocating a toughened approach to EU negotiations. In the December 2019 election, the Conservatives then made a pact with Farage: the Brexit Party wouldn't run candidates in any of the Tories' 317 seats so long as Johnson promised to fulfil their Brexit vision. Flying on Farage's coat-tails, the Conservatives coasted to victory.

Johnson has always been adept at the Conservatives' balancing act: keeping the far right at a distance with one arm and close by with the other. Johnson's early journalism is littered with casual prejudice that the fruitcakes, loonies and closet racists could lap up. He claimed that young people in Britain have 'an almost Nigerian interest in money', described black people as 'piccaninnies' with 'watermelon smiles' (echoing some of Powell's language in his infamous speech, where he also spoke of 'piccaninnies'), and said of Africa: 'The continent may be a blot, but it is not a blot upon our conscience. The problem is not that we were once in charge, but that we are not in charge any more.' While editor of the *Spectator*, he published an article stating that 'blacks have lower IQs'. The list could go on. But Johnson's speciality is in appealing to two sides simultaneously, appearing as both liberal and reactionary at the same time. When he described Muslim women who wear burqas as 'looking like letter-boxes' in 2018, for example, he did so in an article that actually defended their right to wear them – endearing himself with the far right and affirming his supposed liberalism at once. (In a 2007 interview with *Pink News*, as Johnson tried to court the gay vote in his campaign to be mayor of London, he appeared to acknowledge this as a deliberate tactic. He dismissed a range of offensive things he had previously written about the gay community, saying: 'I am on record with loads of provocative articles about loads of things, but if you take the article as a whole, they always amount to robust common sense.')

Johnson maintained this double act throughout the campaign to leave the European Union in 2016. He dismissed the idea that the Brexit campaign was inciting xenophobia by saying that he was personally very pro-immigration, at the same time as he implied that Turkey's imminent (and imagined) member-ship of the EU was an existential threat. This lie, with its tacit warning of a sudden influx of millions of Turkish citizens, had clear racist undertones. The Leave campaign exploited it unashamedly: they put it up on billboards and, a week before the vote, Johnson and Michael Gove wrote a public letter demanding that Cameron 'guarantee' that Turkey would never join the European Union.

Johnson, whose great-grandfather was Turkish (as he pointed out while mayor of cosmopolitan London between 2008 and 2015), was actually one of the biggest proponents for Turkey joining the EU before the referendum. 'What are we saying if we perpetually keep Turkey out of the European Union just because it's Muslim?' he said in 2006. 'It sends out the worst possible signal to moderates in the Islamic world.' After the referendum, he once again expressed his support for Turkey's membership.

In 2019, as the Conservatives made their pact with the Brexit Party, Johnson's flirtations with Farage were decried by many Conservatives as a betrayal of the party's moderate tradition. But Johnson always knew Farage's true tribe. 'He's in our constituencies, wooing our audiences, nicking our votes,' Johnson had written in the *Daily Telegraph* in 2013, during UKIP's rise. But panic, he said, was premature. 'We Tories look at him – with his pint and cigar and sense of humour – and we instinctively recognise someone who is fundamentally indistinguishable from us,' Johnson wrote. The alarm was simply that 'of a man confronted by his doppelganger' – 'he's a blooming Conservative, for heaven's sake'.[30]

While their election masks may differ, the Faragist dream for Britain buried within Brexit is the same one that has excited Conservatives for nearly half a century: of a nation loyal to both profit and a mythologised past; at once enclosed in a unique, sovereign territory and exposed to the homogen-ising market forces of a globalised world; open for business, closed to foreigners; a Singapore-on-Thames, steeped in sepia tones. Thatcher was the first to make this contradictory vision real, bringing Little England and Global Britain together. But, in many ways, Enoch Powell was the project's true pioneer. History has allotted them different roles: Powell, the xeno-phobe; Thatcher, the free-marketeer – but, much like Johnson and Farage forty years later, their political personas were always two sides of the same coin. As Powell coyly reflected in 1988, 'that which used to be called Powellite has recently been redesignated Thatcherite'.

All in all, the Conservatives command an unwieldy coalition of conflicting concerns and promises, standing for monarchy and meritocracy, harmony and hierarchy, diversity and exclu-sion, prosperity and hardship, and England and the Union – all delivered through a rhetoric that combines 'One Nation' overtures with 'divide-and-conquer' strategy. There is no point in trying to flatten out or rationalise these contradictions – the Conservatives thrive because of them. 'In our intellectual way,' Stuart Hall wrote in 1987, as he tried to make sense of Thatcherism's seeming ideological incoherence, 'we think that the world will collapse as the result of a logical contradiction: this is the illusion of the intellectual – that ideology must be coherent, every bit of it fitting together, like a philosophical investigation.'

For the Conservatives, if not the country, this trademark mix of market freedom and state force, national optimism and nationalist fear, has delivered huge success. But it could never have been achieved alone. The Conservatives are aided by a generous political force that, much like Farage and the far right, often does the Tories' dirty work, saying the quiet part out loud. It hounds political opponents, turns them into pariahs and focuses minds on a familiar cast of scapegoats on which to blame society's ills. It loves to position itself as a bastion of free speech and patriotism, bravely representing the interests of the public. It would be better described as a bastion of the Conservative cause – one that holds the Tories to account only as a way of influencing its internal politics and, if anything, trying to push the party even further to the right. Enter the Tory Press.

6

THE TORY PRESS

'You cannot hope to bribe or twist, thank God! the British journalist. But, seeing what the man will do unbribed, there's no occasion to.'

Humbert Wolfe, 'Over the Fire', 1930

'Many a foreign Government would be prepared to pay large sums for the support it gets gratis from incorruptible British journalists.'

Wickham Steed, *The Press*, 1938

'I am so rooting for you tomorrow, not just as a proud friend but because professionally we're definitely in this together.'

Text message from Rebekah Brooks, CEO of News International, to David Cameron, 2009

On 10 June 1987, the *Daily Mail*'s editor, David English, sat with Prime Minister Margaret Thatcher in Downing Street, anticipating the next day's general election results. Thatcher's third victory in a row seemed almost certain, and English asked her what the *Mail*'s celebratory headline should be. She suggested 'Thatcher set for a winning treble', and, sure enough, the following morning her words appeared in block capital letters on the paper's front page – without inverted

151

commas. English sent over his congratulations. 'Well, we certainly agreed the right headline on Wednesday night!' he wrote. 'It gave me great pleasure to put it in type after you wrote it. In fact, you not only wrote it, you worked for it, you earned it and you deserved it.'[1]

Needless to say, a prime minister writing her own headlines is far from the idealised image of the free press. Journalists are supposed to bravely hold the powerful to account, investigating their actions and exposing any scandals to public scrutiny. They put their own political beliefs and allegiances to one side, as they pursue corruptions of power regardless of who is culpable, or whose interests their stories might serve or foil. As they shine a light on injustices in society, the work of journalists should also awaken a sense of empathy among the public. All this performs a vital role in any democracy, which is why a free press is held (and often holds itself) in such high regard. Citizens are empowered to see their society more clearly. Those with power know they must watch their step. 'Democracy dies in darkness' as the famous slogan of the *Washington Post* goes.

Perhaps it would be unrealistic to expect the media in any country always to live up to this ideal. No newspaper could ever fill its pages solely with investigations and in-depth exposés, nor would most readers want that: people read newspapers not only for politics (or even especially for politics), but for entertainment and information – sports coverage, celebrity gossip, film reviews, recipes and so on. Nonetheless, we might at least hope that journalism maintains a basic sense of its responsibility: that journalists should never deliberately mislead the public, inflame prejudices or cultivate a distorted view of society. As far as politics goes, their role is to scrutinise those in power rather than to protect them,

152

to punch up not down. After all, if newspapers continuously gave their readers a warped sense of the world, or sought to obfuscate rather than illuminate the workings of power and privilege, then journalism's prized place in a democracy would be harder to justify. We might all agree that something had to change.

In Britain, we are at such a point. Taken as a whole, the media landscape is so tilted in the right's favour that it is more useful to the interests of the Conservatives than to the health of Britain's democracy. The partisan nature of the British press becomes most pointed at election time, when most news-papers abandon all pretence of independence and effectively become extensions of the Conservative Party's election oper-ation. Journalists and editors see their role not as reporting the election but as winning it for the Tories; they aren't clar-ifiers or commentators, but combatants. 'It was all-in wrestling, hand-to-hand fighting, commando stuff,' the *Daily Express* editor said of the paper's 1945 election campaign. 'We must hit back! We must hit back!' a *Daily Mail* editor declared during the 1987 campaign, after a good day for Labour. A *Mail* reporter said the newsroom felt like a part of Tory HQ.[2]

There are countless examples, ancient and contemporary, of this partisanship in practice. During the 1979 election, the *Daily Mail* splashed a front page that was literally written by Thatcher's own spin doctor. The Tories then reproduced the front page – headlined 'Labour's Dirty Dozen: 12 Big Lies They Hope Will Save Them' – as an election poster, giving the attack an illusion of independence.[3] In the same campaign, the *Daily Express* published an anti-Labour front page that was later framed at Conservative Central Office. In 1992, the *Sun* infamously boasted that its virulently anti-Labour, pro-Con-servative election coverage had secured the Tories their majority: 'It's The Sun Wot Won It'. In 2015, the *Daily Telegraph* breached privacy regulations by sending hundreds of thousands of registered readers an email urging everyone to vote Conservative. In 2017 and 2019, the relentlessness of press attacks on Labour only reached new heights.

Such antics are the exact opposite of how a free press should behave. It's not unusual for a newspaper to endorse a particular party or candidate – what is unusual is the extent to which British newspapers let it colour their coverage during campaigns. Yet this is such a standard part of British politics that we rarely recognise how peculiar – and, in the context of democracy, how damaging – it is. Elections are the most important moment in a democracy, and a free press is the chief means by which the public is informed. What happens to a democracy when a 'free press' consistently and unsubtly allies with one side during elections? As long ago as 1704, Daniel Defoe could comment that 'since this nation is unhappily divided into parties, every side ought to have an equal advantage in the use of the press'. Rarely has such a reasonable notion seemed so implausible.

The balance of the British press has waxed and waned over time, but it has never leaned more left than right. In 1834, *The Times* – Britain's paper of record – helped to launch the Conservative Party when the editor, Thomas Barnes, advised Robert Peel on the Tamworth Manifesto, widely regarded as the party's founding document.[4] For much of the nineteenth century, the Conservatives owned the newspapers that supported them. Even with the rise of the popular press from the 1890s onwards, when newspapers became mass products for the first time, Conservative loyalists were leading the charge. Alfred Harmsworth tried and failed to become a Conservative MP in 1895 before he launched the *Daily Mail* a year later and then became Lord Northcliffe. Max Aitken, soon to be Lord Beaverbrook, was already a Conservative MP when he quietly bought the *Daily Express* in 1916 and made it the most popular newspaper in Britain. Lord Rothermere's son, the 2nd Viscount Rothermere, was also a Conservative MP before he formally took over the family business in 1932.[5]

Today, of Britain's eleven major newspapers, six can be said to make up the so-called 'Tory Press': *The Times*, *Daily Telegraph*, *Daily Mail*, the *Sun*, *Daily Express* and *Evening Standard* are all reliably pro-Conservative, with only *The Times* and *Sunday Times* seeming to aspire towards some impartiality in their political reporting (an impartiality that is unevenly applied at the best of times, and tends to evaporate during elections). These newspapers vastly outnumber the two in Labour's corner, the *Guardian* and *Daily Mirror*. The final three lean right but aren't loyal to either party: the *i*, *Daily Star* and *Financial Times* were all neutral in the 2019 election. Most of these newspapers are owned by billionaires with close ties to the Conservative Party, namely Rupert Murdoch, Lord Rothermere, Lord Lebedev and the Barclay family.

Even as print numbers nose-dive, the chasm in readership and influence is huge. The Tory Press's combined daily circulation was over seven times that of the *Guardian* and *Daily Mirror* combined in 2020. While the disparity narrows on the internet, it's still pronounced, with about two to three times the readership. And even these figures don't reflect their different abilities to set the political weather. Not only does the Tory Press pursue its political agenda with far more intensity than the mild-mannered *Guardian*, for example, but television and radio also have a habit of following the print press. The Tory tilt of newspapers thus ripples throughout the media. This is particularly significant in the case of the BBC, by far the loudest and most listened-to voice in the public conversation. In the name of neutrality, the BBC's news content is largely based on what the national press reports, so the imbalance of the press then becomes part of the BBC's own 'balanced' coverage, which then filters down to its massive monthly online readership and flagship television and radio broadcasts. (Next to the extreme partisanship of the Tory Press, it is no surprise that the BBC's attempts at neutrality nonetheless strike the Conservatives as 'left-wing bias'.)[6]

The 2019 election demonstrated how effectively the Conservatives can hijack the news cycle. On 9 November, for example, a month before polling day, the Conservatives published a warning that Labour would spend £1.2 trillion over five years if elected. The figure was pure fiction: the Labour Party was yet to even release its manifesto. But the *Mail on Sunday*, *Sunday Telegraph* and *Sunday Times* all dutifully splashed it on their front pages, as if it was an independent finding rather than party propaganda. The *Mail* said Labour would 'cost every UK household £43,000'; the *Telegraph* headlined it as 'Scale of Labour's "reckless" spending revealed'; the *Sunday Times* said it would 'bankrupt the UK'. 'Conservative Central Office will be delighted because their analysis of Labour spending hits front page after front page after front page,' Andrew Marr said on his flagship BBC show, which began with a review of the papers. He then read out each headline, one by one. While he later acknowledged that the figure was 'bogus' and 'dodgy', it was too little, too late. 'By then the agenda had been set,' as the political commentator Gary Younge noted. 'For the rest of the day you could either decry Labour's £1tn folly, deny its £1tn folly, contest its £1tn folly or explain its £1tn folly. Either way you'd be discussing it – which means the two things that will cut through the noise are "Labour" and "£1tn". But this is not the product of genius messaging; it's the gift of loyal stenographers.'[7]

Measuring the precise influence of the Conservatives' loyal stenographers in keeping the party in power is notoriously difficult: there is no way of knowing exactly how much influence the press wields in the messy terrain of politics, and both editors and politicians like to claim that the press either follows public opinion or shapes it as it suits. In some moments, the press is an all-powerful political actor that must be kept on side. In others, the press is passé: *who even reads newspapers any more?*

Yet the press, whether online or in print, still wields a remarkable amount of power, even with its circulation figures in seemingly terminal decline. In a more hostile media climate, many pillars of the Conservatives' success would probably collapse. The party wouldn't be able to reinvent itself so freely, or to frame its elitist agenda in terms of 'the national interest' so convincingly. The party's populist credentials would ring hollow, as the disconnect between the needs and wants of the wider public and their great ventriloquists – the Tory Press – became clear. Any account of Tory dominance would be incomplete without the story of the British press. As a brief history reveals, the press might claim to be a bastion of free speech, but it would be more accurate to call it a bastion of the status quo – and that usually means keeping the Conservatives in power.

For the first half of the nineteenth century, newspapers were a niche industry and *The Times* commanded a unique authority. Its ties to the ruling classes were unparalleled; its reporting team was better trained and better resourced than any other publication; its technologies for production – first with the Koenig steam-powered press in 1814, and then the Applegarth press in 1827 – outpaced those of any rival. Its sales figures towered at around ten times the size of any other daily.[8]

But the relative ascendancy of *The Times* masked a more modest reality: the paper's circulation was minuscule by later standards. By 1840, *The Times* was still selling only 23,000 copies in a population of 18 million – and that was after almost a fivefold rise since 1815. This tiny number of readers was ensured, even encouraged, not just by the paper's price – it could amount to almost a third of a worker's daily pay – but also by its lofty dullness. Parliamentary reports would often stretch up to around 15,000 words and MPs speeches were quoted verbatim, at arduous length, all delivered in long, grey, pictureless prose.

The inaccessibility of *The Times* was no accident: it was part of a broader political plan to make newspapers, and the ideas they contained, the preserve of the elite. A tax, known as the stamp duty, helped to ensure newspapers and other publications were prohibitively expensive for most of the public. John Cresset Pelham wasn't the only MP to praise this 'eminently useful' arrangement which, as he explained, placed newspapers 'under the control of men of wealth and character who, for their own sakes, would conduct them in a more responsible manner than was likely to be the result of a pauper management'. The hope was that if the government could prevent the supply of radical ideas there would be no demand for them either. An inflated cover price and higher production costs would, another MP explained, 'prevent the circulation of the most dangerous doctrines'.

The reality was more complicated. The stamp duty essentially created two media realms: one legal, another illegal. A wealth of underground publications known as the 'radical press', clamouring for reform, flourished in these hostile conditions. Because these papers dodged the stamp duty and other press taxes, which they attacked as 'taxes on knowledge', anyone involved faced imprisonment. But for the same reason they were also the most affordable publications available. This alone ensured their relative popularity. It's thought that one such paper, the *Political Register*, sold up to 60,000 copies during 1817's winter of discontent, ten times the number for *The Times*. Their influence also far exceeded the number of copies sold, because articles were often read aloud in taverns and at rallies, and copies were shared among workers and friends.

Conservatives and Whigs were right to be worried. Society seemed increasingly unstable, and the threat of revolution was in the air. As workers began to imagine a better world, the radical press only encouraged them. 'Those infamous publications . . . inflame [workers'] passions and awaken their selfishness,' one MP complained in the Commons, 'contrasting their present conditions with what they contend to be their future condition − a condition incompatible with human nature, and with those immutable laws which Providence has established for the regulation of civil society.' Some in parliament began to wonder whether the success of the radical press proved that the taxes on knowledge weren't working. Rather than preventing these ideas from being published or read, they realised, it gave them a free run. It followed that the way to challenge their dangerous doctrines wasn't through bans, but competition. Affordable establishment newspapers, led by trustworthy figures, would enlighten the public into peaceful, enthusiastic acceptance of the status quo.

Edward Bulwer-Lytton was one of the leading voices of the campaign. A Whig MP who would later switch to the

Conservatives, a close friend of Disraeli, Bulwer-Lytton saw newspapers as one of the few ways besides religion to influence the minds of the masses. He believed that a cheap establishment press would do away with 'those superficial and dangerous notions of the injustice of the divisions of property, which men who are both poor and ignorant so naturally conceive'. Ignorance wasn't bliss, but dangerous: only the press could educate workers into acceptance.[9]

Bulwer-Lytton was also a renowned writer and playwright in his day, and coined the aphorism 'the pen is mightier than the sword'. While this has become a pithy paean to the power of words to change the world, the meaning appears in a different light given its author's politics: as an ode to the submissive, rather than liberatory, power of the press. Bulwer-Lytton assured Conservative leader Benjamin Disraeli that 'a penny journal containing moderate Conservative opinions . . . would do more to popularise Conservatism than half the party speeches we make in the House'.

These are the conservative origins of Britain's 'free press'. The idea was motivated not by liberal or radical impulses, but by conservative ones: the aim was never to challenge or disrupt the status quo, or to revel in the anarchic wonders of free speech, but, rather, to preserve society as it is. 'The only question to answer, and the only problem to solve,' Lord Brougham, then the Lord Chancellor, summarised in 1834, 'is how [people] shall read in the best manner; how they shall be instructed politically, and have habits formed the most safe for the constitution for the country.' Fears about a free press remained: that the state, by permitting the distribution of radical ideas, could sow the seeds of its downfall. But these were eventually displaced by a growing confidence among the ruling classes that the instinctive 'common sense' of the British

160

public was on their side. In 1855, the stamp duty was finally abolished. Britain's free press was born.

The reform went to plan. In the following decades, most radical papers either closed down or were absorbed into the mainstream, while circulation trebled between 1855 and 1860, doubling again in the following decade. New local dailies proliferated and, as it became obvious that ownership of a newspaper was an easy way to wield influence, they were snapped up or launched anew by leading industrialists or affiliates of the major parties. The line between press and parliament blurred. Between 1851 and 1887, the number of Conservative- and Liberal-affiliated newspapers rose from 189 to 707 publications, with a particularly sharp spike in the 1860s. The number of press proprietors sitting in the House of Commons went from four in 1857 to thirty in 1892. These papers were useful mouthpieces for the major parties, and the Conservatives soon gained the lead. By the start of the twentieth century, the Conservatives had gained a clear advantage over the Whigs or Liberals in terms of press support for the first time.[10] With the sole exception of the Blair years, they have maintained this ascendancy over their opponents ever since.

The early expansion of the press proved politically useful in other ways: it helped to make possible the emergence of Britain as a modern nation state. Bulwer-Lytton was among those who realised the formative power of newspapers. 'The newspaper is . . . the common reservoir into which every stream pours its living waters, and at which every man may come and drink,' he said in the 1830s. Newspapers brought people together, focusing their fears on common threats and defining shared interests − 'the familiar bond that binds together man and man'. They also broadened their readers horizons. As future US president Woodrow Wilson put it in 1889, the press 'makes men conscious of the existence and interest of affairs lying outside of the dull round of their own daily lives: It gives them nations, instead of neighbourhoods, to look upon and think about.'

What kind of community was being imagined at the turn of the century? It would still be a while before newspapers would play a central role in answering that question: the British press was still a marginal affair, and it was only in 1932 that national dailies outsold local ones. But the press's national scope and influence was taking shape. The invention of the Linotype machine in 1886 dramatically accelerated newspaper production, simultaneously increasing the upfront costs of starting a newspaper and encouraging production on a mass scale. Trains made newspapers swiftly transportable across the country. Meanwhile a period of rising wages, falling working hours and improving literacy rates meant the public's time and appetite for newspapers was growing. What would be the first paper to meet the new demand?

The *Daily Mail*, launched in 1896, was Britain's first popular newspaper, and its founder, Lord Northcliffe, born Alfred Harmsworth, was Britain's first press baron. Born in Dublin in 1865, the eldest of fourteen children, Harmsworth's passion for newspapers began at a young age. When he was eight, a next-door neighbour (and editor) gave him a printing set, and he'd soon set up a school magazine. By the time he was fifty, amid the First World War, he was the most powerful press baron on the Continent. He controlled almost half of both the morning and evening newspaper circulation, and owned one in every two newspapers read in London, a level of dominance that remains unmatched.[11]

Harmsworth was also a staunch Conservative. In 1894, he had endeared himself to the party faithful by buying one of their struggling papers, the *London Evening News*, to save it from falling into Liberal hands. A year later, he tried to become a Conservative MP, standing in Portsmouth and buying a local paper along the way to help his campaign. While he lost the election, he soon discovered that he could hold more influence outside parliament than inside it.

The *Daily Mail* became the bedrock of his success. At a halfpenny per copy, it was affordable. With an editorial motto of 'explain, simplify, clarify', it was accessible. There were to be no more 15,000-word accounts of proceedings in parliament – the *Daily Mail* was, in its own words, 'the busy man's journal'. The paper filled its pages with a broad range of stories and a stronger, more opinionated editorial line. 'The British people relish a good hero, and a good hate,' Harmsworth liked to say. The *Mail* delivered on both fronts: it was both rabidly pro-Empire and rabidly anti-German. When one journalist wondered aloud whether they were playing up to readers' prejudices, Harmsworth replied: 'Prejudices? Well, most of the ordinary man's prejudices are my prejudices – if you want to call them that – and are therefore the prejudices of my newspapers.'[12] His ideal readers were aspirational individualists at heart: 'He likes reading news about people who have succeeded,' Harmsworth explained. 'He sees himself as one of them eventually and he's flattered.'

Harmsworth had found a winning formula. Within a few years, the *Daily Mail* was selling half a million copies, and it hit a million after a few more. As his power grew, so did the Conservatives' compliments bestowed on him: he was knighted in 1904, and received his baronetcy a year later, becoming Lord Northcliffe. By 1907, he'd added *The Observer*, Britain's oldest surviving Sunday paper, and *The Times*, still then considered by foreign powers to be the official voice of government, to his store.

A new type of power player had arrived in British politics: the press baron. Northcliffe wasn't the only one. As newspaper circulation figures soared, ownership became concentrated in fewer hands. While some newspapers were still officially (if discreetly) tied to political parties, such arrangements were increasingly rare. In 1910, a 30-year-old Canadian businessman named Max Aitken, soon to be Lord Beaverbrook, moved to London, and quickly allied himself with the Conservatives; by 1916, helped by the party, Aitken was the proprietor of the *Daily Express*, another new Conservative daily founded in 1900. Northcliffe's brother and business partner Harold, who became Lord Rothermere, was also growing in stature, and became the leading figure of the family dynasty upon Northcliffe's death in 1922.

But for all the popular press's Conservative sympathies, many of the party's patricians were unhappy with these developments. In their eyes, only the landed gentry, with their deep roots in society and their sense of aristocratic obligation, were qualified to lead public opinion. The 'cheap press' was vulgar; its style, they thought, appealed only to the nation's baser instincts. Lord Salisbury dismissed the *Mail* as 'run by office boys for other office boys', a riff on the newspaper described in Thackeray's *Pendennis*, 'written by gentlemen for gentlemen'. (In private, Salisbury also sent a telegram to Harmsworth congratulating him on the first edition.) In his diary, Lord Crawford, another Tory grandee, derided Beaverbrook as 'a dishonest man' and the *Express* as 'a vile newspaper'. He labelled Rothermere a 'scoundrel' and a 'traitor'. This was a time when, for many Tories, the

word 'commercial' was still a dirty word, with all its conno-
tations of 'profit' and 'progress'. The press was equally
ghastly. As the historian A. J. P. Taylor put it, it stood as a
symbol 'for all the corrupting forces which were at work in
British society'.[13]

As time went on, the press barons only amassed more
power, becoming an ever-more unruly force. They sought to
topple prime ministers and reinstate new ones. They tried to
dictate party policy and select members of cabinet in exchange
for their support. During the First World War, partly to keep
his newspapers on side, Lloyd George's coalition appointed
Northcliffe as Britain's director of propaganda and brought in
Beaverbrook and Rothermere as well. But the vast wealth of
the press barons meant their loyalty was all but impossible
to pin down: no sooner was one demand met than another
one was made.

Under such boisterous proprietorship, the press was in
many ways more 'independent' than ever before, but it was
a peculiar type of independence that – much like the original
case for a free press – still seemed designed to protect the
powerful rather than scrutinise them. 'Freed' from political
parties, newspapers became both more aggressive in defending
the vested interests of elites in some ways – determined to
crush any political movement that threatened their power and
wealth – and more volatile, as wealthy proprietors pursued
their own specific political ambitions and beliefs. The result
was not censorship but, as George Orwell would lay out in
his essay 'The Freedom of the Press', something more insidious: a bias that presented itself as free and democratic. 'The
British press is extremely centralized, and most of it is owned
by wealthy men who have every motive to be dishonest on
certain important topics,' Orwell wrote. 'Unpopular ideas can

be silenced, and inconvenient facts kept dark, without the need for any official ban.'

The Conservatives and the press clashed as never before. But it was not the clash of journalistic accountability, of a press holding politicians to account: it was a fight for control over the Conservative agenda. Some press barons began to believe that they could do a better job leading the country, and that the Conservative Party was betraying its cause. Beaverbrook and Rothermere tried to push the party further to the right, fielding their own candidates to stand against Tories in by-elections and launching campaign groups. In 1929, when Labour became the largest party in parliament for the first time and formed a government, the pressure only increased. Two years later, the embattled Conservative leader Stanley Baldwin fought back, denouncing the press barons in a famous speech:

> The papers conducted by Lord Rothermere and Lord Beaverbrook are not newspapers in the ordinary accept-ance of the term. They are engines of propaganda for the constantly changing policies, desires, personal wishes, personal likes and dislikes of two men. What are their methods? Their methods are direct falsehood, misrep-resentation, half-truths, the alteration of the speaker's meaning . . . What the proprietorship of these papers is aiming at is power, and power without responsibility – the prerogative of the harlot throughout the ages.

Baldwin's words still resonate, even if today's press barons are rather different. They are more corporate and less interfering than their predecessors. Beaverbrook, for example, once quipped that he ran the *Daily Express* 'purely for the purpose of making propaganda, and with no other motive'. He was infamously meddlesome. 'The policies were Lord Beaverbrook's job, the presentation was mine,' his long-standing editor Arthur Christiansen recalled.[14] Rupert Murdoch, who rose to power in the late '60s, initially acted like an old press baron rein-carnated but over time he and his contemporaries have been happy to keep more distance from their editors. They know that too many reports of interference will lead to scrutiny and scandal, with consequences on the bottom line. But while editors enjoy relative freedom to pursue their chosen political agendas, they are usually selected to align with the proprietors' own interests. 'Most Murdoch editors . . . think: what would Rupert think about this?' David Yelland, former editor of the *Sun*, explained. 'It's like a mantra inside your head, it's like a prism. You look at the world through Rupert's eyes.'[15]

The result is that, amid all the transformations of the news-paper industry, so much has stayed the same. There have been moments when the Conservatives' monopoly on the press was less severe. The left's media power peaked around the Second World War, as the harsh realities of the conflict heightened awareness of social inequalities and led to greater press regu-lations. The *Daily Mirror* became increasingly left wing and was soon the most popular paper in Britain. Another influential newspaper, the *Daily Herald*, then controlled by the Trades Union Congress, was constitutionally committed to the Labour cause. Even Conservative-supporting newspapers decried the levels of poverty in Britain.

But this rare window – which, as we shall see in the next chapter, coincided with Labour's greatest period of electoral success – only reduced, rather than reversed, the Conservatives' media dominance. Between 1924 and 1945, Labour's share of circulation went from 5 to 35 per cent, while the Tories' share fell from 72 to 52 per cent.[16] After the rise of Rupert Murdoch in the late 1960s, when he bought the *Sun* and turned it into a tabloid, the press resumed its natural course: an overwhelming, unflinching, right-wing bias. Within nine years of its rebranding, Murdoch's *Sun* had overtaken the *Mirror* as the most popular newspaper in the country. The Tories won the next four elections, buoyed by a frenzy of media support akin to 1924 levels. By 2019, the Conservatives could once again count on the support of over three-quarters of press circulation – while Labour received only a tenth.

The 'Tory Press' moniker might not be as literal as it once was. Over the course of the twentieth century the ties between press and party loosened, culminating in 1997 with a number of influential press barons doing what would once have been inconceivable: they supported Labour. Schmoozed by Tony Blair's Labour relaunch – which was happy to let anyone become 'filthy rich', in the words of Peter Mandelson – the Tory Press became the 'Tony Press': he had almost the entire stable of newspapers on his side. But this fleeting change in allegiance said much more about Blair's Conservative credentials than any newfound radicalism among the press's wealthy proprietors. As the 3rd Viscount Rothermere explained in 1997, remarking on the paper's past policy of quasi-official Conservatism: 'Well, it was a different world, and a different sociology in those days – different everything. The world has changed again; that's why I'm supporting Tony.' The billionaire press baron – the ninth richest person in Britain at the time – described Blair as 'like a breath of fresh air, a new spirit'.[17]

The fact that the media's fondness for Blair coincided with New Labour winning three elections only reinforced perceptions about the power of the press. But the speed and ease with which the press resumed its usual intimacy with the Conservatives under David Cameron also made clear where their natural loyalties lie. Beyond an enduring camaraderie between the press's wealthy proprietors and the Tories, newspaper editors and leading writers are often close friends (or more) with Conservative MPs; or future party advisers; or, like Boris Johnson, future politicians themselves.

As prime minister, Johnson's close team was filled with former journalists and their kin: Michael Gove, often his most trusted minister, was a leader writer at *The Times* before he became a Conservative MP (and was, until 2021, married to Sarah Vine, star columnist at the *Daily Mail*); his former chief of staff, Dominic Cummings, previously worked as online editor at the *Spectator* (his wife, Mary Wakefield, is the magazine's commissioning editor, and has written for *The Times*, *Telegraph*, the *Sun* and *Mail*); his chancellor, and eventual successor, Rishi Sunak, was the best man at the wedding of James Forsyth (political editor at the *Spectator*, columnist at *The Times* and, as of December 2022, Sunak's political secretary), whose wife, Allegra Stratton, was briefly Johnson's spokesperson before she had to resign over 'Partygate' in 2021. Another Johnson loyalist, Jacob Rees-Mogg, is the son of William Rees-Mogg, editor of *The Times* between 1967 and 1981. Johnson's wife Carrie, whom he married in 2021, is of a piece: her former boyfriend, Harry Cole, is political editor at the *Sun*, and her friend Alex Wickham, another influential journalist, is reported to be the godfather of their son.[18]

A free press is supposed to be independent. This has been self-evident from the start. 'To perform its duties with entire independence,' *The Times* declared in 1852, 'and consequently with the utmost public advantage, the Press can enter into no close or binding alliances with the statesmen of the day, nor can it surrender its permanent interests to the convenience of the ephemeral power of any government.'

Most journalists, editors and proprietors still like to pay lip service to such ideals. But in reality, modern British politics now takes place within a web of media connections – what Johnson once called the 'journalistico-political complex'. Journalists, editors and politicians attend the same parties and send their children to the same schools. The media are rewarded for their fidelity not only with access and favourable policies but also knighthoods and peerages. The career path of Northcliffe, from press proprietor to the House of Lords, remains well trodden. Within his first year alone, Johnson appointed two editors, two columnists and a press baron to the Lords – and they joined more than thirty other members of the trade. Officially, media figures receive their awards in recognition of their 'services to journalism'. It might be more accurate to say they receive them in recognition of their services to the Conservatives.

According to Dominic Cummings, Johnson was 'about a thousand times too obsessed with the media' and referred to the *Telegraph* as 'my real boss'. But his fondness for the press merely continued a treasured Tory tradition: reward your friends when you win. Thatcher knighted Larry Lamb (editor of the *Sun*), John Junor (editor of the *Sunday Express*) and David English (editor of the *Daily Mail*) in her first term alone. Victor Matthews, who owned the *Daily Express* between 1977 and 1985 and made a large corporate donation to the Conservatives in 1979, received his peerage a year later. ('I have the papers in which to give my views, but I think the

House of Lords will be better,' he said. [19]) William Rees-Mogg, a contemporary of Thatcher's at Oxford, became a Lord in 1988. Thatcher was in no doubt as to why she received such adulating press coverage. 'Because I've been so kind to them,' she said.

But as Baldwin discovered, it would be wrong to see the press as mere Tory sidekicks. Despite their shared aims and close ties, the bond is based on pragmatism rather than loyalty: you scratch my back and I'll scratch yours. In exchange for Murdoch's support, for example, Thatcher blocked a referral to the Monopolies and Mergers Commission that could have stopped him adding *The Times* and the *Sunday Times* to his media empire. When Blair persuaded Murdoch to switch to Labour, it was on a similar premise: 'If Murdoch were left to pursue his business interests in peace, he would give Labour a fair wind,' Blair's staffer Lance Price later recalled. [20] (Next thing Blair knew, he was the godfather to Murdoch's child.) David Cameron also knew the score. Soon, the links between News International and Cameron were so close – with the executive editor of *The Times*, Daniel Finkelstein, reportedly speaking to George Osborne 'six or seven times a day' (he received his peerage in 2013) – that Rebekah Brooks, CEO of News International, reportedly quipped that she was 'running the government now in partnership with David Cameron'. [21]

The failure of the British press to fulfil its independent role is perhaps best symbolised by a message Brooks, running the most powerful media conglomerate in Britain, sent to Cameron in 2009. Brooks enjoyed a close bond with Blair and Gordon Brown – the latter attended her wedding to Charlie Brooks in 2009 – but her relationship with Cameron was even closer: they were neighbours in the Cotswolds, and she had had an affair with Cameron's adviser (and former

News of the World editor) Andy Coulson, who resigned in 2011 as part of the phone-hacking scandal. Her husband also knew Cameron from Eton, and Cameron often dined at the Brooks's home at weekends, regularly attending their annual New Year's Eve party. In 2009, ahead of Cameron's speech at the Conservative conference, Brooks texted him a message of support: 'I am so rooting for you tomorrow, not just as a proud friend but because professionally we're definitely in this together. Speech of your life. Yes he Cam!'

That isn't to say that the Tory Press never scrutinises or criticises the Tories – at times, it can be ferocious in its attacks on Conservatives. But the aim is often to influence the Conservatives' agenda, to prod it in a particular direction or change its personnel. When push comes to shove, the Tory Press and party are united against a familiar threat: a Labour government. The papers and party put their differences aside and make sure that it's Labour in the line of fire. The likes of Rothermere and Beaverbrook would easily recognise the more recent attacks on Labour. Like the best myths, the same fearmongering stories and inventions about Labour are simply reapplied and retold. Here the Conservative Party – in all its three guises: patriotic, prosperous and nasty – and the Tory Press sing from the same hymn sheet.

In the Tories' telling, for example, no matter its leader, Labour is always dangerously unpatriotic. This narrative was pushed by the *Daily Mail* from the moment Labour became an electoral threat. 'The British Labour Party, as it impudently calls itself, is not British at all,' the *Mail* declared in November 1923, shortly before the election that led to the first Labour government. The following year, during a snap election, the Conservatives leaked a forged letter to the *Mail*, purporting to prove that Labour was working with the Communist International. The 'Zinoviev letter', as it came to be known, was only disproved decades later, long after the damage had been done. The *Mail* reported it with glee. 'For the safety of the nation every sane man and woman must vote on Wednesday, and vote for a Conservative Government which will know how to deal with treason,' the *Mail* declared. The *Daily Mirror* ran the front-page headline 'Vote British, not Bolshie', asking its readers: 'Do you Wish to Vote for Leaders of Law, Order, Peace and Prosperity or to Vote for the Overthrow of Society and Pave the Way to Bolshevism?' When the Tories won, the *Mail*'s editor claimed that 'the effect of the publication was, I think, unequalled in all the history of general elections. No single event that I have ever heard of produced such direct and definite reaction in the public mind.' Rothermere, the *Mail*'s then owner, boasted to Beaverbrook that it was probably worth a hundred seats. [22]

A century later, this remains the basic typology of every election in the press's framing. To paraphrase Cameron's infamous tweet in 2015, Britain always faces a simple and inescapable choice – stability and strong government with the Conservatives, or chaos with Labour. When there are no facts to stoke fear, innuendo and invention must do. Struggling to paint a figure like Clement Attlee as an extremist in 1945, for example, the *Daily Mail* merely remarked that he bore a resemblance to Vladimir Lenin. The *Daily Express* happily reported one of Churchill's outlandish claims as fact: 'GESTAPO IN BRITAIN IF SOCIALISTS WIN'. In 1979, the *Telegraph* insisted that Labour's manifesto was 'a mandate for . . . a totalitarian socialist state'. In the 1980s, the *Sunday Times* accused Labour leader Michael Foot of being on the payroll of the Soviet KGB, before withdrawing the accusation following a libel suit. In

1992, the *Sun* published a mock endorsement of Neil Kinnock by Stalin's ghost. Even the mild-mannered Ed Miliband was called a 'class war zealot', nicknamed 'Red Ed' and chastised by the *Mail* for having a socialist father 'who hated Britain'.[23]

Later, the press accused Miliband's successor, Jeremy Corbyn, in even more shrill and fanciful terms: for being a Russian spy, an ally of Islamic extremists, an existential threat to the Jewish community, a terrorist sympathiser, and of conducting 'purges' of his party. In the attempt to 'expose' Corbyn, truth and fact were often relegated from the discussion completely. When Corbyn attended a Remembrance Sunday ceremony, for example, the *Sun* and the *Mail* compiled photographs of him walking along with a war veteran in such a way as to claim that he was doing a disrespectful jig.[24] The day before the 2017 election, the *Daily Mail* published a thirteen-page spread 'proving' that Corbyn and his team were 'APOLOGISTS FOR TERROR'. The *Sun* called on its voters to 'Vote Tory, unless you want a friend of terrorists'. In 2019, no doubt running out of material, the *Sun* sank to a new low: the paper's then political editor, Tom Newton Dunn (the son of a former Conservative MEP), published an 'exclusive' claiming that a group of former British intelligence officers had uncovered a 'hard-left extremist network' at the heart of the Labour Party. When it was revealed that the sources of the story included neo-fascist conspiracy websites, the story was swiftly removed from the *Sun*'s website without comment.[25] Meanwhile, the *Daily Telegraph* happily splashed a Boris Johnson column on its front page, claiming that Corbyn's Labour 'point their finger at [wealthy] individuals with a relish and a vindictiveness not seen since Stalin persecuted the kulaks'.

Like the Conservative Party, the Tory Press positions itself as the nation embodied – playing up its patriotism while also vilifying scapegoats and fuelling prejudices against minorities. The aim is twofold: to generate controversy, thus boosting circulation, and to concoct an endless array of moral panics to which the Tories can then pose as the solution. Beaverbrook used to sing 'Sow the seeds of discord, sow the seeds of discord' down the telephone to his staff, to the tune of 'The more we are together . . .'. 'We must make the readers cross', instructed an internal memo at the *Sunday Express* in 2003. The papers never let the facts get in the way of a good fury. The same method is tirelessly applied: fabricate, exaggerate, aggravate – and then summon the Tories as the nation's saviour.

The Tory Press's proprietors may have their own financial reasons for championing the Conservative Party's economic agenda. There are certainly curious, recurring inconsistencies in their newspapers' concern for the state of public finances: their scorn for welfare cheats is matched only by their indifference to tax avoidance. The Tory Press has always obsessed over alleged government profligacy, seeking lower state spending and lower taxes. Welfare policies are always deemed too generous, wasting taxpayers' money and rewarding bad behaviour. The early *Daily Mail* railed against 'wastrels' in local government and so-called 'squandermania'. (As discussed in Chapter 5, this fixation even fuelled the *Mail*'s interwar flirtation with fascism, as the paper praised Mussolini for 'rationing departments in money and officials, and doing precisely what the *Daily Mail* has suggested a hundred times should be done by government departments here'.[26])

Along with refugees and the far left, welfare claimants are among the right's favourite scapegoats, attacked as 'scroungers', 'frauds', 'cheats' and 'parasites' who live off the hard work of others. Labour is cast as their malign defenders. After the 2008 recession, the press repeated this narrative ad nauseum, justifying the Conservatives' programme of austerity. The levels of disinformation were such that, by 2013, a YouGov poll found that people on average thought 41 per cent of the welfare budget went on the unemployed (the true figure was 3 per cent) and that over a quarter of the welfare budget was claimed fraudulently (the government's own figure was 0.7 per cent).[27] The Conservatives happily exacerbated and exploited these misperceptions – just as it does again now. After twelve years of austerity, which has given Britain one of the stingiest and most punitive welfare systems in the developed world, Home Secretary Suella Braverman still complained at the party conference in October 2022, at an event hosted by the *Daily Telegraph*, that Conservatives needed to clamp down on 'benefit street culture' to save the economy.[28]

The press still likes to play the role of responsible guardian of the public purse. The duplicity that drives this performance can be seen in its utter indifference towards another form of government waste: tax avoidance and tax evasion. The state loses around £35 billion a year to tax non-payment, avoidance and fraud, according to official figures in 2021, which dwarfs the £3.5 to £6.5 billion losses estimated on benefit fraud.[29] Yet most of the press – so easily outraged in other regards – is unstirred by this gap in state finances. More than that, on the few occasions when tax avoidance and evasion have become the subject of public debate, the Tory Press has often worked to actively downplay its significance.

In 2016, for example, the Panama Papers revealed that the father of then prime minister David Cameron was using an offshore tax haven, potentially to the financial benefit of his son. Most of the press treated the story with obfuscation. At the *Sun*, Tom Newton Dunn said there was nothing to see here: it was just 'a boring investment fund set up in the Bahamas to buy things in dollars, as the Caribbean islands are within the dollar area'. The *Daily Mail* agreed: 'The truth is that there are no parents in this country, of any income bracket, who do not want their children to do better than themselves and to give them a leg-up in life.' The *Daily Express* responded to Cameron's statement on the controversy with the headline: 'PM backs your right to pass on wealth'.[30] The same pattern played out when it was revealed that the wife of the chancellor Rishi Sunak was registered as non-domicile. Dan Hodges, for the *Daily Mail*, immediately took to Twitter to denounce those pushing the story as sexist, suggesting they believed that a wife should 'order her tax affairs in a way solely designed to further her husbands [sic] career'.[31] (It is worth pausing to consider the reporter's reflex here: a story breaks about an important Conservative minister, and the journalist's instinct is to jump to their defence.) The *Sun*'s headline framed the story in Sunak's favour: 'Rishi Sunak's wife Akshata Murty defends non dom tax status and blasts claims she's a tax dodger', while the *Daily Express* merely included the revelation in a more general story about Sunak's plummeting popularity.

Why such indifference? It's impossible to be sure, but the Tory Press's softness on tax avoidance may say less about media deference towards the Conservatives, and more about the shared interests underpinning their relationship. Not only do Tory journalists and politicians alike tend to be united in a conviction that all taxes are bad (so who can be blamed for avoiding them?), but the companies behind most Tory Press proprietors are notorious tax dodgers themselves. A report claims that Murdoch's News Corporation effectively avoided paying any UK corporation tax between 1988 and 1999, despite making over £1 billion in profits;[32] News UK, a branch of News Corp, reportedly had more than 150 companies in tax havens revealed by the Panama Papers.[33] (In 2015, the Australian Taxation Office placed News Corp in its highest risk category for tax avoidance – the only company included there.) The Barclay family, owners of the *Daily Telegraph*, use offshore trusts to control their businesses.[34] Lord Rothermere inherited the *Mail* from his father through a Jersey trust, who achieved 'non-dom' status after telling a friend: 'It's absolutely essential [I leave], otherwise I'll be virtually ruined by taxation, and I feel terribly strongly about keeping the empire together.' The *Daily Mail* and General Trust's parent company is Rothermere Continuation Limited (RCL), based in Bermuda. Companies linked to Richard Desmond, who owns the *Daily Express* and the *Daily Star*, also have long histories of tax avoidance.[35] All the while, these newspapers purport to be the most patriotic of them all.

The paradox of the Tory Press is therefore much like that of the Tory Party itself: a force performatively opposed to the establishment and yet embodying it to the core, speaking for the 'man on the street' while residing in multimillion-pound mansions – one foot in the pub, another in the penthouse, offering a pastiche of public service as they bravely face down phantom threats. The Tory Press and the party attack the left by inventing affiliations with extremists and accusing it of wasting taxpayers' money, at the same time as they cosy up to the far right and hide their money offshore; they revel in calling out hypocrisy at the same time as they privately pursue their own political agendas for personal gain.

This populist façade was as true of the first press barons as it is now: the likes of Murdoch, Rothermere, Lord Lebedev and the Barclays control about three-quarters of Britain's newspaper circulation, position themselves as brave defenders of the little man, and all enjoy close links with the Conservatives. Murdoch – the privately educated son of a knighted media tycoon and an Oxford graduate – might be the master of the art. But it's a role that many Conservative politicians also know well.

Far from inspiring any grave concern, however, the bias of the press is accepted as part of the basic architecture of British politics. Left-wing complaints about the media are dismissed as sour grapes, or recast as the patronising assertion that the Tories only win because voters have been brainwashed by the press. Perhaps there is a strain of left-wing thought that does see the power of the media in such simplified terms. The balance between what people read and what they do isn't so simple. Neither the media nor marketing departments can dictate how people think or act. A realistic account of how and what people believe politically will always be more nuanced. As the sociologist Arlie Hochschild has written, 'purchased political influence is real, powerful, and at play . . . but as an explanation for why any of us believe what we do, duping – and the presumption of gullibility – is too simple an idea'.[36]

This is no doubt one of the reasons why it's easy to avoid discussing the role of the press in keeping the Conservatives in power: determining the precise extent of its influence is impossible. Do people inherit their political views from newspapers, for example, or simply choose their newspaper based on their political views? The long-standing disparity between the Conservative-supporting proportion of newspaper circulation (often over 70 per cent) and the Conservative-supporting proportion of voters (usually between 30 and 43 per cent) might suggest that the press doesn't matter: people vote for whatever party they want anyway. Then again, we simply can't know for sure how either the Tories or Labour would fare in a more representative media environment.

There are obvious limitations on the press's power in Britain today. In the 1990s, 4 million people were reading the *Sun* alone, in a population of 55 million. Now 4 million people don't even buy the *Sun*, *Mail*, *Mirror*, *Express*, *The Times* and *Guardian* combined. Trust in the media has also plummeted. Journalists usually rank among the least trusted professionals in Britain, and a recent study suggests that the relationship between the press and the public is worse than elsewhere: the nation's media is the least trusted by its citizens in Europe by some way.[37] When people don't believe what the press writes – when indeed they read it all – what power can the press realistically wield over the public in this context?

Clearly the press is not omnipotent, but nor does it need to be. As long as those in Westminster continue to believe in the press's power, then it will continue to wield undue influence over British politics. This belief shows no sign of waning. As Boris Johnson put it many years ago, in a rare moment of introspection: 'We politicians can be sometimes so consumed with vanity that our very existence, our self-definition, our self-esteem depend on how we think we are portrayed in the media.' According to Ken Clarke, the idea that 'if you want to win an election you have got to have the *Sun* and if you want to keep in power you have got to have the *Daily Mail*' is a basic tenet of Westminster thinking. Meanwhile, the metaphors and analogies through which leading Labour figures often describe the press speak to their sense of fear. Blair, who had friendlier media relations than almost anyone, likened the media to 'feral beasts' that 'hunted in a pack'. Explaining his desire to charm and work with the press, he said: 'It is better to ride the tiger's back than let it rip your throat out.' The former Labour politician Tom Watson has described the media as 'like a mafia'. According to Alastair Campbell, a former *Mirror* journalist and Blair's spin doctor, 'if the public knew the truth about the way certain sections of the media operate, they would be absolutely horrified'.[38]

No one can say that the current state of the British press is the sign of a healthy democracy. It is not enough just to defend the value of a free press in the abstract. A free press that hounds civilians for trivial misdemeanours and stokes prejudices against those at the bottom, while leaving those in power safe from scrutiny, shouldn't be celebrated or defended simply because it is free. Nor can it be passed off as representative of society – as supply simply meeting demand. Even during the Tories' 'thumping' win in 2019, they were far from receiving 75 per cent of the vote, and Labour were comfortably above the 10 per cent of backing they received in the press. The British press cannot claim simply to represent public opinion.

The enduring success of the Conservatives, combined with the press's rabid cheerleading, points to a more obvious reality: that the press exists in society not as a check on the Conservatives' dominance, but as a scaffold of support – another imposing pillar of the Tory Nation. The press's effectiveness in achieving its aims may not be easy to measure, but even if its stories aren't always believed by readers, the daily drip feed of Toryphilia, xenophobia, left-baiting and jingoism lets the Conservative Party convincingly claim to reflect – rather than shape – the national mood. Laying blame for society's ills elsewhere – on immigrants, minorities, welfare cheats, the unpatriotic left – is a shared passion and serves a common purpose: keeping the left out of power, and the Conservatives in.

7

'PERMANENT OPPOSITION': THE BRITISH LABOUR PARTY

'If a man were asked to name the greatest single achievement of the British Labour Party over the past twenty-five
years, he might well answer, the transformation of the
British Conservative Party.'

> Labour MP John Strachey, quoted in *The Labour
> Government and British Industry, 1945–1951*, 1955

'Tony Blair and New Labour. We forced our opponents
to change their mind.'

> Margaret Thatcher, when asked what her greatest
> achievements were, 2002

'They say I hate this party and its traditions. Well, I don't.
I love this party. There's only one tradition I ever hated:
losing.'

> Tony Blair, Labour Party conference speech, 2006

On a weekend in mid-July 1995, Tony Blair, Labour's new
leader, flew to Hayman Island, situated within Australia's Great
Barrier Reef, to meet Rupert Murdoch and his army of newspaper executives and editors. Blair was soaring in the polls
and already regarded as Britain's prime minister-in-waiting.
An endorsement from Murdoch – a Thatcher loyalist and

owner of *The Times*, the *Sun* and their Sunday editions – would surely seal his victory. The invitation was too good to turn down. 'The country's most powerful newspaper proprietor, whose publications have hitherto been rancorous in their opposition to the Labour Party, invites us into the lion's den,' Blair later recalled in his memoir, *A Journey: My Political Life*. 'You go, don't you?'[1]

Blair's decision to accept the invitation received fierce criticism from those Labour figures still bruised by Murdoch's Labour bashing during the 1992 general election. But Blair was on a grand tour of the Tory Nation, aimed at reassuring various poles of power that they had nothing to fear from a Labour government. On his Murdoch stop, he pledged to be different from Labour's 'unelectable' leaders of the past, lampooning the left's indifference to 'the family and individual responsibility' and casting Thatcher as 'a radical, not a Tory', to whom Blair was the natural heir. He spoke of a 'new Labour Party'. 'The old solutions of rigid economic planning and state control won't work,' Blair declared.

Blair was on the attack – and his target was his own party. Earlier, in April, he had managed to ditch Clause IV from Labour's constitution, which committed the party, at least nominally, to nationalising key industries. In its place, Labour now celebrated 'the enterprise of the market and the rigour of competition'. 'His strategy is simple,' a critic noted at the time. 'Get your betrayals in early. He is not waiting for power before confronting the party with its realities.'[2]

What were these realities? Namely, that by the time of the next election, Labour would have been out of power for almost two decades, having suffered four election defeats in a row; that Thatcher's eleven-year reign had rewritten the terms of British society and politics. For Blair, the upshot of these hard truths was clear: Labour had to reinvent itself; the party's traditional platform of equality, welfare and national-isation was obsolete; it needed a new mission, a new purpose, a new language.

In the early 1900s, few would ever have imagined that it was the then new Labour Party that would need to 'modernise' itself. Labour was the self-declared 'party of the future'. It was the Tories, the outdated representatives of the old ruling class, with roots stretching back to the seventeenth century, that would surely need to repudiate its roots, forsake its founding principles and adopt a new name as time went on. But in a dramatic reversal, through a combination of Thatcher, the fall of the Berlin Wall and the seeming triumph of liberal capitalism around the world, socialists ended the century as Britain's dinosaur race. And Labour, which always enjoyed an uneasy relationship with socialism at best, was at least guilty by association. Labour was ordered to cut all remaining ties.

Tony Blair's task was to make Labour relevant again. As a public school-educated Oxford graduate, with Tory tendencies and a devout Christian faith, he was well suited to making new friends of old foes: the bankers and the plutocrats, and the newspapers that spoke for 'Middle England', the meto-nymic heart of the Tory Nation. Blair promised to safeguard the economic consensus of the past two decades, matching Conservative spending commitments for at least his first term, but with a twenty-first-century twist. Imagine the Tories, Blair seemed to say, but with a defence of multiculturalism, minority rights and a concern for the 'less fortunate' — Conservatism, but with less sleaze, better looks, bigger hearts, more Europhilia. Blair even had a tough law-and-order agenda for all those who feared that New Labour's optimistic, lovey-dovey liberalism might be a light touch. Playing into moral panics

185

about delinquent youths, early New Labour policy proposals included 'fast-track punishment for persistent young offenders' and a 9 p.m. curfew on all unaccompanied children. 'The vast majority of parents are as appalled as I am at seeing children on the streets on their own at nine, 10 or 11pm,' Jack Straw, Labour's shadow home secretary, explained.[3] He also promised to 'reclaim the streets from the aggressive begging of winos and addicts'. Cool Britannia and Cruel Britannia marched as one. What was there not to love?

In 1997, buoyed by Murdoch's support, Blair accomplished his task: Labour won its biggest ever parliamentary majority, sinking the Tories to their worst result since 1832. Blair became the youngest PM in almost two centuries, and the first one with a public school education since the 14th Earl of Home in 1963–4. It was the beginning of an unprecedented and disorienting ascendancy for the Labour Party. Before Blair, only one Conservative leader had failed to enjoy at least a brief stint as prime minister.[4] By the time Blair left office in 2007, there were three more: William Hague, Iain Duncan Smith and Michael Howard all acquired this unhappy honorific. The Tories had met their match, in more ways than one.

There can be no denying Blair's electoral achievements. But his significance in political terms is harder to decipher. Blair pitched himself as unideological, neither Labour nor Conservative, somewhere above 'the bitter struggles of left and right that have torn our country apart for too many decades'. But in reality there was broad agreement among observers as to where the main thrust of his policy agenda came from – and it wasn't from the left. 'Under the guise of left/right arguments having little meaning, New Labour has swerved so sharply to the right that it is in danger of crashing through the central reservation,' *The Observer* rued in 1996.[5] 'The presentational spin is that policy should be tough and hard choices should be made; but the direction of the toughness seems always to involve a concession to the right.'

Blair's lurch to the right only accelerated in office and left little space for the Conservatives: the party of patriotism, prosperity and nastiness struggled to contend on all fronts. 'We have faced an entirely new phenomenon in British politics: a party willing to say anything to get elected, to speak, in many ways, the language of the Conservative Party,' William Hague declared. (Hague wouldn't have meant it as such, but the insinuation that until Blair it was only the Tories who would say anything to get elected was also apt.) Just as Disraeli once described how Peel caught the Whigs bathing and walked away with their clothes, now the Tories saw themselves suffering the same cruel trick. 'You go for a swim in the sea,' John Major said. 'When you come back a man has taken your clothes. He has put them on. He looks like you. When he talks, he sounds like you. He has taken your identity. But if he is you, who are we?'

Drawing a meaningful distinction between Labour and the Conservatives became increasingly difficult. On issues of immigration and race, talk from leading Labour figures about asylum seekers 'swamping' British schools, echoing Thatcher and Powell, and denouncing the Muslim veil as a 'mark of separation' delighted the right-wing tabloids. 'Our tolerance is part of what makes Britain, Britain,' Blair said. 'So conform to it, or don't come here.' On fiscal matters, *The Times* marvelled at Blair's combination of 'Thatcherite means with social democratic ends', urging its readers to re-elect Labour because it had 'consolidated many elements of Thatcherism'. In fact, by introducing tuition fees to universities in 1998, many on the right praised Blair for out-Thatchering Thatcher herself. By 2001, he boasted the support of almost every newspaper: *The Times*, the *Sun*, *Express*, *Mirror*, their Sunday editions, the *Guardian* and the *Observer*. This meant that a remarkable 71 per cent of total print circulation was behind Blair, a level of media dominance by a government not seen since the 1930s.[6]

For all Blair's Thatcherism, the left still had reasons to celebrate: the Conservatives were out of power, wages were rising, and poverty, if not inequality, was in decline. The Belfast Agreement secured peace in Northern Ireland, and devolution to Wales, Scotland and Northern Ireland suggested at the least the possibility of a happy future for the Union. Hundreds of new schools and hospitals opened, and a minimum wage raised the earnings of those at the bottom. But the early feelings of unease – the sense that, when Blair entered the lion's den on Hayman Island, he'd found his true tribe – were hard to shake. 'We're intensely relaxed about people getting filthy rich,' Peter Mandelson, one of New Labour's architects and Blair's consigliere, declared in 1998. And then three years later: 'we're all Thatcherites now'.

In 2003, Blair's fateful decision to follow America into invading Iraq only compounded the left's disillusionment and estrangement. 'I will be with you, whatever,' Blair wrote to George Bush, America's right-wing Republican president, seemingly unfazed by how his own citizens felt. The war in Iraq, and a similarly ill-fated invasion of Afghanistan, would implicate both Blair and Britain in the deaths of over 500,000 people. Such blind faith seemed to reflect all of Blair's worst traits: his mix of spin, missionary zeal and destructiveness; his habit of making friends with all the wrong people. Rupert Murdoch was another enthusiastic supporter of the invasion, and he and Blair were in close contact on the subject. 'The greatest thing to come of this for the world economy, if you could put it that way, would be $20 a barrel for oil,' Murdoch stated publicly.[7] 'That's bigger than any tax cut.' Remarkably, for a proprietor who claims to apply no editorial control over his newspapers, each of his 175 newspapers – along with, one might say, at least three of his prime ministers/presidents, in Britain, the US and Australia – joined him in cheering on the invasion.[8]

All of this marked a new phase for the British left: they had endured countless election defeats before; now they suffered a spiritual one. Their beloved party, the historic vehicle of radical, progressive politics in Britain, the pioneer behind the NHS, the welfare state and equal rights, had put a conservative warmonger in power. 'This is a Labour government?' John Lanchester wondered out loud in the *London Review of Books* in 2004. 'This is what we were looking forward to for those 18 years of Tory rule? War, tuition fees, house arrest, wholesale subservience to American foreign policy, talk of services being "swamped" by refugees, the deliberately manipulative use of fear, the introduction of ID cards, the suspension of habeas corpus – and these are the good guys. What happened?'[9]

For Lanchester, like many others, New Labour represented the opposite of everything Labour was supposed to stand for. But in a way this was unfair on Blair: the traits Lanchester listed – 'left of centre, socially liberal, anti-authoritarian, anti-American, pacifistic, anti-big-business, keen on benefits for the poor, and in favour of nationalisation' – have only ever been one side of Labour's platform, whether in power or in opposition. A wider and more realistic reckoning with Labour's past reminds us that 'what happened' under Blair

— his rightward drift and party betrayal — was not the anomaly that many took it for. He was exceptional in his record of victory, but his deference to the old Tory order had a rich Labour history to draw upon. Since the party's beginnings in 1900, radicalism has always competed with more conservative instincts. Labour's evolution is as much a product of the Tory Nation as a threat to it.

No revolution, an unruffled ruling class, a popular monarchy: for the left at least, Britain wasn't supposed to be this way. During the nineteenth century, Karl Marx believed that Britain's early industrialisation made it riper than anywhere else for a workers' revolution. 'In no other country has the war between the two classes that constitute modern society assumed so colossal dimensions and features so distinct and palpable,' Marx declared in 1854.[10] About four in every five people belonged to the working class. Britain was, he said, 'the most important country for the workers' revolution'.

But the prophesied revolution never happened — in part, for the very reason that Marx thought it would. Britain's early and accelerated industrialisation, which created for a moment the largest working class in the world, inadvertently proved a boon for the old governing class. The mere fact that it was 'unprecedented' meant that workers had no precedent to draw upon, no outside experience or blueprint to follow, no history to inspire them. Perry Anderson calls it 'the tragedy of the first proletariat': Britain's working class 'had to invent everything — tactics, strategy, values, organisation — from the start'.[11] The anti-capitalist thought and practice pioneered by Marx and Engels arrived too late to shape working-class consciousness in Britain — indeed, it was often formulated from the British experience.

The Labour Party bears the imprint of this tragedy. The world's largest working class was among the last to organise as a national political force. By the time that the Labour Representation Committee launched in 1900, renamed the Labour Party in 1906, Germany's Social Democratic Party had been around since 1863, the French Workers' Party (a socialist organisation set up by Marx's son-in-law) since 1880, Sweden's Social Democratic Party since 1889 and Italy's Socialist Party since 1892.

The contrasting names of these various left-wing parties is also telling. Whereas a Social Democratic or Socialist Party suggests an alternative vision of society, and while a 'workers' party' posits a collective identity, 'Labour Representation Committee' suggests something tamer. Labour was effectively conceived of as a pressure group: the aim was to boost the representation of workers in parliament and assist the fight of trade unions against their bosses for better pay and working conditions.

The absence of the word 'socialist' or 'social democratic' from Labour's title was deliberate. Theory was often frowned upon as 'foreign': the British people were too matter-of-fact for all that. 'I would sooner have the solid, progressive, matter-of-fact fighting trade unionism of England than all the harebrained challenges and magpies of continental revolutionists,' militant unionist Ben Tillett explained in 1893, at the launch of the Independent Labour Party (ILP), a small radical group that was later absorbed into Labour.[12] 'It is not so much socialism, nor the absence of it, which wins elections, as the fact that the candidate is representing a party which the average man who does not indulge over-much in theories, understands and approves,' the ILP's founding chairman Keir Hardie, later Labour's first parliamentary leader, declared.[13]

In the 'broad church' of the Labour Party, Hardie and the ILP always represented its most radical faction. Born in 1856 in Scotland, the illegitimate son of a farm servant, Hardie was working as an errand boy by his eighth birthday and had started down the mines at ten. He was living proof of how cruel the Tory Nation could be. Like many others, he often worked a six-day week that included a four-hour shift on Saturday mornings – a schedule that was so rare elsewhere that the French called it *la semaine anglaise* and the Spanish *la semana inglesa* or *el sábado inglés*.[14] (Legislation introduced in 1850 mandated factory-work to finish at 2pm on Saturdays – hence the enduring footballing tradition of the 3pm kick-off.) Hardie's talent for public speaking, learned through church, saw him quickly rise to be a union leader by the age of twenty-three. He entered parliament in 1892, standing as an independent in Essex.

Hardie's admittance into the ruling class's lair did nothing to dampen his contempt for them. He saw how his comrades and predecessors tended to lose their radicalism amid the pomp and ceremony of parliamentary politics. 'If the truth be told, the working-man representative has not been much of a success in Parliament,' Keir Hardie said in 1887. 'As a rule, he is afraid to offend the proprieties by being considered extreme. He desires to be reckoned a gentleman, fit to take his place as a member of the "finest club in the world".'[15] Hardie was determined not to repeat their mistakes, and wore his cap and grey woollen suit as an act of defiance. He remained both a staunch republican in parliament – famously causing consternation among the Tory benches with a diatribe against the monarchy – and a proud champion of direct action, giving the suffragette movement and strikers his full backing.

But alongside the trade unions and Hardie's radicalism, there was a third major influence at the Labour Party's heart, one that would eventually become the most important: the Fabian Society. Led by Sidney and Beatrice Webb and George Bernard Shaw, first launched in 1884, it called for the 'reconstruction of Society in harmony with the highest moral possibilities'. It was a transformational intellectual project, committed to changing minds, lifting living standards, abolishing poverty and raising the competence of government. The name was taken from the Roman military general Fabius Cunctator ('the delayer'), who had famously overcome Hannibal's more powerful army by avoiding direct combat and attacking supply lines instead, exhausting the enemy in a long war of attrition. The Fabians would supposedly do the same, achieving political transformation without confrontation. Their key terms were 'permeation' (infusing major political parties, not just Labour, with their ideas) and 'the inevitability of gradualness' (a conviction that the arc of the universe bends towards justice, equality and expertise). At least initially, the Fabians believed that the Conservatives and Liberals could be brought around to their ideas. No doubt, they saw some common ground: a faith in the neutrality of British institutions, a distrust of the unions and direct action and an elitist condescension towards workers whom Beatrice Webb deemed 'stupid and in large sections sottish, with no interest except in racing odds'.[16] All talk of revolution was out of the question. These views would go on to play a formative role in Labour's future.

Sidney Webb joined Labour in 1915 amid the First World War and, in 1918, helped to draft the party's new constitution. It was a radical document, Clause IV of which infamously committed Labour to 'the common ownership of the means of production, distribution and exchange'. The devastations of battle had emboldened Labour's cause: normalising a high level of state intervention in the economy and raising the status of working men and women, most of whom were rewarded with the vote in the 1918 Representation of the People Act (all men over twenty-one and all women over thirty). For the first time, Labour presented itself as a 'national party': 'the party of the future', committed to the interests of not only the working class but 'all those who are dissatisfied with the old political parties'.

In 1924, Labour fulfilled its destiny far earlier than anyone in the party ever imagined – far earlier, perhaps, than they had ever wanted. The circumstances of the first Labour government were strange: in the December 1923 election, Labour were the second largest party in a hung parliament with 191 seats, sixty-seven fewer than the Tories. But when the Tories were unable to organise a workable coalition, Labour were invited to form a minority government. Many in Labour harboured doubts: they knew governing without an absolute majority would be difficult, even impossible, and potentially self-destructive. But Sidney Webb warned of the 'calamitous . . . effect on public opinion and on the party itself . . . if, when it was offered office, it flatly refused to accept the responsibility'.[17] Others agreed; Labour accepted and entered Downing Street.

Labour's leader at the time was Ramsay MacDonald, a working-class man and former Fabian with Liberal inclinations. He had sought to become a Liberal MP in 1894, only to be rebuffed. 'There must be co-operation and not conflict between labour and capital,' MacDonald insisted. His faith in British institutions was all but total, and saw no need for strikes, demonstrations or direct action. 'The weapon is to be the ballot box and the Act of Parliament,' he declared.

In January 1924, MacDonald became Britain's first Labour prime minister. While the mere idea of a 'socialist' government terrified many, the fact that the party had so few seats, and were led by a figure as moderate as MacDonald, reassured the old governing class that any Labour danger would be minimal. Many figures of the British establishment also saw it as an opportunity to welcome Labour into the fold in a controlled setting, to teach them the ways of the Tory Nation on a tight leash. The Conservative leader Stanley Baldwin was among them. 'I know I have been criticised, and criticised widely, for being too gentle in my handling of the Labour Party,' Baldwin explained in July 1924. 'But I have done it deliberately, because I believe it has been a good thing for this country that that Party, comprising as it does so many citizens of this country, should learn by experience what a great responsibility administering an empire such as ours really is.'

The patronising tone of Baldwin's comment spoke to the Tories' enduring sense of superiority and ownership: they were the parents of British politics, who let Labour govern in the same way a benevolent father might let their child have a turn at the steering wheel of the family car, knowing deep down whose car it really was and that, if the child either made a mistake or tried anything unruly, the father could always reclaim control of the vehicle. MacDonald could 'gain some experience of administration with his wings clipped', the editor of *The Times*, Geoffrey Dawson, assured Lord Robert Cecil in private. The Liberal leader Asquith agreed: 'If ever a Labour government is to be tried in this country, it could hardly be under safer conditions.'[18] (These lofty pronouncements also disguised baser self-interest: the Liberals hoped MacDonald's brief spell in government would expose Labour's divisions and so strengthen the Liberal Party; the Tories hoped that a more powerful Labour Party would weaken the Liberal vote.)

MacDonald did not let his masters down, prioritising respectability over radicalism and leaving the old social order unscathed. It was a dramatic anti-climax, best symbolised when Labour was sworn into government at Buckingham Palace and MacDonald arrived, clad in full ruling-class costume: gold-braided tailcoat, knee breeches, sword, the lot. MacDonald's cabinet was also replete with the old guard, including former Tories and Liberals with aristocratic roots. Even Beatrice Webb lamented how her former Fabian's cabinet included 'too many peers': 'JRM [MacDonald] oddly enough does not like the plebeian element and chooses as his intimate associates not the workman but the lawyer or big administrator with the manner and attitude of the ruling and thoroughly comfortable class.'[19]

But MacDonald's contrived attempt at continuity was never going to be enough to placate the Tory Nation for long. Within nine months, mounting scare stories and scandals around Labour's supposedly 'Communist' or 'Soviet' sympathies, actively stoked by the same Conservative Party that had propped Labour up in power, forced MacDonald to dissolve parliament and call a fresh election. At the heart of the subsequent Conservative campaign was the notorious 'Zinoviev letter', a fiction concocted by Tory HQ, the Foreign Office and the *Daily Mail*, alleging to show Labour as part of an international Communist cabal. The Conservatives won the election on a landslide, with 412 seats to Labour's 151. MacDonald understandably felt himself the victim of a conspiracy: 'It is a most suspicious circumstance that a certain newspaper and the headquarters of the Conservative Association seem to have had copies of [the forged letter] at the same time as the Foreign Office, and if that is true how can I avoid the suspicion – I will not say the conclusion – that the whole thing is a political plot?'[20]

The 'Zinoviev letter' brought an end to the first Labour government but marked the start of a lasting pattern. Nominally committed to a radical agenda, the Labour Party ultimately proved more concerned with affirming its establishment credentials than its radical ones, only to be hounded for a phantom radicalism nonetheless. MacDonald stayed on as leader and, despite witnessing the dark arts of the British establishment first-hand, his faith in the state never wavered. Sidney Webb's insistence on 'the inevitability of gradualness', first declared in 1923, resonated widely within the party: Labour's ultimate victory was sure to arrive eventually.

In 1929, Labour returned to power with 287 seats: still shy of a working majority, but at least as the largest party in parliament. Such an enlarged mandate might have emboldened Labour in their second stint in government. In the end, it proved an even more feeble affair than the first.

Labour were unlucky with events. In the autumn of 1929, months after taking office, the Wall Street Crash plunged the global economy into crisis. In Britain, between January and December 1930, unemployment almost doubled from 1.5 million to 2.7 million, while spending on unemployment benefits – first introduced by the Liberals in 1911 – rose tenfold, from about £12 million in 1928 to £120 million in 1931. The old establishment – the Tories, the Liberals, the City and the press – combined to deliver strict instructions to Labour on how to balance the books. MacDonald, lacking an absolute majority in parliament, had few paths available to him: the policies he was told to pursue – slashing welfare spending and reducing wages, making the poor and the unemployed pay for the crisis – couldn't command the support of his party, and the policies of his party couldn't command a majority in parliament. But MacDonald's resolution was still breathtaking in its betrayal: encouraged by King George V and the Conservatives, MacDonald abandoned Labour to form a 'National Government', containing a mere three members of his Labour cabinet and the entirety of the Conservative benches. Britain's first Labour prime minister became, almost overnight, a quasi-Conservative one.

The King played a decisive role in convincing the Labour leader to swap sides. 'His Majesty hoped that the Prime Minister, with the colleagues who remained faithful to him, would help in the formation of a National Government, which the King was sure would be supported by the Conservatives and the Liberals,' the King's private secretary wrote in a memo. 'The King assured the Prime Minister that, remaining at his post, his position and reputation would be much more enhanced than if he surrendered the government of the country at such a crisis.' Who could refuse such an entreaty? Not MacDonald, who readily obliged: his establishment credentials enhanced, no doubt, but Labour's left in disarray. 'Tomorrow every Duchess in London will be wanting to kiss me,' MacDonald reportedly joked after making his decision.[21]

It was among the most stunning illustrations of the Tory Nation's ability to absorb and assimilate unruly outsiders. As ever, the entry of a new power player into British politics was conditional upon a profound dilution of its danger, transforming the status quo and preserving it at the same time. Labour's closely supervised time in government ultimately flattered, rather than threatened, Britain's gatekeepers, who could praise their own open-mindedness while keeping the real doors to power closed. At the next election in October 1931, Labour's support collapsed, falling from 287 seats to fifty-two. The number of Conservative MPs rose from 260 to 470. Ramsay MacDonald – the hapless victim of one political plot and then the active participant in another – remained prime minister for the next four years. The Conservatives, channelled through the National Government, dominated the decade.

It took the tragedy and trauma of war, once more, to breathe life back into the Labour cause. Even more so than the First, the Second World War transformed Britain's political landscape. Not only were Labour and the Trades Union Congress brought into central government and granted a new level of legitimacy, but the enormous collective effort required of the British people seemed both to soften and illuminate society's divisions. Higher taxes reduced income inequality and suggested a growing spirit of solidarity, while the effects of air strikes – evacuations from cities into the countryside, shared bomb shelters, a collective fear – bound people together, emotionally and physically. 'Hitler is doing what centuries of English history have not accomplished – he is breaking down the class structure of England,' the American journalist James Reston quipped in 1940, in a dispatch for the *New York Times*.

Reston's remark required a degree of creative licence – many of Britain's class inequities survived the Blitz – but it was hard to resist the impression that Britain, and the conceptions of freedom and fairness that underpinned it, would never be the same again. Even *The Times* declared the need for a new social contract. 'If we speak of democracy we do not mean a democracy which maintains the right to vote but forgets the right to work and the right to live,' the paper announced on 1 July 1940. 'If we speak of equality we do not mean a political equality nullified by social and economic privilege . . . The new order cannot be based on the preservation of privilege, whether the privilege be that of a country, a class or an individual.'

This force of collective feeling continued to grow stronger over the course of the war. In June 1941, the government commissioned the Liberal economist and politician William Beveridge, together with a team of civil servants, to address complaints from trade unions about an overly complex benefits system and make recommendations. It wasn't intended to be a radical inquiry, but in the final document Beveridge strayed from his brief and ultimately called for a vastly expanded and centralised welfare state, available to everyone, including a free health service and the redistribution of wealth. 'The object of government in peace and in war is not the glory of rulers or of races, but the happiness of the common man,' the report declared. The national mood had found its manifesto.

The call for wealth redistribution was antithetical to most Conservatives, and they sought to quell Beveridge's report: the Treasury demanded he weaken his recommendations; civil servants were prevented from signing the document; Churchill tried to stop the government publishing it altogether.[22] But Beveridge ultimately prevailed in 1942, and even though the government publicised it as little as it could, the response was electric: over half a million copies were sold in the UK – unprecedented for a 300-page government publication – and it received international renown, with 50,000 copies also selling in the US. Beveridge became the unlikeliest of celebrities, photographed wherever he went, and the press gave the report sustained, glowing coverage. 'All pay – all benefit,' the *Daily Mirror* rejoiced. It was for everyone, 'from Duke to Dustman'.

The enthusiastic reception of the Beveridge Report was also illustrative of another novel change sweeping through society to Labour's advantage: an increasingly progressive press. Paper rationing, introduced in February 1940, roughly halved the size of most newspapers, both reducing production costs and forcing advertisers to distribute themselves more evenly in search of whatever space they could find. This led to a surprise boom for the entire sector. The *Daily Mirror* was among the biggest beneficiaries. Already leaning increasingly left in the run-up to the war, the *Mirror* was further radicalised as the battle progressed. By 1945, the *Mirror*'s daily circulation reached 2.4 million and rising, having been at 700,000 copies just ten years earlier. Other Liberal and Labour papers also saw their circulation soar.[23]

Overall, by the end of the war, Labour could claim the support of 35 per cent of national daily circulation against the Tories' 52 per cent – a dramatic change from 1924, when the comparative figures had been 5 and 75 per cent respectively.[24] When a new general election was called in July 1945, the conditions could hardly have been better for Labour: never before in British history had the left competed against the right on such even terms.

On 5 July 1945, these various factors combined to catapult Labour to power. Labour secured 393 seats to the Conservatives' 213, with 47 per cent of the vote. It was the greatest electoral shock for the Tories since 1906. 'My present feeling is not so much one of depression as of waking up bewildered in a world completely strange to me,' James Stuart, Conservative chief whip, said of the election result.[25] 'I feel that my entrails have been pulled right out of me.' Labour politicians barely believed it themselves. James Chuter Ede, a veteran Labour MP, recalled how he 'began to wonder if I should wake up to find it all a dream'. Hugh Dalton, Labour's post-war chancellor (and an Old Etonian), described a mood of 'exhilaration among us, joy and hope, determination and confidence. We felt exalted, dedicated, walking on air, walking with destiny.'[26]

Labour's past forays into government had taught the party that only an absolute majority in parliament could realise their ambitions. Now they had it. Would they waste it? In the context of British history, the reforming successes of Labour's first majority government exceed those of any other govern-ment ever: welfare provision was radically expanded in line with the Beveridge Report, over a million new houses were built, key industries were nationalised, working-class politi-cians enjoyed unprecedented power and in the National Health Service, finally ushered in in 1948, British society changed for ever – a pillar of the nation was now Labour's legacy to claim. It was the Tories' turn to adjust.

The NHS symbolised the defining ethos of Labour's radic-alism: the principle of universalism, which held that public services should be the first choice for everyone, rich or poor, available without discrimination or favour. This both ensured higher quality services and stripped them of any stigma: people didn't turn to the state when they were 'less fortunate' or 'in need' – they did so proudly, as the citizens of a socialist society.

The health secretary, Aneurin Bevan, was among the leading Labour figures who made the NHS a reality, against fierce opposition from the Tories and the British Medical Association. As a working-class trade unionist from Wales who grew up in poverty, his fight for the NHS carried a personal resonance. His father had suffered pneumoconiosis, a lung condition caused by a life working in the coal mines, yet received no healthcare compensation for it because it wasn't officially recognised as a work-related illness under the Workmen's Compensation Act until 1942. Bevan never forgot the pain his father went through. 'No attempts at ethical or social seduction can eradicate from my heart a deep burning hatred for the Tory Party that inflicted those bitter experiences on me,' Bevan declared in 1948. 'So far as I am concerned they are lower than vermin. They condemned millions of first-class people to semi-starvation.'

Bevan's break with the gentlemanly civility of British politics was part of a wider attack on the Tory Nation. Labour's leader Clement Attlee also ridiculed the Conservative claim to be a 'national' party. 'You have only to run through the list of Conservative members in the House of Commons and their candidates running for safer seats to see that they belong to two classes only: those who are born rich and those who have achieved riches,' he said. 'You would look in vain for anyone from the wage-earning classes.' The Conservatives represented a minority masquerading as the majority. Labour defined the Tories as unpatriotic and un-British, as the vessels of factional interests; amplified by what was now Britain's biggest newspaper, the *Daily Mirror*, the message cut through. The Conservatives were at a loss. 'It looks as though those bastards can stay in as long as they like,' Churchill complained.

But for all Bevan's irreverence and Attlee's nous, the 1945 Labour government still didn't represent a complete break from the Tory Nation. Attlee himself was a proud public schoolboy from Haileybury, a boarding school famed for its strong imperial tradition, who 'favoured anyone who came from Haileybury', as Denis Healey recalled in his memoir. In 1946, Attlee visited his alma mater to offer personal reassurance that the public school system was safe in his hands.

'He saw no reason for thinking that the public schools would disappear,' *The Times* wrote in a summary of his speech. 'He thought that the great tradition would carry on, and they might even be extended.'[27]

In a similar vein, the House of Lords, where Tory peers effectively agreed to pass Labour's manifesto in exchange for the chamber's survival, was left untouched; the monarchy received Attlee's full support; and besides finally securing one-person-one-vote in 1948, revoking the rights of property owners and university students to vote twice, Labour's agenda for election reform was non-existent: the party's interest in proportional representation evaporated amid the thrill of an inflated, first-past-the-post majority – 47 per cent of the vote earned them 61 per cent of the seats. Labour even redrew constituency boundaries to the Tories' advantage.[28] The party's top brass seemed simply to assume that, regardless of the fine print, the future was still on Labour's side. 'We are the masters at the moment, and not only at the moment, but for a very long time to come,' one Labour politician famously declared in the Commons.

Labour's failure to modernise Britain's antique political system ultimately set the stage for its fall. In 1950, having completed a full term of government for the first time, Labour fought a fresh election and saw their majority fall from 146 seats to five. In October 1951, only eighteen months after the last election, the Palace made another political intervention. King George VI was concerned about the instability of Labour's small majority and its mounting internal divisions as the Cold War took root. The King was about to embark on a six-month tour of Africa, and he told Attlee that he'd like the matter resolved before he left: a fresh election would do the trick. Attlee obliged.

In the resultant 1951 election, Labour won more votes than any political party in British history – but it still wasn't enough to beat the Tories. Thanks partly to Attlee's reforms, the Conservatives won more seats with fewer votes. But rather than lament this failure of democracy or the vagaries of a flawed electoral system, some senior Labour figures instead rejoiced at their impressive vote share and reasoned that, in this uncertain period, it was probably for the best being in opposition for a term. An imminent return to power was certain. 'The election results are wonderful,' Hugh Dalton wrote privately. 'We are out at just the right moment.'

Such complacency, so characteristic of Labour's history, proved woefully misplaced. The Conservatives stayed in power for the next thirteen years, winning three elections in a row. Labour never returned to the heights of 1945. What was supposed to be a launchpad for the British left ended up being a climax, a summit to which it never returned. Over the subsequent decades, the party occasionally reclaimed power, spending a total of eleven years in office between 1951 and 1979, but the sum legacy of all those Labour governments was less than Labour's first five-year spell in charge.

How to explain this record of failure? It is not so much Labour's inability to achieve office, but, rather, the lack of ambition that afflicts it once it does, that remains the most confounding enigma of the party. MacDonald had reasoned that once Labour became an accepted part of the political landscape, then its radical intent could be unleashed. But the opposite seemed to happen. The more time Labour spent as Britain's other major party, the more its ambitions softened, tamed by the very status quo that it once sought to overthrow. Whether the reason has been the party's underlying ideology, fear, deference, or faith in the 'inevitability of gradualness' remains a matter of debate. But for the most part, Labour have been happy to play second fiddle to the Conservatives, maintaining their status as what Orwell once dubbed 'the Permanent Opposition'.[29]

There should be no downplaying of the forces allied against Labour. 'When a Conservative government is in power, it is an integral part of a continuous landscape which extends in a smooth, unbroken space around it,' Perry Anderson wrote in 1964.[30] 'When a Labour government is in power, it is an isolated, spot-lit enclave, surrounded on almost every side by hostile territory, unceasingly shelled by industry, press and orchestrated "public opinion".' More recently, David Edgerton has put the point even more bluntly. In the twentieth century, Labour 'was always subservient or in opposition to greater political powers. The Labour Party was in office from time to time; the industrial, military, financial and professional arms of the Liberal and Conservatives parties were in power all of the time.'[31] The same point could easily be put in the present tense.

But it's also true that Labour have often been active participants in their own subjugation. They have tended to agree with MacDonald's tepid assumption that all talk of constitutional reform is a distraction, a sideshow, more trouble than it's worth. The fact that it took almost a century for Labour even to *reform*, let alone abolish, the House of Lords, and that this reform neither democratised the chamber nor removed all the hereditary peers, speaks to the party's quasi-truce with Toryism. In general, Labour politicians seem keener on receiving the blessings of the current system – a peerage, a knighthood, a royal invitation – than democratising it.

No doubt, the historic dominance of the Tories over Britain leaves Labour in a difficult position. Out of 'patriotism', Labour are forced to pay their allegiance to the nation's institutions and customs, which are simultaneously entwined with both the ruling class and Britain's popular identity. But those same institutions and customs – the Lords, the monarchy, Empire, the cult of common sense, stoicism – also tend to reinforce a Tory vision of Britain, fuelling the image of an ancient, traditional nation, impervious to change and new ideas. Labour then faces a choice: either it accepts – even champions – these Tory-inflected institutions and customs, achieving an easier ride but jeopardising any radical destination, or it seeks to challenge these institutions and customs, aiming for a less hostile environment for the left in the long term but exposing the party to accusations of being un-British in the here and now. Labour usually opts for the former, the path of least resistance, with varying degrees of reluctance and enthusiasm.

This predicament explains the charge most frequently laid against the Labour left: its purported lack of patriotism. There is no more favourite attack line among Conservatives or indeed Liberals than that the left hates its country. As the socialist George Orwell once wrote, in words that Conservatives love to recall, 'England is perhaps the only great country whose intellectuals are ashamed of their own nationality': 'In left-wing circles it is always felt that there is something slightly disgraceful in being an Englishman and that it is a duty to snigger at every English institution, from horse racing to suet puddings.' In some ways, the left's discomfort with national pride might simply reflect the international dimension of socialist thought more broadly: worker solidarity is elevated above nationality, or at least it is supposed to be. But in other ways, Labour's patriotic malaise might also reflect the precise nature of Britain's national identity: the absence of a revolution in modern times, the dominance of the Tories, combined with an imperial history, makes it hard to know what the left should celebrate. The historian Hugh Cunningham goes so far as to say: 'In the age of imperialism it was impossible to demarcate a patriotism of the left; the language had passed to the right and those who employed it did so too.'[32]

But there are other stories to be told about Britain. As the historian E. P. Thompson explored in his classic *The Making of the English Working Class*, published in 1963, there is a rich history of radicalism to draw upon. In this alternative history of the nation, Thompson describes working-class triumphs, republican uprisings, dissident traditions, a terrified ruling class and windows of time when revolution was both wanted and plausible. But this narrative isn't just a romantic recollection of lost causes and missed opportunities – it's a reminder that Britain benefited from their legacy.

Such histories of Britain are essential for the left. But for the Tories they must remain in the margins: their fairy-tale Britain – as the peaceful, stable nation with the kindest, wisest ruling class – cannot be undermined. This is why the Conservatives have sought throughout Labour's existence to portray the party and its platform as fundamentally alien to national character and interests, as if Labour itself was an interloper in British history. Neville Chamberlain called on Conservatives to emphasise the distinction between the 'steady . . . patriotic . . . conservative trade unionist' and 'the socialist visionary with a foreign, international, anti-British point of view'. At the 1946 conference, one Conservative described how 'liberalism and "Conservatism" have grown out of the life and experience of the British people', while socialism was 'no more rooted in English soil than a toffee apple on a Christmas tree'.[33] The more ordinary insults flung at the left, new and old, are just as revealing: what words like 'intelligentsia', 'literati' and 'bourgeois' share, along with more playful insults like 'champagne socialists', 'Bollinger Bolsheviks', 'wokerati' and 'Corbynistas' is the attempt to make left-wing people foreign. For something as peculiar as a left-wing person in Britain, it seems, a traditional English word just won't do.

In 1945, Attlee was well suited to rebutting the trope of the unpatriotic left. He had been wounded during the Second World War, and so his patriotism could not be questioned. But Labour leaders have rarely benefited from such a ready defence at hand. Instead, they find themselves jumping through endless hoops, ostensibly to prove their love of country, but in reality designed to divide the party and usher it along Conservative lines.

Nowhere is this seen more than on the issue of immigration. For the left, capitalism rather than immigration – greedy bosses rather than foreigners – is to blame for low wages. But the Tories say this simply shows that the left cares more about the needs of other nationalities over those at home – only they will put British interests first. Labour tries in vain to prove the Conservatives wrong without betraying the party's multi-cultural, egalitarian principles. Blair's private memos on wanting to look 'tough' by punishing asylum seekers, Brown's call for 'British jobs for British workers' and Miliband's mugs stamped with 'controls on immigration' – all pursued in the name of 'patriotism' – are just some illustrations of where these contortions can lead. The party's past is filled with them. After Enoch Powell's incendiary speech in 1968, for example, it was actually Labour that responded with tougher immigration controls, barring Commonwealth citizens from freely entering Britain for the first time. 'We don't want any more blacks in Britain,' James Callaghan, then Labour home secretary and soon-to-be prime minister, declared. Hence race scholar

Ambalavaner Sivanandan's wry assessment that 'what Enoch Powell says today, the Conservative Party says tomorrow, and the Labour Party legislates on the day after'.[34]

After the dizzying heights of 1945, Labour spent much of the post-war decades on the defensive. In 1951, the party split over plans to take free dental care and eyewear off the NHS, leading to Bevan's resignation. The siren call of the centre ground grew louder. Many in the party believed that, as society became wealthier and more people became middle class, Labour's old brand of politics – which had only recently secured the largest number of votes of any party ever – would no longer resonate. In 1955, the *Economist* told Labour to leave 'the age of Keir Hardie' behind. Hugh Gaitskell, who replaced Attlee as leader that year, tried and failed to have Labour ditch Clause IV from its constitution. In 1959, Douglas Jay, another influential Labour MP, called on the party to sever its links with the unions. 'We must now all learn to be middle class,' the labour minister Anthony Crosland declared.[35]

The heyday of Britain's progressive, or at least politically diverse, press was also coming to an end. As wartime regulations and paper rationing receded, normal competition resumed and several left-leaning newspapers folded. The decline of the *Daily Herald*, once a champion of the suffragettes and anti-colonial movements with ties to the trade unions, was a particularly sad story. In 1924, it had been the only daily newspaper to question the authenticity of the 'Zinoviev letter'. In 1964, struggling to make revenue, it relaunched as the *Sun* and was later bought by Rupert Murdoch.

The same year the *Sun* was born, 1964, Labour returned to government, now under Harold Wilson's leadership. Wilson, while no doubt more radical, shared certain similarities with

Blair: a slick image, popularity with the press and a modern vision of Britain that mocked the Tories as old-fashioned. 'We are living in a jet age, but we are governed by an Edwardian establishment mentality,' he said. (Wilson was also the first PM since Ramsay MacDonald not to have had a private school education.) He passed a wave of laws that extended civil rights and freedoms, including the abolition of the death penalty, lowering the voting age to eighteen, increasing welfare benefits and legalising homosexuality and the right to abortion. The economy continued to grow, and inequality continued to fall, but quietly the parameters of post-war politics were shifting. A sprawl of new, innocuously named think-tanks were teaming up with the Tories to sow the seeds of a counter-movement. Most influential of all were the Institute of Economic Affairs, an 'anti-Fabian society' created with the help of Friedrich Hayek in 1957, and the Centre for Policy Studies, set up in 1974.[36]

These opaque institutions, dedicated to usurping the age of collectivism with the age of individualism, cultivated ties with newspapers like the *Telegraph*, *The Times* and the *Financial Times* and with multinational companies like Barclays and British Petroleum. Under Thatcher, the Conservatives were finally transformed in their image – and after her victory in 1979, both Labour and whatever was left of the post-war consensus were swept aside. A new consensus was in the making, and Labour would never look the same again. David Edgerton acidly refers to James Callaghan, who had replaced Wilson in 1976 and then lost to Thatcher in 1979, as 'the last Labour prime minister'.[37]

In 1997, after eighteen years of Tory rule, Blair brought Labour back to power – in body, if not in soul. He had found a winning formula. Privatise state services, set the financial sector free, drum up patriotic feeling, tack right in the culture war and boost public spending to reduce poverty levels. 'A spoonful of sugar helps it all go down', as Blair memorably put it. Even the *Economist*, which had backed 'the real Tories rather than possible Tories' in 1997, was impressed, later conceding that Blair was 'the only credible conservative currently available'. The Conservatives were in a rut, divided over a fringe obsession – Britain's then uncontroversial membership of the European Union – and unsettled by their own admiration for Blair. 'I can't fight my feelings any more,' the then journalist Michael Gove wrote in *The Times* in 2003. 'I love Tony.'

But Blair's dominance was always slightly misleading. Not only did Britain's capture by the Labour Party reflect, in a deeper sense, Labour's own capture by the Conservatives – Thatcher famously called Blair and New Labour her greatest achievements – Labour's election wins were also less convincing than they looked. In 2001, voter turnout had fallen to a record low of 59 per cent, after never having dropped below 70 per cent since the First World War. By 2005, when Labour was re-elected on a similarly low turnout, the party had shed more than 4 million supporters, mostly among the working classes in the North of England. 'They have nowhere else to go,' one of Blair's senior advisers said. And so nowhere they went.

These shifts laid the ground for future Labour defeats, but the nature and extent of the Tories' revival could not yet be foreseen. In the 2010 election, when Labour sunk to its lowest share of the vote in a hundred years, many Labourites welcomed the Conservatives' return to power.[38] The complacency was familiar: a spell in opposition would apparently do Labour some good, allowing the party to regroup before returning to power soon; in the aftermath of the recession, the Conservatives' coalition with the Lib Dems was hardly

likely to be successful or popular. Capturing this spirit of
stoical good cheer, not to mention the chumminess of British
politics in general, Labour's departing chief secretary to the
Treasury left a note to his Conservative successor: 'Dear Chief
Secretary, I'm afraid to tell you there's no money left.' The
Tories gleefully wielded it against Labour as proof of its callous
incompetence.

In power, riding this narrative of Labour's recklessness, the
Conservatives heralded 'a new age of austerity': Blairism, but
without the spoonful of sugar to help it all go down. Labour,
now led by Ed Miliband, immediately went on the defensive.
At least, in following Thatcher, Blair was compromising with
a prime minister who'd won three elections and been in power
for eleven years – here, Labour rushed to adapt themselves
to the Conservatives' post-recession consensus, with the Tories
only having scraped back into government through a coalition
after thirteen years in the wilderness. It was an unedifying
spectacle: as the Tories insisted that their ideologically motivated austerity agenda was simply clearing up Labour's mess,
Miliband's shadow cabinet offered little challenge. 'My starting
point is, I am afraid, we are going to have to keep all these
cuts,' Ed Balls, Labour's shadow chancellor, rousingly declared.
Rachel Reeves, the shadow welfare secretary, swore to be
'tougher' on benefit fraud than the Conservatives.

This time, however, Labour's self-flagellation was unsuccessful. In the 2015 election Cameron became the first prime
minister to increase both his party's share of the vote and its
tally of seats in the Commons after serving a full term – an
unexpected reward for five years of painful austerity policies.
But Cameron's victory came with a generation-defining
concession: to absorb the rise of the UK Independence Party
(UKIP), led by Nigel Farage, he had committed to a simple

remain/leave referendum on EU membership. Cameron knew it was dangerous: such a referendum, he said in private, 'could unleash demons of which ye know not'.[39] But with an insouciance characteristic of the old governing class, Cameron went ahead with it anyway, undertaking one of those leaps into the dark that Conservatives love in times of crisis. The date for the referendum was set for 23 June 2016. A new word was to enter British politics: Brexit. The demons were unleashed.

8

A LEAP INTO THE DARK: TORY NATION IN CRISIS (2016–PRESENT)

'When a regime has been in power too long, when it has fatally exhausted the patience of the people, and when oblivion finally beckons – I am afraid that across the world you can rely on the leaders of that regime to act solely in the interests of self-preservation, and not in the interests of the electorate.'

Boris Johnson, writing in the *Daily Telegraph*, 2011

'Do-dooo-do-do.'

– David Cameron, humming to himself after announcing his resignation, 2016

'Look what you made me do . . . #trouble.'

Liz Truss, sharing a selfie with Taylor Swift on Instagram, 2019

Before 2015, Jeremy Corbyn, a Labour MP for Islington North since 1983, was well respected in activist circles and parodied in parliamentary ones, but hardly featured in the public's imagination. Between 1997 and 2010, under the Labour governments of first Tony Blair and then Gordon Brown, Corbyn voted against his party an unrivalled 428 times. No one paid much attention. When Blair reportedly quipped, in a 1996 interview affirming his own New Labour credentials, that 'you really don't have to worry about Jeremy Corbyn suddenly taking over', the wisecrack never got published, because the reporter reasoned, quite rightly, that nobody would know who this Corbyn person was.[1]

All this changed when Corbyn suddenly did take over. It happened almost by accident. In the Labour leadership race that followed the party's defeat in 2015, Corbyn was allowed to run, not as a genuine candidate, both he and his colleagues implicitly agreed, but as a relic: a melancholic reminder of Labour's socialist roots as it chose another ex-Blair or -Brown cabinet minister. 'It would be good for the left of the party to see just how few votes would be cast,' a senior Labour figure told the *Spectator* at the time.[2]

But then the relic came alive. Corbyn received more votes from Labour members than his three opponents combined, running on a campaign against the Conservatives' austerity agenda. Against the wishes of 206 of the 220 Labour MPs, Corbyn was declared leader of the Labour Party, with the largest mandate of any modern equivalent. For his supporters, it heralded the rebirth of the British left. For his critics, Labour had suffered a second death, dooming itself to electoral oblivion.

Mixing both moods, Conservatives delighted in Corbyn's disastrous unelectability, eagerly anticipating a new age of dominance. 'Sign up today to make sure the bearded socialist voter-repellent becomes the next Labour leader – and dooms the party forever,' the *Daily Telegraph* urged its readers during the leadership campaign. Other Conservatives started a #ToriesForCorbyn hashtag on Twitter. Corbyn seemed to offer Conservatives the perfect foil, a socialist scapegoat come to life: he was a scruffy leftie, with internationalist and anti-imperial sympathies, who was not only a republican but a vegetarian, with a degree from neither Oxford nor Cambridge, nor indeed any university at all. When he decided not to kneel before the Queen during his induction into the Privy Council, it only affirmed his status as an alien outsider. In one early Prime Minister's Questions exchange, Cameron reprimanded Corbyn with a headmaster's condescension: 'Put on a proper suit, do up your tie and sing the national anthem!' It was the kind of advice that is written into the walls of Westminster, but rarely said explicitly.

Looking back at the shock of Corbyn's victory, the various convulsions that it triggered in the British political establishment seem almost quaint compared to what was to come a year later, with the Brexit vote. What's equally striking is how little the question of Europe came up in the Labour leadership debate, despite Cameron confirming that the referendum would be held the following year. Labour had actively condemned Cameron's referendum promise as irresponsible during the 2015 election, and the membership was overwhelmingly pro-EU. But the Labour membership seemed to assume, like most of the country, that the Brexit verdict would be a mere blip before Britain moved back to more important matters. On the one occasion that EU membership did come up during the leadership debates, Corbyn did not hide that, unlike his three opponents, he had his doubts. The veteran critic of the EU won regardless.

While Euroscepticism remained a fringe issue within Labour, the party harboured their own hopes for the referendum: that the carnival of Conservative infighting would doom their opponents. The conflict unfolded as expected, but little else went to plan. Rather than leading to the implosion of the Tory Party, as Labour hoped, or resolving the issue of Euroscepticism for Tories, as Cameron wished, the referendum initiated a stunning Conservative-isation of British politics. The demons were unleashed. The political terrain opened up. The Tory Nation's roots, and their interlocking tensions, were exposed like never before: its establishment and anti-establishment identities, its delusions of grandeur and its vested interests.

The combined effect of Brexit and Corbyn was to provide, in effect, an X-ray of the Tory Nation, revealing the surprising array of friends and allies committed to its upkeep, their shared priorities and underlying rivalries, the flimsiness of its demo-cratic institutions and the hollowness of some of its founding myths. The Conservative Party achieved a confounding ascend-ancy, built upon a familiar template: changing shape, stoking fear and division, and veiling elite interests in the lure of patriotic adventure. But success came at a cost. Tales of Britain's essential stability, pragmatism and moderation – its impervi-ousness to radicalism and its reputation for prudent leadership – would never quite sound the same again. We are still living in the aftermath.

The Brexit referendum transformed the political landscape. In 2010, less than 1 per cent of Brits named EU membership as their most important concern, according to the British Election Study.[3] Through the referendum, Brits were soon talking about nothing else. Brexit became the issue that defined British politics on the right and the left. 'Leaver' and 'Remainer' surpassed party allegiance as the primary way people identi-fied politically. It split not just the country, but the British establishment, causing all kinds of chaos.

On the one side, Cameron and his chancellor George Osborne campaigned for Remain, joined by other senior

Conservatives, almost all of Labour, and a rare alliance between business leaders and the trade unions. On the other side, the Leave campaign was spearheaded by the likes of Boris Johnson, Michael Gove and Nigel Farage, boosted by the Tory Press, influential libertarian think-tanks and various big hedge funds and donors.

Remain was the favourite to win, but Leave had one major advantage on its side: the question itself. Voters were asked: 'Should the United Kingdom remain a member of the European Union or leave the European Union?' They could then tick one of two boxes: 'Remain a member of the European Union' or 'Leave the European Union'. The former essentially meant the status quo; the latter could mean anything and everything: more funding for public services, a bigger state, a smaller state, lower taxes, stronger workers' rights, weaker workers' rights, less immigration, more non-EU immigration, a stronger economy, a more harmonious society, a return to the past, a leap into the future. 'Outside the EU we can become richer, safer and free at long last to forge our own destiny – as America, Canada, Australia, New Zealand and many other great democracies already do,' the *Sun* declared.[4]

For the Tory Press, EU membership had long represented many bugbears rolled into one: more regulation of the private sector, more immigration, an affront to Britain's sovereign greatness, and, perhaps most importantly, a legislative power unbeholden to their influence. As an infamous (and potentially apocryphal) quote from Murdoch has it: 'When I go into Downing Street, they do what I say. When I go to Brussels, they take no notice.' The *Sun* went so far as to register as an official campaign group for Leave. Richard Desmond, owner of the *Express*, had already given £1.3 million to the right-wing UKIP in 2014–5.[5] With the exception of *The Times* (but not the *Sunday Times*), all of the Tory Press fought for Leave. This meant that more than 80 per cent of those who bought a daily newspaper during the referendum campaign read a title that favoured Brexit.[6]

For Conservatives campaigning for Remain, this represented an alien situation. Suddenly their usual allies were hostile. They were subjected to the same cynical strategies that, only a year earlier during the 2015 election, they had thrived on: misrepresentations, hit pieces, absurd fearmongering and witch-hunts. 'We're discovering what it's like to be Ed Miliband,' David Cameron's communications chief reflected.[7] They suffered a similar fate. On 24 June, the results were confirmed: Leave had won by 4 points, 52 to 48 per cent. The Brexit-backing press lapped it up. 'So much for the waning power of the print media,' the *Sun*'s then-editor Tony Gallagher, who now edits *The Times*, cooed.

The atmosphere of uncertainty was only heightened when, hours after the result came in, the chief instigator of the disorder, David Cameron, announced his departure: his oft-declared commitment to 'clearing up Labour's mess' did not apply to his own. Cameron had always feared that holding the referendum would threaten his leadership, since it would galvanise the Brexit wing of his Conservative Party. 'The only person this will help is Boris Johnson, who is clearly after my job,' he reportedly told a colleague in the build-up. But the speed of Cameron's resignation surprised everyone, not least Johnson. He had never expected to win the referendum. And when he did, he did not expect Cameron to quit so quickly.[8]

Johnson found himself exactly where he wanted to be. The country was in disarray, but his Brexit-cum-leadership campaign had been, personally, a great success. He stood as the immediate and obvious favourite to replace Cameron.

Theresa May, who backed staying in the EU but remained tactfully taciturn throughout, was a distant second. In the days that followed, Johnson assembled his Brexit 'dream team', with Michael Gove as manager and their fellow Brexiteer Andrea Leadsom alongside them. But then Johnson's leadership chances collapsed as quickly as they converged. First Leadsom withdrew her support – unconvinced by Johnson's promises, she decided to run herself – and then Gove, incredibly, did the same. It remains one of the great personal betrayals of British politics, and among the most brutal moments of Johnson's career: Gove was supposed to be Johnson's closest ally, the team behind the dream. Johnson withdrew from the race, aware his support no longer added up. Gove and Leadsom blundered. May became Britain's first 'Brexit prime minister', almost unopposed.

Theresa May, the state-educated daughter of a vicar, pledged to launch a new kind of Conservatism, one that was aware of the disillusionment and resentment buried within Brexit, and that escaped the ruling-class insouciance of Cameron, Johnson and Co. 'The government I lead will be driven, not by the interests of the privileged few but by yours,' May said in her opening address in Downing Street. She swiftly summoned George Osborne, a key member of Cameron's Bullingdon Club clique, to fire him from his post. 'Her advice was that I needed to go away and get to know the Conservative Party better,' Osborne later recalled. Instead, he went and became editor of the *Evening Standard* and an adviser at BlackRock, earning £650,000 for about fifty days of work a year: its own type of Tory education.[9]

May forged her name as a fearsome, authoritative leader, adored by the tabloids for taking on the Brexit beacon with glee: 'Brexit means Brexit,' she famously declared. The Tory Press saw in her a resurrection of their darling leader, Margaret Thatcher, another Iron Lady attuned to the hearts and minds of Middle England. With Labour beset by internal fighting – in the wake of the referendum, Labour MPs had blamed Corbyn for the result and resigned en masse, only to see Corbyn re-elected with an even bigger mandate – May enjoyed the happiest of honeymoons. She had higher popularity ratings than almost any prime minister before her. Her party sailed to a twenty-point lead in the polls. The Conservatives were ascendant. Labour seemed destined for catastrophe.

May initially resisted calls to hold a fresh election. It was obvious, she said, that Britain's departure from the European Union required stability, a spell free from the demands and distractions of an election campaign when 'the will of the British people' – a phrase she was fond of using – could be fulfilled. But as the Brexit stalemate began to set in, the prospect of a bigger parliamentary majority became too tempting to turn down. It was time to, in the words of the *Mail*'s front cover, 'Crush the Saboteurs'. (Months earlier, the *Mail*'s political editor, James Slack, had become May's communications chief.) The election date was set: 8 June. Tories salivated over their predicted majority – 200 seats, by some counts.

May's campaign was to centre around a single question: who do you want to lead the Brexit negotiations? Her team put out a familiar slate of slogans that offered an easy, unthinking answer. She offered *Strong and Stable Leadership*, while a government led by Labour Party leader Jeremy Corbyn would be a *Coalition of Chaos*. These were the party lines to be repeated ad infinitum, ritual-like, a sort of rain dance with the promise of electoral nirvana. The words 'Conservative Party' barely appeared on banners or on buses; the vote was for 'Theresa and her team'. The plan was to absorb voters who had backed Brexit and yet still harboured ancient hostilities towards the Tories, capitalising on May's broad appeal as a woman who 'gets the job done'.

But then it all started to unravel. May's problems began with what many saw as her first campaign policy: a bizarre declaration to bring back fox-hunting, revoking a ban that eight out of ten Brits supported keeping in place. Soon followed a U-turn on an unpopular manifesto pledge, dubbed the 'Dementia Tax', related to social care. She never recovered her poise. The Tory Nation's spell of strength and stability had been broken. The Irony Lady 2.0 had melted into the air.

The election resulted in a hung parliament, with the Tories as the biggest party. They lost thirteen seats; Labour added not only thirty seats but also 3.5 million new votes – its share of the electorate rising from 30 to 40 per cent, the party's biggest leap between elections since 1945. Corbyn supporters celebrated the narrowness of the defeat as a victory: dismissed as unelectable, the bearded voter-repellent socialist – assailing austerity, inequality, tuition fees – had attracted a larger portion and number of the electorate than Blair in 2005, or Cameron in either 2010 or 2015. And Corbyn did so without either of their chummy ties with the press.

Both the Tory Press and the Tory Nation had thrown everything at him. The *Sun*, the *Mail*, the *Express*, *The Times*, their Sunday papers and the *Financial Times* were all pro-Conservative. Attacks on Corbyn were torrential and, according to research by Loughborough University, unprecedented in their intensity. The military had issued anonymous briefings about a Corbyn government, warning of a coup if he carried out 'any plans to emasculate and shrink the size of the armed forces'. 'The army wouldn't stand for it,' a serving general said.[10] 'People would use whatever means possible, fair or foul, to prevent that.' Even parts of the Labour Party were against Labour. Blair advised voters to consider voting Lib Dem and even Conservative in some constituencies.[11] Leaked exchanges showed how senior officials actively sought to thwart Corbyn's campaign and were then dismayed by its success. 'Opposite to what I had been working towards for the last couple of years!' one official wrote on an anti-Corbyn Labour WhatsApp group.[12] Of the newspapers, only the *Daily Mirror* backed Labour with any conviction (and even they had called for his resignation the previous year), while the *Guardian* came around reluctantly towards the end of the campaign.

Corbyn defied them all. Labour's membership swelled to almost 600,000 people, making it about four times the size of the Tories and the biggest party of the left in Europe, energising a generation of young people. May, by contrast, seemed increasingly trapped in a living nightmare. As if held hostage to some higher force, barraged on every side, she tried and failed to build a Brexit consensus within her party, never mind parliament or the country. There were weekly cabinet rifts, monthly resignations and in January 2019, when May finally, belatedly, put her Brexit deal before parliament, it was voted down by 230 votes – the largest defeat for a government in history.

British politics stood at a chaotic impasse, engulfed by a strange mix of paralysis and pandemonium – everything changed and nothing changed. Brexiteers couldn't agree on what they wanted; Remainers couldn't settle on how to respond; the very idea of compromise was unthinkable to either side – an all-or-nothing atmosphere had set in, antithetical to the Conservative ideal of level-headed compromise, and actively stoked by Theresa May's hostile rhetoric: 'No deal is better than a bad deal,' she said, legitimising the harshest, fastest and most damaging rupture with the European Union available.

This was the context in which, in April 2019, Nigel Farage – City trader, Conservative influencer, Britain's most dangerous demagogue – decided to launch the Brexit Party to contest the European elections the following month. It stood on a single policy: a no-deal Brexit. Every credible economic forecast predicted that it would crash the British economy. But for Farage 'it would make us proud of who we are as a nation once again, and you can't put a price on that'. Farage's newly born party won the EU elections comfortably, and the Conservatives sunk to fourth place, a historic low. May's time was up. 'I have done everything I can,' she said, in a tearful resignation speech on 24 May 2019. 'It is, and will always remain, a matter of deep regret to me that I have not been able to deliver Brexit.' Farage had ousted one Conservative leader – and he knew who he wanted as the next one.

It is sometimes said that Boris Johnson defies 'the usual rules of political gravity'. In fact, Johnson embodies the closest thing British politics has to a law of gravity: an alumnus of Eton and Oxford who joined the Conservative Party and became prime minister. Even Johnson's performative unseriousness – his ruffled hair and slapdash style – had an ancient Tory lineage to draw upon. When Bonar Law was unexpectedly chosen as leader of the Conservatives in 1911, a veteran backbencher advised him: 'You're not very well known to our fellows, and you must get yourself popular. What you want to do is drink a bottle of Champagne a day, and look as if you did.'[13] Bonar Law, a teetotaller, couldn't take the advice, but Johnson seems to have done so.

Johnson, who spoke as a young boy of becoming 'World King', became a Conservative MP in 2001, by which point he was also the editor of the *Spectator*. He rose quickly within the party. At a time when most British politicians seemed bland and one-dimensional, Johnson mastered the art of holding multiple identities at once – a man of so many masks that, one stacked upon the other, they granted him an illusion of depth. At the heart of his appeal was his sense of humour. He found that the truth matters less if you can make people laugh. Your words and your actions are forgotten, but your name and your face are remembered, smilingly. Johnson's self-deprecating jests protected him from the usual charges laid against politicians, especially those he exhibited to a more extreme degree: evasiveness, selfishness and hypocrisy.

Johnson's decision to cast his lot with the 'Leave' campaign during the 2016 referendum was almost certainly made with his leadership ambitions in mind: backing Brexit gave Johnson an unprecedented publicity run and the chance to position himself as the unlikely opponent of the British establishment. Johnson eventually turned himself into the Brexit dream embodied, its most inveterate advocate, a man whose Brexit belief could never be questioned. But when David Cameron called the referendum, Johnson was one of the last to decide which way he would campaign.

Johnson announced his decision on a Sunday afternoon, 21 February 2016. The following day he published a column in the *Daily Telegraph* explaining his decision. The message was typically convoluted, suggesting that voting to leave the EU, rather than Britain actually leaving the EU, was the aim: 'All EU history shows that they only really listen to a population when it says No.' Months later, it emerged that on the same weekend that Johnson wrote those words explaining why he was backing

Leave, he wrote a separate article, explaining why he was backing Remain. 'Shut your eyes,' he wrote in the unpublished column, later leaked to the *Sunday Times*. 'Hold your breath. Think of Britain. Think of the rest of the EU. Think of the future. Think of the desire of your children, and your grand-children to live and work in other European countries; to sell things there, to make things there and perhaps to find partners there. Ask yourself: in spite of all the defects and disappoint-ments of this exercise – do you really, truly, definitely want Britain to pull out of the European Union? Now?'

You can almost picture Johnson on that decisive, late-winter weekend in February, a mask in either hand, wondering to himself: which one shall I wear? Perhaps he knew that, which-ever one he chose this time, he wouldn't be able to take it off.

By the summer of 2019, when May formally stepped down, the quest to leave the EU had descended into boring bureau-cratic debate, weighed down by a growing awareness that, whatever Brexit might mean, Britain would be worse off than before. Johnson swooped in to lift the nation's spirits, vowing 'to get this country off the hamster wheel of doom' and 'bring us together'. The combination of his past career in journalism, spanning *The Times*, the *Telegraph* and the *Spectator*, and his passionate conversion to the Brexit cause, meant the press showered him with devotion. He sailed through the leadership contest. 'NOW BRING US SUNSHINE', the front page of the *Daily Mail* sang. The *Sun* showed a yellow ball with Johnson's face inside, surrounded by rays of light, beaming down from the sky: 'JOHNSUN: New PM promises a "golden age"'.

Not all Conservatives shared this enthusiasm. Some saw in Johnson's baseless bravado, his cynical opportunism and decep-tion and his indifference to parliamentary norms and etiquette a betrayal of the Conservative tradition. In his first few months alone, he prorogued parliament, kicked out twenty-one Conservative MPs who opposed his Brexit strategy, attacked the courts and was accused of lying to the Queen.[14] Some Tories said that they could no longer support a party that behaved so recklessly. 'I'm still not sure whether I left the Conservative Party, or whether it left me,' Rory Stewart lamented in October, announcing his departure.[15] 'The Tory party has crossed their Rubicon,' Matthew Parris mourned in *The Times* on 1 November, announcing that, after fifty years of loyalty, he would now vote for the Lib Dems.

But after a decade of disruption and destruction, such crises of conscience among Conservatives were hard to understand. Cameron, after all, had revealed his own recklessness by calling the referendum in the first place, and his own dogmatism was plain to see through his ruthless programme of austerity. Certainly, Johnson represented a break from Theresa May, a moral purist whose most scandalous transgression was, in her words, running through fields of wheat as a child. But even she had embraced nakedly populist rhetoric, pitting parliament against 'the will of the people' and pandering to Faragist fantasies about a no-deal Brexit. Johnson simply carried on where she left off.

In many ways, Johnson stood as a remarkable composite character of the Conservative tradition. He had Peel's eagerness to expand the party's base, Disraeli's shape-shifting ability, Balfour's air of effortless superiority, Bonar Law's disregard for the constitution, Churchill's myth-making grandeur, Thatcher's media celebrity and Cameron's entitlement. The Conservatives liked to see themselves as unideological – in Johnson, whose only guiding 'ism' is narcissism, they had the most unideological of leaders. With no obvious ideal other than his own self-image, Johnson's convictions are more like crutches, carrying him to the next career goal where they can be replaced with new ones. He was an artefact that only the Conservative Party could have produced.

Johnson called a new election on 6 November 2019, to be held the following month. He framed his campaign in terms of freedom: after years of gridlock and dreary debate, Johnson would finally 'Get Brexit Done', liberating the nation from the stalemate of the past three years. His entire pitch played on the public's frustrations, impatience and longing for swift solutions. The word 'unleash' was used seventeen times in his manifesto. In one election stunt, he drove a digger marked 'Get Brexit Done' through a wall of polystyrene bricks.

The Conservatives won a majority of eighty seats, their largest tally since 1987. Labour lost sixty seats, leaving them with their worst result since 1935. While the division in voting between young and old was still stark, Conservatives had happier demographic shifts to boast about: for the first time ever, more people on low income voted Conservative than Labour, with many seats in the North of England turning Tory for the first time.[16] 'We have changed the political map of this country,' Johnson announced. He chose a fitting place to deliver his victory speech: the old mining town of Sedgefield, Co. Durham, which had turned Tory for the first time since 1934 – and was the twenty-four-year parliamentary base of Tony Blair.

Perhaps it was inevitable, given the arc of British history, that the nation's self-proclaimed liberator would arrive in the form of an Old Etonian who had once edited the *Spectator*. That, at least, was the impression from the result's media reception. Johnson was hailed as a Conservative hero whose celebrity appeal had energised an unprecedented coalition of voters and brought the entire nation together. The reality was less grand. Johnson, after all, had barely received more votes than Theresa May two years prior: 13,966,454 to 13,636,684, about 1 per cent difference. The great rise in Conservative voters actually happened under May's leadership. Between 2015 and 2017, the Conservative vote rose by over 2.5 million.

Neither May nor Johnson redrew the political map of the UK. Brexit did. The referendum's high turnout of 72 per cent – well above the 63 per cent average of the previous four elections – introduced, and reintroduced, many voters into the fray. The largest rise was among the working classes, two-thirds of whom voted Leave, in regions where disillusionment under New Labour had deepened. Many of these voters had left Labour long ago. Brexit, and its resonant 'Take Back Control' slogan, was the gateway drug they needed to finally turn Tory. At least the Tories, unlike Labour, called the referendum, and could count a decent number of authentic Brexiteers in their ranks (Johnson was not among them). Johnson's success lay in simply holding on to May's Brexit coalition, and watching Labour's implode.

What happened to Labour? The most obvious difference between Labour's two election campaigns – in which it lost 2.7 million votes – was its Brexit stance. In 2017, Corbyn's manifesto promised to uphold the referendum vote. In 2019, under concerted pressure, Labour backed a second referendum. Leave voters fled en masse. Of the sixty seats Labour lost, fifty-two had pro-Brexit majorities in 2016. Overall, almost half of Labour's Leavers in 2017 had deserted the party by 2019, compared to a fifth of its Remainers. Across the North, the Midlands and in Wales, Labour's vote share sank back to its 2010 level, falling from 50 per cent in 2017 to 39 per cent in 2019.[17] Meanwhile the only seat Labour won spoke volumes: the prosperous west London constituency of Putney, which voted overwhelmingly for Remain.

Labour's self-defeating Brexit policy had many causes: the indecisiveness of Corbyn and his close team, some sly manoeuvring from senior Labour figures like future leader Keir Starmer (who, as shadow Brexit secretary, went rogue at the 2019 party conference by unilaterally declaring Labour's commitment to a second referendum), a small group of MPs that theatrically left Labour to form a new party, Change UK, generating much controversy before quickly collapsing, and an effective strategy from Johnson and his chief adviser Dominic Cummings that pushed Labour into a tight spot. But perhaps most of all, the failed policy reflected the elemental rift that the Brexit vote, for all its Conservative roots, created in Labour, one that any leader would have struggled to surmount. The referendum vote cut the country in two, traversing traditional party lines, and, for Labour, landed especially awkwardly.

Amid all the furore around Corbyn's character and (lack of) tactical acumen, it was easy to miss the magnitude of Labour's predicament. The vast majority of the party wanted to remain in the EU: only ten of the 230 Labour MPs in 2016 voted to leave, while around nine-tenths of the membership and two-thirds of Labour voters wanted to stay. But partly because support for the EU clustered in major cities, the third of Labour voters who backed Brexit were estimated to have accounted for almost two-thirds of Labour's parliamentary seats in 2017. What's more, Labour knew that thirty-five of its top fifty target seats in 2019 — those requiring minor swings to switch to Labour — were Leave constituencies.[18]

This compromised state complicated many of the moral tenets of so-called Corbynism: that the principled path should be pursued over political expediency; that the membership should be empowered to decide party policy; that the interests of young people – Corbyn's most reliable voting base and mostly Remainers – would be at the centre of his agenda; that Corbyn's humanitarianism would counter decades of hostile immigration policies, so emboldened by Brexit and previously appeased by both Blair and Brown. Corbyn's leadership also promised to reingratiate the party with lost heartlands in the North and in Scotland, as it did in the 2017 election, but then, with the former broadly wanting to leave and the latter to remain, they stood opposed to each other.

Besides Brexit, Corbyn's 2019 election campaign was paralysed by a second crisis: the anti-Semitism allegations that featured throughout Corbyn's leadership, but especially from 2018 onwards. It is a difficult matter to write about. The evidence that many Jews in Britain genuinely felt threatened by his leadership is clear. The evidence that Corbyn actually posed that threat is far less conclusive, to say the least. Anti-Semitism undoubtedly existed, and still exists, within Labour, as it does throughout society, including in the Conservative Party. But the main thrust of the allegations posited something much more damning than this: that Corbyn turned a blind eye to anti-Semitism, that he posed 'an existential threat' to British Jews, that in fact Labour anti-Semitism – sometimes, it seemed, anti-Semitism in general – started and ended with Corbyn. Before becoming leader, Corbyn had a long history of supporting Jewish causes, along with combatting other forms of racism and xenophobia as well. But according to an illustrative resignation letter from one disgruntled Labour MP, Joan Ryan, who joined Change UK in 2019, all previous Labour leaders '[stood] up to racism in all its forms', while anti-Semitism 'simply did not exist in the party before [Corbyn's] election as leader'.

232

This notion is clearly false: Labour have not always stood up to racism, nor been magically immune to anti-Semitism. But the fantasy contained a seed of truth: the anti-Semitism *crisis* within Labour never existed before Corbyn's election as leader. As research by the late theorist David Graeber showed, in 2015, there was only one reference to 'Labour anti-Semitism' in the British press. Between 2016 and 2019, there were over 13,000 mentions. (Over the same period, 'Tory anti-Semitism' or 'Conservative anti-Semitism' received one mention.)[19]

Consider the delayed commotion over a foreword that Corbyn wrote in 2011 for *Imperialism*, by J. A. Hobson, a book first published in 1902. Hobson was an influential British intellectual and *Imperialism* frequently appears on university syllabuses. Blair and Brown have both invoked Hobson positively.[20] In 2015, the *Guardian*'s former political editor Michael White described Corbyn's foreword as 'a perfectly decent introductory essay'.[21] But on 30 April 2019, *The Times* 'uncovered' this foreword, pointing out clear examples where Hobson had published anti-Semitic tropes which Corbyn had failed to mention or call out: a silence that was taken as implicit endorsement for or indifference towards the anti-Semitism.[22] What's important isn't whether the outrage was justified, but the evident double standards. Not only was the foreword uncontroversial before Corbyn became prime minister but similar expressions of anti-Semitism from popular Conservative figures in the same period – not least Winston Churchill, as we have seen – have never prompted the same guilt-by-association controversy for supportive Tories. (Nor does the widely recognised anti-Semitism in Edmund Burke's *Reflections on the Revolution in France* – which, in the words of one scholar, 'deemed the Jews' financial dealings and their presence in Britain as a threat to Britain's national solidarity'[23] – taint contemporary Conservatives who claim it as their foundational text.) In Corbyn's case, however, his foreword became a national scandal; *The Times* story drew follow-up reports in all the major newspapers along with the BBC, and led to a strongly worded statement from the Board of Deputies of British Jews expressing 'grave concerns'.

Such inconsistencies were standard fare. The coverage of Corbyn featured the usual fabrications and sensationalist misrepresentation that the Tory Press is known for, and this time it wasn't just the typical newspapers that saw Corbyn as a threat. Much of the 'respectable' left press like the *Guardian* and the *New Statesman*, along with national broadcaster the BBC, also treated Corbyn as less legitimate than past Labour leaders: it wasn't simply that they disliked or disagreed with him, it was that his leadership and supporters were deemed to have no place in serious British politics. A study by the London School of Economics in 2016 found that three-quarters of print stories failed to accurately present Corbyn's views.[24] An analysis of the BBC's coverage revealed that Corbyn's critics received airtime as his supporters.[25] Indeed, aside from the anti-Semitism charges, Corbyn's election posed the BBC in particular – with its commitment to 'impartiality' – a problem. Writing in 2015, the author Paul Myerscough explained:

> Because its notion of political balance between left and right is defined by the Labour and Conservative Parties, its spectrum of opinion has narrowed and its fulcrum drifted to the right in concert with New Labour. Corbyn has reopened the gap, but the BBC has not adjusted. So far as it is concerned, with his election the Labour leadership has put itself beyond the pale. Its norm remains a 'balance' between the Tories and the Labour right.[26]

234

The patterns of reportage continued throughout Corbyn's leadership. By the 2017 election, the levels of press hostility against Corbyn were already unprecedented. By the 2019 election, Loughborough University's analysis found that it had doubled again.[27] These distortions inevitably impacted the way the anti-Semitism allegations were reported as well.

In the end, these two themes dominated the 2019 election campaign: Brexit and the purported racism of the Labour Party, even as the Conservative Party – already a decade in power – made an election pact with Nigel Farage, a man who that very year was accused of purveying anti-Semitic conspiracy theories in his speeches about 'globalists' trying to create 'a new world order'.[28] In this topsy-turvy world, even the *Daily Mail* could describe Labour as 'institutionally racist' as it waged war on the left. Rarely can the maxim of political strategist Karl Rove – attack an opponent's strengths, not their weaknesses – have been implemented with such ruthless success. By the time of Johnson's election win, Corbyn and anti-Semitism were so conflated as to be synonymous: to defeat one was to defeat the other. A politician who had sat in parliament for almost forty years, regarded mostly as a principled activist not to be taken too seriously, was now a pariah, a racist and a wannabe dictator whose mere presence in the Labour Party was beyond the pale.

After the 2017 election result, the left had been allowed to dream of a victory that went beyond New Labour compromises. By 2019, those dreams were deemed morally reprehensible, akin to the delusions of 'fellow travellers' that could be soberly compared – in the *Guardian*, no less – to the evils of Nazism. 'At least we are finding out who would have hidden us in their attic,' the columnist Rafael Behr quoted a Jewish friend saying during the election campaign.[29]

'We laughed,' Behr reflected, 'because it wasn't even a joke.' Where this non-joke left Jewish people who supported Corbyn was left unsaid. Tom Bower, esteemed Conservative commentator and Corbyn biographer, had one answer: earlier in 2019, when debating a Jewish journalist defending Corbyn on ITV, he called him a 'self-hating Jew'. 'You must be,' Bower insisted. There could be no other explanation.

Corbyn's conversion into an existential threat, witnessed in real time, was a confounding spectacle to behold. It relied on much more than Labour's usual opponents: the Conservative Party, the City, the Tory Press, Farage and the far right. Other influential participants included US politicians, members of the security state, parts of the centre-left press, and once again, perhaps most crushingly, parts of the Labour Party itself. 'It could be that Mr Corbyn manages to run the gauntlet and get elected,' Mike Pompeo, then US secretary of state, said in a leaked recording in June 2019.[30] 'It's possible. You should know, we won't wait for him to do those [anti-Semitic] things to begin to push back.' This talk of a US intervention into UK politics joined a stream of similar-spirited stories coming from the national security state at home: overall, the investigative journalist Matt Kennard found at least thirty-four examples of people within the national security state – the military, MI5, MI6 and other intelligence agencies – briefing the press about the threat posed by Corbyn.[31] When a video leaked of soldiers using a picture of Corbyn as target practice at a shooting range, the bulk of the press barely blinked.

For many in Labour, meanwhile, Corbyn's leadership always stood as a mistake that needed correcting: he wasn't one of them, and the idea that he now 'led' them was intolerable. They took their revenge through an unending barrage of negative press briefings, leaked documents, concocted scandals and public criticisms. One MP, Ian Austin, who resigned from Labour in early 2019, went so far as to call on all 'decent, traditional, patriotic Labour voters' to back Johnson during the 2019 campaign. An indication of what might have motivated this explicit Conservative endorsement – which went well beyond calling on Labour voters simply to support other progressive parties or abstain – became clearer later on. When Johnson secured victory, Austin was swiftly ennobled as Baron Austin of Dudley, entering the Lords along with two other former Labour MPs who campaigned against Corbyn. The Tory Nation still had its charms.

The Labour figures who preferred a Conservative win to Corbyn extending his stay as party leader achieved their ambition. 'People might ask me in 30 years, "what did you achieve in your time in politics?"' Gavin Shuker, a former Labour MP who left to join Change UK and now works as the CEO of a credit card company, reflected a few months after the election, as the coronavirus pandemic was unfolding. 'I will be able to say I helped prevent Jeremy Corbyn from leading us through a huge national crisis. And to be honest, I'll take that.'[32]

Johnson's boosterish bravado, coupled with his indifference to the details, made him an ideal leader for Britain in the age of Brexit – a realm of fantasy where the details, with all their real-world consequences, were swept aside, and all the nation needed was a bit of self-belief. Johnson offered Britain an escape — from Europe, seriousness and self-doubt. What he lacked in a sense of direction he made up for with his boundless optimism and sense of humour. Punchlines could take the place of policy, raising spirits if not wages. Johnson would set Britain free.

But a very literal type of containment awaited Britain, putting the purported captivity of EU membership in perspective. On 31 January 2020, as Britain formally left the EU, it quietly recorded its first two cases of Covid-19. On 11 March, the World Health Organization declared a global pandemic. While it is hard to imagine a cause more suited to Johnson's strengths than Brexit — twin forces that disguise narrow self-interest in national renewal — it is hard to imagine a cause less suited to Johnson than a pandemic. The need to follow restrictions, to listen to experts, to lead by example, combined with the life-or-death stakes, are all antithetical to his character. But history had decided: Britain's self-proclaimed liberator would have to be the one to lock the nation down.

For a fatal few months Johnson utterly failed to adjust to his new role. He seemed structurally incapable of accepting the seriousness of the virus. He boasted about shaking hands with Covid-19 patients and, according to Dominic Cummings, wanted to have himself injected with the virus live on television, to show the nation that there was nothing to worry about. He pushed a policy of herd immunity, which really meant no policy at all: the idea, as Johnson explained on national television, was that 'you take it all in one go, and allow the disease to move through the population'. Later, an official government report described the initial response to the pandemic as 'one of the most important public health failures the United Kingdom has ever experienced'. It is thought to have led to tens of thousands of avoidable deaths.[33]

Many assumed that Johnson's own hospitalisation with the virus would be a turning point: surely now he must treat it seriously. But his government continued to bungle their way through with a cavalier indifference: lockdowns consistently arrived too late, only to last longer as a result; Covid contracts worth billions of pounds were assigned to Tory Party donors and friends without oversight; mixed-messaging was rife and often tragicomic. Testing was the order of the day, and then it wasn't (and then was again). Masks were not to be worn, until they were (and then only sometimes). People were told not to go to work, unless they could. Schools could safely return, and then they couldn't. Britain would have a 'world-beating' tracing system, except it wouldn't. And so on, for everything from quarantining new arrivals to following that early policy of 'herd immunity', which the government now denied ever pursuing.

By March 2021, the UK had lost over 120,000 lives to the virus, the highest per-capita death rate of any country with more than 12 million people, earning it the unhappy nickname 'plague island'.[34] It had also suffered the second-worst economic downturn in the OECD and experienced the third strictest lockdown globally.[35] It was a devastating triptych. Johnson had said throughout the pandemic that compromises must be made between safety, liberty and economic prosperity. Under his leadership, Britain failed on every front: more lives lost, longer lockdowns and a steeper economic decline.

But Johnson's ability to not just survive career-ending calamities but thrive on them was legendary, earning him nicknames like 'Teflon Johnson', 'Houdini' and, less flatteringly, 'the greased piglet'. As the pandemic receded into the background, he appeared to have conjured up another great escape. It was an unprecedented situation, much of the press and public seemed to agree, and Boris did his best. Meanwhile, a successful roll-out of the vaccine, which initially outpaced the European Union, allowed him to recast the tragedy as a triumph. 'It all seems to be worryingly hitch-free,' Johnson could muse at the Conservative Party conference in October 2021, with his party comfortably ahead in the polls once again.[36] 'We will need to concoct some sort of diversion or row.'

Johnson got his wish. Beginning in late November, revelations that he and his team attended parties during lockdown, flouting the very rules they imposed, angered his party, the public and the loyalist press as never before. The details of 'Partygate' – gatherings of forty people, 'wine time Fridays', suitcases used to sneak booze into the building, debauchery on the evening (and early morning) of Prince Philip's funeral – jarred with memories of a time when socialising was forbidden, people couldn't visit dying relatives in hospital and mothers gave birth in isolation. While Johnson's other misdemeanours could be cast as him mocking the establishment – breaking rules that the public didn't believe in anyway – the flouting of lockdown only made a mockery of the public, who often took pride in abiding by the pandemic's call to duty.

It was an impossible scandal to spin, a joke that couldn't be laughed off: the British public were the punchline. The Conservatives fell further behind Labour in the polls than at any point since 2013. Johnson's own popularity plummeted to its lowest-ever level. On 16 December, the Conservatives fought a by-election in North Shropshire – a seat in the West Midlands region of England that the Tories have held almost continuously since 1832 – and lost. Johnson persevered as leader, ready to weather yet another storm, as he always did. But there would be no great escape this time.

On 6 July 2022, after months of will-they-won't-they commentary, catalysed by reports that Johnson had turned a blind eye to sexual harassment allegations within the party, the Conservatives ousted Johnson. A record-breaking number of

Conservatives resigned from government. When Johnson appointed replacements, they turned on him, too. Across three days, Britain had three different education ministers. Some saw in all this the signs of a healthy democracy. 'We are watching a still-functioning democracy dispatch its bombastic populist leader because his amorality and narcissistic dishonesty were simply too much,' Michelle Goldberg wrote in the *New York Times*. But Conservatives dispatched Johnson simply because they realised that his amorality and narcissistic dishonesty could no longer win them votes. The decisive moment was when, two weeks earlier, Johnson had lost two by-elections in one day: the first in a traditional Tory area in the South, the second in a post-industrial seat in the North. The double defeat proved that Johnson's magic had worn off: he had redrawn the political map against himself.

When Johnson resigned on 7 July he left behind an embittered nation, its divisions and disillusionment deeper than ever. His passionate promises to 'level up' the country had proved to be old Tory tricks. Analysis suggested that, in practice, 'levelling up' simply meant channelling money from poorer areas to shore up Conservative seats, with some of the wealthiest parts of England receiving ten times more per capita than the poorest. Rishi Sunak confirmed as much on the campaign trail, as the former chancellor vied to replace Johnson. 'We inherited a bunch of formulas from Labour that shoved all the funding into deprived urban areas and that needed to be undone,' he said, on a visit to Tunbridge Wells.[37] 'I managed to start changing the funding formulas to make sure areas like this are getting the funding they deserved.' (Conservatives cringed at Sunak's naked articulation of their method, which he was hardly the first to pioneer.)

Throughout his prime ministership, Johnson had been criticised for filling his cabinet with mediocrities to secure his authority. This, too, was an old Tory trick. 'As every political captain knows, only mediocrities can be counted on for loyalty,' the Austrian economist Joseph Schumpeter had observed in the 1940s, singling out Disraeli as an example.[38] With Johnson on his way out, the mediocrities now queued up to claim control of the ship. Of the eleven initial contenders, only two had been in parliament before 2010: one of them, Grant Shapps, withdrew before he could be nominated, and the other, Jeremy Hunt, had already tried and failed for the leadership in 2019. Liz Truss and Rishi Sunak swiftly moved to the head of the pack, and on 20 July, it became a two-horse race.

The contest had the drawn-out feeling of a general election – obsessive coverage, interviews with candidates on national television and radio, leader debates, grandiose promises, personal barbs – where the public could have any leader they liked, so long as they were Conservative. Not that their preferences made any difference in the end. Only Tory members were eligible to vote: that 175,000-odd rank-and-file, overwhelmingly white, over-fifty and Leave-supporting.

In the name of leading the nation, Truss and Sunak prostrated themselves at the feet of this eccentric fringe. They promised the most efficient economy, the toughest ever culture war, the greatest ever country. Truss's tax proposals were so extreme that even Sunak deemed them irresponsible. Then two of Sunak's more out-there policy suggestions – that asylum seekers should be housed on cruise ships rather than hotels and that 'hatred of our country' should effectively be criminalised – allowed Team Truss to pose as the Sensible Conservative.

Both ultimately offered versions of the same clichéd script: deliver economic growth, protect the nation against evil threats (left-wing activists, 'trans ideology', asylum seekers), and undo the damage that malign forces (not the Conservative government, of course) had inflicted upon Britain since 2010. Sunak said he would 'restore trust, rebuild the economy and reunite the country', but didn't dwell on why these 're' prefixes were needed. With a hint of nostalgia, he invoked 'Labour's irresponsible management of the economy', just to see if the old hits could still land. But such banalities were nothing compared to Truss's inordinate pick-and-mix of platitudes. 'Turbo-charging our economy, unleashing the potential of Britain, keeping taxes low, being pro-business, that's what my campaign is about,' she said. She inherited Johnson's anti-establishment mask and tried to make it fit. But she couldn't even convince herself with her performance. In a hustings interview with Tom Newton Dunn, she attacked 'the media' several times. 'For the record, that's the third time you've attacked the media – a lot of which supports your campaign,' Newton Dunn pointed out, not enjoying being portrayed as the pantomime villain on stage. After the talk, apparently unaware her microphone was still on, Truss apologised: 'I am sorry I was mean about the media, Tom.' Newton Dunn, wounded, replied: 'It's cheap and you know it.'[39]

In the end, neither Truss nor Sunak could assert themselves as the dominant Conservative of the campaign. That honour fell to Margaret Thatcher, whose ghost haunted the contest like none before. It became clear that the winner was to be decided not by their own leadership credentials, but by who offered the most convincing Thatcher impression. This suited Truss, who had been cultivating her Thatcher tribute act for years: wearing similar outfits, conducting copycat photoshoots and echoing her language. Truss also had Thatcher's free-market think-tanks – the IEA and the CPS, in particular – on side.[40]

On 5 September, Truss's victory was confirmed. The Tory Press did their best to rally the troops. 'Cometh the hour, cometh the woman,' the front page of the *Daily Mail* declared, going through the motions. 'Put Faith in Truss to Deliver for Britain', implored the *Express*. But it was possible to detect exhaustion even among the Conservatives' most dependable cheerleaders: only so many new dawns can be celebrated before spectators start to yawn. The Conservative Party, bastion of strength and stability, was now on its fourth leader in six years, claiming the direct mandate of 0.15 per cent of the voting population. The front page of the *Mirror* was the most striking of the day's offerings: images of Cameron, May, Johnson and Truss side by side, morphed together into a single, eight-eyed beast, with the caption 'Same old Tories'.

On 6 September, Liz Truss travelled up to Balmoral to meet the Queen and become the fifteenth leader of Her Majesty's seventy-year reign. Truss was also to be the last. Two days later the Palace announced the Queen's death at the age of ninety-six. The nation descended into mourning, and Truss retreated into the shadows. Britain's soul took the stage.

The mood of reverence and melancholy was overwhelming: eulogies blanketed every media outlet; mourners flocked to Buckingham Palace; supermarkets turned down the beeps on their scanners out of respect; the nation came to a stop. Commentators spoke with one voice about how much Britain had changed under her reign, but how she alone had stayed the same: so dutiful, dignified and eternal – the people's Queen. What a tough job it was, they said, and how stoically she had endured it. References to the Queen's 'special sense of humour' were compulsory. 'The Queue' – the hundreds of thousands of people, rich and poor, who waited in line to walk past the Queen's casket – became a symbol of national pride and a performance to the outside world. Rumour had it that you could see it from space, curling along the Thames and through the streets of Central London. Britain seemed, once again, the centre of the universe.

The royal funeral was an intricately choreographed affair, planned and rehearsed over decades, offering the Tory Nation in full bloom: the sceptre and the orb; the diamond-studded crown on its own little cushion; the vast symphony of staff, each with their own special title and costume. Around 100 world leaders were in attendance, from all continents of the globe. No one else – no*where* else – could attract such a crowd, everyone agreed. It was quite simply, one Conservative MP declared, 'the most important event the world will ever see'.[41]

There could be no doubt: Britain was great again – or, rather, Britain had always been great, but now the rest of world received the reminder that they needed. Over ten days of mourning, the Queen's funeral offered Britain a fairy-tale distraction from the dullness of its domestic challenges: low wages, low growth, rising poverty, surging inflation and a worsening cost of living crisis. But Britain could only look away for so long. By 20 September, the funeral was over, and Truss's prime ministership properly began. Had Truss been a Conservative leader with 'One Nation' inclinations, there would have been a clear opportunity to harness the mood of togetherness, compassion and pride that the Queen's death had unleashed. Truss had other ideas.

On 23 September, Truss announced a 'mini-budget', a package of fiscal policies designed to make her mark on government and awaken the British economy. Instead of a pay rise for struggling workers, the government announced that it would toughen welfare, scrap a planned rise in corporation tax, end caps on bankers' bonuses and abolish the top rate of income tax completely: someone who was earning £50,000 a year would now pay the same amount of tax as someone earning £1 million. Pitched as 'Big Bang 2.0', in reference to Thatcher's deregulation of the financial sector, Truss's policies made Britain the most economically right-wing country in the developed world.[42]

Many pillars of the Tory Nation rejoiced. 'At last! A true Tory budget!' the front page of the *Daily Mail* declared. 'This was the best budget I have ever heard a chancellor deliver, by a massive margin,' wrote Allister Heath on the front page of the *Daily Telegraph*. 'The tax cuts were so huge and bold, the language so extraordinary, that at times I had to pinch myself to make sure I wasn't dreaming.' 'I have long tried to fine-tune our criticism of Conservative governments for not being radical enough,' Mark Littlewood, IEA director general, said. 'Now they're being more radical than even we are requesting.'[43] The *Daily Express* joined the chorus: 'In the space of just 26 minutes, Kwasi Kwarteng tore up decades of conventional economic thinking to put Britain firmly on a path to growth.'

Rarely was the gap between the public's self-appointed ventriloquists and the reality of public opinion so glaringly exposed. Contrary to the Tory Press's celebrations, most people saw the budget for what it was: a boon for the rich and a pittance for the rest. Overall, reductions in income tax meant that, while someone earning £200,000 would have an annual tax saving of almost £4,500, a worker on £20,000 a year saved £218 — a sum that was easily usurped by inflation, rising bills and uncapped rent.[44] Most damaging of all, however, was the backlash from establishment institutions – not just in Britain but around the world – to the extreme tax cuts. Expressions of disapproval came from everywhere: the left and right of the Labour Party, the International Monetary Fund, the Bank of England, Germany's ambassador to the UK, and even the US president. The pound fell to an all-time low against the dollar, while the Conservatives fell by twenty to thirty points in the polls. Electoral extinction loomed. 'This is the most dramatic polling shift in my lifetime,' said Chris Curtis, head of political polling at Opinium.

Truss and her entourage struggled for survival: they cited the Queen's funeral and Putin's invasion of Ukraine as reasons for the instability; some suggested that the woke mob had taken over the financial markets, hence their negative response; others ventured that the real source of the financial panic was actually the growing prospect of a Labour government. Truss reversed her plans and offered the sacking of her chancellor, Kwasi Kwarteng, as a human sacrifice. It was no use; the Tories were in freefall, carrying the nation down with them.

After only six weeks in office, much of which was taken up by the Queen's funeral, Liz Truss was forced to announce her resignation. 'Don't worry,' she told her shell-shocked Downing Street staff. 'I'm relieved its over . . . at least I've been Prime Minister.'[45]

Boris Johnson was watching all this unfold from the Dominican Republic on a family holiday. He saw his opportunity and flew back to Britain with the hope of resuming the leadership. He had significant support within the party, but not as much as Rishi Sunak, who quickly emerged as the favourite. There would be no membership vote this time: in a return to tradition, this leader would be selected solely by MPs.

247

Despite internal differences and all the chaos the party had caused, the Tories' infamous survival instincts showed themselves again. Liz Truss resigned on Thursday; Boris Johnson dropped out of the race on Sunday;[46] and on Monday, Rishi Sunak was declared Britain's new PM: the first ever with Asian heritage, and the wealthiest party leader since at least Lord Salisbury.[47] Surely no other prime minister in British history can have boasted such an impressive real estate portfolio, either: a £7 million, five-bedroom townhouse in Kensington with a nearby apartment as well; a £2 million Georgian manor house in Yorkshire, currently undergoing a £400,000 renovation, replete with tennis court and swimming pool; and a £5.5 million penthouse in Santa Monica, California. Together with his chancellor, Jeremy Hunt – another one of the Conservatives' wealthiest politicians – Sunak announced that a new era of austerity beckoned. George Osborne was brought into the Treasury's team for good measure.[48]

It was a historic moment. Besides Sunak's identity, there had now been more Conservative prime ministers in the last seven years than Labour PMs in the last seventy years. 'A new dawn for Britain,' the front page of the *Daily Mail* declared. The Tories had been kicked out – now it was the Tories' turn to rule the country.

The autumn had offered Conservatives a bewildering mix of emotions: the glorious, elevating nostalgia of Queen Elizabeth's funeral; the exhaustion and embarrassment of Truss's failures; the fantasy of an eternal England channelled through a new King; the fear of the Conservatives' terminal collapse. But as Sunak took charge, it was possible to detect, lingering in the autumn air, a hint of Tory hope, of revival: the Conservative Party's fate was not sealed; they were still in power; victory at the next election – which would represent an unprecedented fifth in a row — was still within reach. The Conservatives had bounced back from defeats before. The beauty of their most recent ordeal was that the humiliation of Truss's leadership *felt* like a defeat but didn't involve leaving Downing Street: it provided the shock of an election loss without the cost. The Conservatives found themselves, once again, in a familiar state: ambitious, anxious, focused and fearful, suspended somewhere between the dread of annihilation and the possibility of an ever-more total ascendancy — one foot in the grave, another on the throne, right where the Conservatives are most at home.

CONCLUSION

Since 2010, the wealth of the UK's ten richest people has almost quadrupled, to £182 billion a year. The Conservatives have received record-breaking sums in big donations, while the rest of the country survives on wages that, for the most part, haven't risen at all.[1] Connect the dots and it's hard to resist the impression that, under Tory instruction, the commons have been plundered for private gain.

The Conservatives have been described as 'an alliance of the City and the mob', denoting their ability to appeal to both elite interests and the masses, the southern stockbroker and the Sunderland factory worker – wrapping up the pursuit of profit and the protection of privilege in the Union Jack.[2] What this label obscures, however, is which of these two forces is the more prone to pillaging. Since 2010, the Conservatives' finance-first agenda has left a ruinous trail in its wake: ransacking communities across the country by slashing state funding; pushing the National Health Service to breaking point, to the point where Brits now have the worst healthcare access in Europe;[3] and overseeing the mass closure of public spaces, whether in the form of libraries, youth centres, or sold-off parks and squares.

Despite much ado about the party's populist turn, the Tories' ties with the City remain as strong as ever. A 2022 report found that the finance industry gave £15 million to political parties between 2020 and 2021, and more than three-quarters of it went to the Conservatives.[4] Since 2010, all but one of the Conservatives' seven chancellors have had backgrounds in finance and consultancy, George Osborne being the only exception (who quickly made amends at BlackRock after leaving office). The leaders' backgrounds are equally illustrative. David Cameron comes from a family of stockbrokers stretching back centuries, and after resigning as prime minister he went to work for financial services company Greensill Capital, lobbying the Conservative government he once led. Theresa May spent twelve years at the Bank of England before becoming a Conservative MP. Rishi Sunak, who spent fourteen years in the financial sector and whose wife is a billionaire heiress and venture capitalist, brings an even greater level of intimacy with the City to Number 10.

Johnson's prime ministership was also illustrative. While claiming to lead 'the people's government', he maintained a secretive 'advisory board' whereby elite donors received monthly meetings with the prime minister or the chancellor to share their views and interests, often in exchange for upwards of £250,000 donations to the party.[5] It was telling that when Johnson's resignation appeared increasingly inevitable in July 2022, one of the few voices leaping to his defence was a group of twenty-two wealthy Conservative donors. 'We need Boris Johnson to remain as our Prime Minister,' they wrote in an open letter. Nine of the names were on the Sunday Times Rich

List, with a combined net worth of £35.3 billion. The full set had collectively donated over £20 million in recent years.[6] We can only guess why they were so devoted to Johnson – but presumably it wasn't his dedication to 'the will of the people'.

The Conservatives' appeals to 'the mob', through xenophobia and culture war, are ever crueller and more theatrical. Even as Sunak promises a return to sensible politics, he has made defeating 'woke nonsense' and deporting asylum seekers to Rwanda key priorities. The hope seems to be that if Britain can only send enough asylum seekers into the sky, the nation's more mundane problems – collapsing living standards, overstretched public services, falling wages – might be carried away with them, too. Sunak took the controversial step to reappoint Liz Truss's hard-line home secretary Suella Braverman to her post, even though she had been forced to resign only a week earlier for breaking the ministerial code. Braverman increasingly stands as the self-appointed commander-in-chief of the Conservatives' culture war, railing against human rights and an immigration 'invasion of our south coast'. 'I would love to be having a front page of the *Telegraph* with a plane taking off to Rwanda,' a grinning Braverman said at the Conservative Party conference in October 2022. 'That's my dream. That's my obsession.'

The very way Braverman framed this dream, however – not as a policy but as a front page, conceived to satisfy the cruelty-lust of the Tory Press – also poses questions about who the culture war is really for: the mob or the media? The newspapers certainly do a lot of the supposed mob's baying. 'Migrants side by side in hotels with public,' the *Daily Telegraph*'s front page declared on 1 November 2022, as Britain's economic skies darkened. 'Nurses paying price of migrant crisis,' the *Daily Mail*'s front page declared two weeks later. Nurses saw it differently: the same day, the Royal College of Nursing voted to strike for the first time in its 106-year history, demanding better pay and working conditions.

As the Bank of England forecasts a second 'lost decade' in a row – an unprecedented economic failure by the Conservative government – Tory attacks on scapegoats are only increasing. The supposed threats to the nation are everywhere: not just the immigration 'invasion' along the south coast – never mind that Britain receives among the fewest number of asylum applications in Europe – but also the transgender community, trade unions, environmentalists, metropolitan elites, loony lefties and former Labour leaders like Ed Miliband and Jeremy Corbyn. Why are such scapegoats to be feared? We're told that they sow division, waste public money, overstretch public services, have little respect for democracy, denigrate the nation's reputation, drag down wages, jeopardise Britain's future and often pretend to be something that they are not. Perhaps it's time we realised that all these threatening forces do indeed exist, and they're coming from inside the house.

In 2010, shortly before the Conservatives returned to power and implemented their austerity agenda, George Osborne delivered a speech that attacked New Labour on its record in government. 'When people ask the famous question "are you better off than you were five years ago?",' he said, in the wake of the Great Recession, 'this will be the first election in modern British history when the answer from the government must be no.'[7]

Since then, the Conservatives have led Britain into three such elections, and seem certain to make it four. On almost every domestic measure, life in Britain has become worse with each Conservative win. The previous thirteen years under New Labour represented no utopia, by any means. Blair and Brown were both enamoured with the financial sector, cultivating the very divisions, disillusionment and economic imbalances that would define the subsequent decade. They shamelessly parroted Tory talking points, and in pursuit of a tough-enough reputation scapegoated asylum seekers and oversaw the highest rate of incarceration in Europe.[8] Welfare use was still stigmatised. Labour MPs started to adopt the Tory (mal)practice of leaving politics to become lobbyists for private companies. To some extent New Labour was simply continuity Conservatism. But Blair's policy achievements far surpassed those of any Conservative leader since: public services ran more smoothly, levels of poverty and homelessness both fell markedly, hundreds of new schools and hospitals opened, and more. Perhaps it can at least be said that, based on his domestic record if not his foreign policy, Blair stands as the best Conservative PM of the twenty-first century.

This isn't to say that the Conservatives would see their track record since 2010 as a failure. The social devastation they have wrought represents its own kind of success: selling off public services and infrastructure, making the welfare state more punitive, increasing inequality and adversity, weakening local government – all of these fulfil long-term Tory ambitions. The instability of Brexit – which merely compounded Britain's economic problems – can't simply be written off as incompetence, either: many Conservatives actively craved a disruptive break with the EU, in the name of creative destruction. But the litany of scandal, deceit and social disregard have taken a heavy toll: both Britain's economic landscape and its democratic faith are in dire straits. Countless studies and surveys have found that trust in Britain's political system and the integrity of its politicians has never been so low.

Britain is far from the only society to suffer such problems. Around the world, countries are witnessing deepening political disillusionment and a rise in reactionary forces. These eruptions are at least partly fuelled by democracy's failed promises: between its ideal form, on the one hand, where people have an equal say in how their society is governed, political parties compete on even terrain, and alternative futures always seem possible; and on the other hand, a reality where inequalities in wealth, education, status and connections ensure that influence is safeguarded from democratic scrutiny, decision-making is hoarded in a few hands and subject to secretive corporate lobbying, and feelings of political impotence are rife.

The widening gulf between these two systems – democracy as it is and democracy as it could be – has received no shortage of attention. Commentary variously focuses on the aftershock of the Great Recession, the rise of social media, the increasingly precarious nature and poor pay of many jobs, and burgeoning tensions caused by climate change. All these factors play their part. But democracy's deficiencies also predate the past decade. They have, in a sense, always been there. 'We get confused because we assume that the fight for democracy was won a long time ago,' the political scientist E. E. Schattschneider wrote in *Semi-Sovereign People*, published in 1960. We lure ourselves into a false sense of complacency by setting the bar for democracy too low, assuming that once a society has universal suffrage, an uncensored press and regular elections, the task is done. These are insufficient guarantors of democracy's ideals; anti-democratic forces are all too compatible with them.

255

The Conservatives' opposition towards democracy is inscribed upon Britain's past and present. Elsewhere, democracy was often achieved by overthrowing old elites and installing a new, imperfect political system based on democratic ideals. In Britain, by contrast, democracy emerged through a series of ruling-class concessions to mounting public unrest. Hence Britain's stuttering path towards universal suffrage: reforms occurred in 1832, 1867, 1884, 1918, 1929 and 1948. Conservatives often praise themselves for being the authors of some of these reforms, but that is much like a landlord praising themselves for fixing a hole in their tenant's ceiling after months, maybe years, of complaints, merely as a way of avoiding a rent strike or tenant revolt. Study any specific example and it's clear that the Conservatives' main aim with expanding the suffrage was never to realise the democratic dreams of the masses, or fulfil a duty to the British people to realise their right to self-rule, but to hold on to as much power and privilege as they could. In this sense, Britain's process of 'democratisation' was always simultaneously a process of ruling-class preservation – and the process succeeded to a greater extent than arguably anywhere else in the Western world.

This historical evolution explains many of the anachronisms of British politics. The House of Lords represents a kind of systematised corruption, where the Tories have enjoyed a majority for almost 200 years and party leaders can curry favour with friends and flunkies, giving any ally – a fellow politician, a family member, a journalist, editor or press baron, or a party donor – a job for life as a legislator, regardless of their suitability, with full state approval. According to a recent analysis, one in every ten Tory peers has given more than £100,000 to the party.[9] In any other context, we would know what to call such a practice. And then there are the public schools. Eton's enduring dominance over British society is just one expression of a national education system that is among the most elitist in the world. Only about 6 per cent of pupils in Britain attend a private school, but for children in the top income bracket — those families who earn upwards of £300,000, or 1 per cent of the population — that proportion rises to 60 per cent. According to Francis Green and David Kynaston, writing in *Engines of Privilege: Britain's Private School Problem*, this represents the starkest education divide of any advanced democracy. Often funnelled through Oxford or Cambridge, the alumni of private schools then dominate the press, parliament, the judiciary, and more. The Conservatives remain overwhelmingly committed to maintaining these engines of privilege. Even as social mobility grinds to a halt, criticisms of private schools are dismissed as 'inverted snobbery' and 'class war', as counterproductive attacks on one of Britain's world-renowned institutions and a case of 'social engineering'.

But the Conservatives have also understood that for things to stay the same they would have to change. The Conservative art of surrender involves knowing not only when to concede, but also how to frame those concessions, transforming potential defeats into proud moments in the party's past, proof of its benevolence and good sense. A Tory-friendly picture of Britain's past emerges irresistibly, where the Conservatives protected Britain from the ruptures of revolution and sagely agreed to an expanded suffrage, according to an eminently sensible timetable. In the same vein, Conservatives didn't fight to preserve the Empire until the dying moments (and beyond), but in fact were always only ever working to raise colonised peoples to political maturity and then free them;

Conservatives didn't oppose the creation of the NHS, but in fact proposed it in the first place; and Conservatives called and championed the Brexit referendum out of a profound commitment to democracy, rather than to paper over their own problems and muzzle the threat of UKIP. These reframings are slowly absorbed into the folklore of the nation, assisted by two old adages that work in the party's favour: not just that history is written by the victors (and the Tories are usually the victors), but also that newspapers write the first drafts of history (and most newspapers support the Tories).

But no matter how many patriotic declarations and rhetorical overtures to 'the British people' Conservatives make, the party remains a fundamentally anti-democratic force. It is wedded to an unrepresentative political system that allows it to frame fine margin victories as towering majorities. Over recent years, it has also sought to ban disruptive protests, weaken unions, prohibit strikes, increase prison terms for anyone caught defacing statues and push through voter-ID under a fictitious threat of voter fraud – a measure that is likely to disenfranchise millions of people, most of them typical Labour voters.

The Tories' ruthless pursuit of austerity since 2010, slashing the budgets of local governments sometimes almost in half, should be understood within this same context. Conservatives have long held fears that local councils could enable municipal socialism, creating progressive pockets outside of Conservative rule, reflecting the wishes of residents. Thatcher abolished the Greater London Council, along with other metropolitan county councils, for just this reason. County Hall, the grand building along the Thames where the council once sat, is now the home of two hotels, Shrek's Adventure and a cluster of co-working spaces for 'climate tech businesses' – a fitting monument to the Conservatives' loyalty to capitalism over democracy.

So, what is to be done?

In a 2011 essay, 'Why Last Chapters Disappoint', the historian David Greenberg reflected on some of the frustrating tendencies of final chapters. 'Practically every example of [the] genre, no matter how shrewd or rich its survey of the question at hand, finishes with an obligatory prescription that is utopian, banal, unhelpful or out of tune with the rest of the book,' Greenberg wrote. 'Hard-headed criticism yields suddenly to unwarranted optimism,' he noted, whether through a vague allusion to 'raising awareness' or a rousing call to action.

There is a long list of potential policies, ranging from the banal to the radical, that are likely necessary to dethrone the Tory Nation. With the caveat that they are far easier to name than enact, these include: restoring greater funding and autonomy to local governments; raising taxation on wealth on the grounds that more equal societies are generally happier societies; ending the charitable status of private schools and levying VAT on private school fees; stripping the monarchy of its tax breaks and public funding, and working towards becoming a republic; democratising the House of Lords; imposing greater limits and transparency on lobbying and political donations; replacing first-past-the-post with a proportional representation system; curbing corporate ownership of the press; and codifying a constitution that will bring an end to Britain's pliable good-chap approach to checks and balances. (The most quintessentially British aspect of Brexit was not the Euroscepticism it revealed, which is visible across the

Continent, but the remarkable casualness with which Cameron could call the referendum.)

If such a list of policies is of little practical use, it's because what's missing is not ideas, nor even popular support for these ideas, but the democratic space in which the popularity of such proposals is conceivable. This is precisely what the Conservatives are committed to stifling. Conservatives may claim the mantle of 'free speech' and 'the will of the people', but ideologically and historically they dislike the idea that people should have an equal say over how society is run. They take affront at non-Conservative viewpoints and ways of life. And they have worked concertedly against the notion that local communities might have control over local policies: one of the main objectives of austerity is not so much to weaken the state but to centralise it, while stripping away its basic public services to let private companies and charities do the rest.

The same scorn for democracy appears when Conservatives feverishly accuse institutions of having a left-wing bias. What they usually seem to mean is that they don't have an unwavering pro-Conservative bias, the absence of which is apparently unacceptable in the Tory Nation. There is no other way of explaining the Conservatives' ever-lengthening list of enemies: not just familiar foes like the Labour Party, trade unions, universities and the BBC, but also corporations, museums, galleries, the Office for Budget Responsibility (set up by George Osborne in 2011), the Church of England, anyone or anything that dares to question Conservative rule. Conservatives often try to bandy many of them together, as if they represented a co-ordinated front, whether as 'the anti-growth coalition' or the 'woke mob'. This anxiety has ancient roots and is tied to the existential fear of losing power.

This final chapter will not provide a step-by-step policy programme for how to make that fear a reality. The book's intention isn't to provide a plan for change, but to reveal the nation we inhabit, how its historical evolution and its most powerful party have shaped our politics and us. The Tory Nation might seem inescapable, but in a sense the implication of this book is the opposite: buried within Britain, suppressed by a political system constructed in the Conservatives' favour, other visions of society – other expressions of national identity – exist. Neither Britain nor even England are fundamentally Conservative. In the absence of a genuinely representative democracy, such conclusions cannot be drawn.

This basic fact – that the Conservatives' record of victory does not correlate with mass popularity – sheds light on one of the more peculiar Tory tendencies witnessed today: the Conservatives' habit of acting like an embattled minority, even when ensconced in Downing Street on the back of four election wins in a row. Their anxiety reflects an undeniable truth: the Conservatives really are an embattled minority, rarely claiming more than a quarter of eligible voters' support and consistently having to fight away other forces for government control. They appear dismayed by the absence of universal Conservative consent, by the persistence of non-Conservative ways of life and thought, by the fact that, for all their efforts, 'Conservative' and 'British' are still not perfectly synonymous. To the despair of Conservatives, cultural and social trends still evolve beyond their control. No matter how many elections the party wins, many British people carry on detesting the Tories, while also behaving in ways that Tories detest, too: they join trade unions, go on strike, haul down statues, laugh at the monarchy, quote Winston Churchill's racism, boo the national anthem, support Scottish independence and Irish unification, and even vote Labour.

Conservatives define these forms of expression as not just un-Conservative but somehow 'un-British', and their political dominance makes this claim more plausible. The idea that Britain might be a 'Labour country' as opposed to a Conservative one – despite similar electoral support for both parties, if not electoral success – would likely strike even the most optimistic of leftists as wishful thinking.

But the Tories speak no more for Britain than the Tory Press does. Far from allowing us to see society more clearly, the bulk of the British press too often colludes in diverting our attention away from where power really lies, making scapegoats out of those who have least, with the aim – by turns covert and overt – of keeping the Conservatives in power, and progressives out. We're often told, as David Cameron said in 2015, that 'Britain and Twitter are not the same thing', the point being that a noisy sub-section of society is not representative of the nation at large and shouldn't dominate the national discourse. The same, and more, can be said of the Tory Press.

Perhaps nowhere is the success of the Tory Nation's conquest of national identity clearer than in the left-wing lament: 'I don't feel English/British.' 'Conservatism' and 'Englishness' in particular can seem so equivalent that to renounce the former apparently requires renouncing the latter as well. But despite the left's well-founded discomfit with nationalism, this conflation should be challenged, rather than surrendered to. As Anthony Barnett has argued, the left needs to embrace some kind of national identity if it is ever going to stop being seen as an outlier in its own home.[10] A rival patriotism can't be centred around military victory, imperial nostalgia or the pomp and ceremony of royal pageantry, nor should it avoid the darker chapters of the nation's past and the demands they place upon the present. It will lie somewhere else – in the Chartists, the trade unions, the suffragettes, the spirit of 1945, the NHS, Windrush. The project of building an honest, progressive past isn't nostalgic, overly romantic or – in its reckoning with historic wrongs – self-flagellating. It is born of an awareness that all identities and movements must have their pasts to draw upon. As the Queen says to Alice in *Alice in Wonderland*: 'It's a poor sort of memory that only works backwards.' And it's a poor sort of politics that only looks forwards, too.

The left can take strength from the fact that British voters seem increasingly to share an appetite for change. For all their differences and conflicting support bases, Corbyn's rise enjoyed a strange synergy with the Brexit vote. Within the space of ten months, between his election as Labour leader in 2015 and the referendum in 2016, both of these one-time fringe political forces upended a status quo that seemed set in stone. Both drew on similar structures of feeling, as well: a sense that, somewhere along the way, Britain went astray, with similar turning points imagined – either Britain's free market transformation under Margaret Thatcher or her decision to join the single market.

Stripped of its malicious xenophobia, the Brexit campaign contained at least the seed of an effective Labour campaign: more money to underfunded public services, overturning an elite consensus and putting power back in people's hands. 'Take Back Control', Brexit's specious slogan, could have been a rallying call for Labour long ago, with its target not Brussels or national borders but an overpowerful corporate sector and the Conservatives' attacks on local government. That this message was instead pushed by Tories and the one-party press, with their own vested interests and rabble-rousing nationalism, only reaffirms just how duplicitous the Brexit campaign really was. But this shared resonance still suggests an opportunity for the left.

It's hard to find such opportunities convincing amid the relentlessness of the Conservatives' 'culture war' narrative, which leaves us with the image of an irreconcilable rift at the heart of British society: between immigration-loving liberals obsessed with identity politics who live, literally or spiritually, in 'north London', and sidelined social conservatives who live – or, rather, are 'left behind' – everywhere else (most emotively in 'the red wall'). These fantasy constructions are now the twin pillars of Conservative rhetoric: the Tories stand for 'real people'; Labour represent an out-of-touch metropolitan elite.

But this image of an irreconcilably divided nation is just that: an image. A spate of polls show that we are not as divided as many would have us think.[11] Views in the so-called red wall are largely consistent with the rest of the country. Attitudes to immigration are far less reactionary than the Tories imply, and have a tendency to vary depending on how a pollster's question is phrased and the media attention the matter receives.[12] Well-funded public services remain widely popular nationwide.[13]

Perhaps the most important point is that the views of the 'British people' are not singular or fixed. Public opinion always reflects wider political, cultural and economic trends, and is shaped by the visions put forward by opposing parties. As the political theorist Nancy Rosenblum has written, in a democracy the clash of beliefs and the interests that underpin them do not arise 'spontaneously': 'Someone must create the lines of division over social aims, security and justice. Party rivalry is constitutive. It stages the battle.'[14] Stuart Hall put the same point more pithily: 'Politics does not reflect majorities, it creates them.'[15]

For now, however, Labour seems uninterested in staging the battle. Keir Starmer follows on from Blair – admittedly the only victorious Labour leader in almost fifty years – by promising a more competent brand of Conservatism. Labour pitch themselves as the party of prosperity and patriotism – defining their platform almost entirely on the Tories' terms, offering little more than a revolution in manners. Cuts will be carried out more competently; immigration controls will be imposed more efficiently; the culture war will be waged more humanely. References to 'making Brexit work' are indulged as par for the course; corporate bosses and privatisation are praised; support for strikes is not just resisted but actively punished. Starmer has expelled Jeremy Corbyn from the party and in the *Economist*'s words, 'purged the party of lefties, with the brutality one used to associate with the Conservatives'.[16] He insists that electoral reform will not be part of his programme, and bills Labour as 'the party of law and order'. There are crumbs to keep progressives on side – an end to private schools' tax exemption, renationalising the railways, a publicly-owned energy company – but they are easy to miss (and distrust) amid the constant courting of the Tory Nation.

As with New Labour, as with Starmer, idealism and hope are scorned in favour of 'pragmatism' and 'common sense'. In contemporary Britain, these twin concepts almost always seem to mean caving to the right. But their substance can change. The decades after the Second World War provide proof that the centre ground does not need to mean low taxes on the rich and cuts to public spending. Back then, for a brief window, common sense and pragmatism leaned left. The result is that if the Conservative Party from the 1950s contested an election today, it would be offering the most left-wing economic programme of any major party, and if New Labour contested an election in the 1950s, it would be the most economically right-wing. The point isn't to return to 1945, but to remember that if the trend was reversed once, it can be reversed again.

A different Britain is possible, but nothing in politics is guaranteed. While it seems likely that the current groundswell of discontent will oust the Tories from office at the next election, it would be a mistake to write them off before or after the result. Some two hundred years of precedent tell us that, whether in government or in opposition, the Conservatives will continue to find ways to adapt, sow division and preserve whatever privileges they can.

Even after over a decade in Downing Street, the Conservatives remain more combative and assertive than Labour: deference is for other people. 'They dream about real cultural power,' Stuart Hall observed. 'And Labour, in its softly-softly, don't-rock-the-boat, hoping-the-election-polls-will-go-up way, actually has in front of it only the choice between becoming historically irrelevant or beginning to sketch out an entirely new form of civilisation.' Amid a dispiriting confluence of crises – political, economic and environmental – the task of rebuilding and reclaiming Britain has rarely felt so pressing, or so great. It can be stated most simply as a struggle for democracy – and it will require more than an election victory to win.

ACKNOWLEDGEMENTS

I remember reading once that the biggest lie in journalism is the by-line: one name usually appears next to the text, giving the impression that it was the work of one person. The truth is that every writer is helped not only by at least one editor – several editors and a fact-checker, if they're lucky – but also scholars and sources who provide time and expertise, the sub-editors and web editors who bring a piece to publication, the work of other journalists, and colleagues, friends and/or family who listen to ideas, offer advice and read through drafts.

All this feels even more true of writing a book: it takes a village to make one. I was lucky to have a wonderful agent in Kat Aitken who first made that daunting, far-fetched notion – writing a book – seem realisable. She nudged, encouraged and refined my proposal into existence, and then – best of all – connected me with Assallah Tahir at Simon & Schuster. Assallah really felt like a co-pilot in the writing process. Her editing and advice were essential and elevating throughout. Both the writing of this book and, I assure you, the reading of this book would have been infinitely more cumbersome without her. My thanks too go to the wider Simon & Schuster team, Sophia Akhtar, Hannah Paget, Sue Stephens, Polly Osborn especially, for helping to bring the book to readers.

I'm grateful to every editor I've had the chance to work

with as a journalist, but there are three in particular I'd like to mention: Siddhartha Mahanta, Tim Schneider and Ryu Spaeth. Besides each making me a better writer, they also gave me the opportunity to write and think about British politics as a young journalist in a way that didn't feel as available at UK publications. They may not have worked directly on the book, but I can't imagine it existing without them. A special thank you goes to Ryu, who commissioned and edited a set of long-reads from me between 2018 and 2022 for the New Republic and New York Magazine, one of which – 'the Sordid Story of the Most Successful Political Party in the World' – spawned this book.

Thank you to all the people I spoke to for *Tory Nation*, both those who belong to the Conservative tradition and those who study it: Sheri Berman, Richard Bourke, John Hayes, Emily Jones, Charles Moore, Anthony Seldon, Sayeeda Warsi and David Willetts. The final stages of writing and editing the book benefited from classes with Ira Katznelson, Michael Schudson, Andie Tucher and Nadia Urbinati at Columbia University, where I began a PhD in September 2022. Ira also generously read through, and brought important nuance to, Chapters 3 and 4. The works of Perry Anderson, Stuart Hall and Tom Nairn were constant sources of inspiration and insight. The historical research of David Cannadine, Linda Colley, David Edgerton, Andrew Gamble and Susan Pedersen were indispensable. The measured scorn and committed prose of Pankaj Mishra, Arundhati Roy and Gary Younge were never far from my mind. Needless to say, none of the names mentioned here are responsible for any claim or mistake made within this book's pages.

For very different reasons, I am grateful to my wonderful late grandparents, Auriol and Eric, who passed away at the open and close of 2021 respectively. Many of my first memories of books are with them: the bed-time stories they read me as a young boy; the walks to Waterstones along the high-street; the infinite shelves that lined the walls of their old home in Guildford. It therefore felt fitting, if also sad, that I wrote much of the early chapters of the book in that same home, where they had lived for almost sixty years. By the time I turned it into a makeshift writing retreat, their cat Tuppence was the sole remaining resident. He kept me company – affectionately, if not always helpfully – and I liked to think that, through Tuppence, they were there too. I'm grateful as well to my auntie and uncles, Wendy, Rod and Patrick, for making that home what it was, and for ensuring its spirit survives on both sides of the equator.

And then there are my friends in and around London. I feel like this book was borne out of decade-long discussions with a few friends in particular: Ash Atighetchi (aka Morpheus), Ben Cross (defiant believer in the socialist heart of Britain), the phenomenological Matt Graham and Lucie Parker, the most avid reader a writer could wish for. Yet there are many others who, for both similar and varied reasons, must be mentioned: Tom Cox (platypus prince), Griff Ferris (angels instead) and Ryan White (journalism's Junya Watanabe); Rosie Brear and Chloe Curry, my forever housemates at Lausanne Road; and Yasmin Bar-Tzlil, Max Bond, David Dabieh, the Diaz family, John Harvey, Flora MacLeod, Moya Lothian-McLean, Maria McLintock, Ella Navot, Claudia Paterson, Lydia Sheldrake and Joe Softley. Along with Adonis, Eat Vietnam, Skehans, Singburi, Thom Yorke, Cloud X, Gellatly, Vittles and Liverpool F.C., you're the reasons why, despite the best efforts of the Tory Nation, England will always be the place I'm proud to call home.

All this and more is true of my partner and best friend,

Olivia Head. Your love, compassion and comedy routines made writing a book a far lighter, and happier, task than it could ever have been otherwise, and that is as true of life beyond the book as well. Our many discussions are also here, while our slightly impulsive foray across the Atlantic means that I'll always remember it as just one chapter in a larger adventure together.

The last, and greatest, thank you goes to Jenny Earle and Judy Wajcman: perennial thorns in the Tory Nation's side, and pioneers I'm lucky to have as my two mums. For your love, wisdom and example – really, for everything – I dedicate this book to you.

NOTES

INTRODUCTION

1 'Britain's Tories are the world's most successful party. Here's why', *Economist*, 21 December 2019.

2 'Key findings: British Social Attitudes in an era of crisis', NatCen, 22 September 2022; 'Poll shows even Tory voters feel austerity has gone too far', *Financial Times*, 1 May 2018.

3 John Ramsden, *An Appetite for Power: A History of the Conservative Party Since 1830*, HarperCollins, 1998, p. 22.

4 Tim Stanley, Twitter post, 23 October 2022.

5 Andrew Atkinson, 'One of World's Least Generous Safety Nets Awaits U.K. Unemployed', Bloomberg, 9 October 2020; 'Public and family finances squeezes extended well into the 2020s by grim Budget forecasts', Resolution Foundation, 9 March 2017.

6 Emily Head, 'Life expectancy declining in many English communities even before pandemic', Imperial College London, 12 October 2021; Patrick Collinson, 'Life expectancy falls by six months in biggest drop in UK forecasts', *Guardian*, 7 March 2019; Anna Cooban, 'UK workers suffer biggest hit to their wages since records began', CNN, 16 August 2022.

7 Daniel Ziblatt, *Conservative Parties and the Birth of Democracy*, Cambridge University Press, 2017, p. 76.

8 Laura Beers, *Your Britain: Media and the Making of the Labour Party*, Harvard University Press, 2010, p. 56.

9 Hugh Cunningham, 'The Conservative Party and Patriotism', in *Englishness: Politics and Culture 1880–1920*, Bloomsbury, 2014, p. 317.

10 Geoffrey Nowell-Smith and Quintin Hoare (eds), *Selections from the Prison*

Notebooks of Antonio Gramsci, Lawrence and Wishart, p. 151. The full sentence the quote is taken from reads: 'Hence it may be said that to write the history of a party means nothing less than to write the general history of a country from a monographic viewpoint, in order to highlight a particular aspect of it.' Abbreviated here for emphasis.

1 TORY HISTORY: SURVIVAL INSTINCTS

1 Matthew Parris, 'The Right has won the argument, so why is it so angry and sour?', *Spectator*, 20 November 2004, p. 28.

2 As part of this clean-up act, he wrote a series of columns for the *Guardian*. The headlines tell their own story: 'What I learnt from my stay with a Muslim family' (2007), 'No one will be left behind in a Tory Britain' (2007), 'We'll change black Britain' (2008).

3 Haroon Siddique and agencies, 'We will match Labour spending plans for three years, say Tories', *Guardian*, 3 September 2007.

4 James Forsyth, 'Turning Brown's happier mood against him', *Spectator*, 13 October 2008.

5 Ziblatt, *Conservative Parties and the Birth of Democracy*, p. 114.

6 Robert Stewart, *The Foundation of the Conservative Party: 1830-1867*, Longman Publishing Group, 1978, pp. 103–4.

7 Another example is Singapore's governing People's Action Party, which has held power continuously since 1965, through many mutations. See 'Singapore's governing PAP returns to power but faces setback', Al Jazeera, 11 Jul 2020..

8 Peter Hennessy, '"Harvesting the Cupboards": Why Britain Has Produced No Administrative Theory or Ideology in the Twentieth Century', *Transactions of the Royal Historical Society*, 4 (1994), pp. 203–19; Lord Hailsham, 'Elective Dictatorship', Dimbleby Lecture, 1976.

9 Nicholas Sowels, 'Living together in an age of inequalities: an overview of economic inequalities and poverty in the United Kingdom', *Observatoire de la société britannique*, 26, 2021.

10 Brett Christophers, *The New Enclosure: The Appropriation of Public Land in Neoliberal Britain*, Verso, 2018.

11 See Tom Crewe, 'Strange Death of Municipal England', *London Review of Books*, vol. 38, no. 24, 15 December 2016; Abbey Innes, 'Corporate state capture: the degree to which the British state is porous to business interests is exceptional among established democracies', London School of Economics British Politics and Policy Blog, 16 April 2021; Peter Geoghegan, *Democracy for Sale: Dark Money and Dirty Politics*, Apollo, 2020.

12 Musa Okwonga, *One of Them: An Eton College Memoir*, Unbound, 2021, p. 32.

13 Ziblatt, *Conservative Parties and the Birth of Democracy*, p. 87.

14 Rab Butler, *The Art of the Possible: The Memoirs of Lord Butler*, Hamilton, 1971, p. 133.

15 Lord Lexden, 'Popular party?' (A letter to the editor), *The Times*, 16 August 2013.

16 M. Rosenbaum, *From Soapbox to Soundbite Party: Political Campaigning in Britain Since 1945*, Palgrave Macmillan, 2016, p. 8.

17 *Ibid.*

18 Charles Dod, *Electoral facts, from 1832 to 1852, Impartially Stated*, Whittaker and Co, 1852, p. 195.

19 See Ron Johnston and Charles Pattie, *Money and Electoral Politics: Local Parties and Funding at General Elections*, Oxford University Press, 2014, p. 27.

20 Peter Geoghegan, 'Cronyism and Clientelism', *London Review of Books*, vol. 42, no. 21, 5 November 2020.

21 E. H. H. Green, 'The Man Who Stood Behind the Man Who Won the War', *London Review of Books*, vol. 21, no. 18, 16 September 1999.

22 In 1924, when Labour first entered government, they actually finished second in terms of seats in a hung parliament, but the Conservatives were unable to form a minority government or find a coalition partner.

23 Allan Silver and Robert McKenzie, *Angels in Marble: Working Class Conservatives in Urban England 1958–60*, Heinemann, 1968.

24 *Ibid.*

25 Andrew Gamble, *Conservative Nation*, Routledge, 1974, p. 202.

2 WHAT CONSERVATIVES BELIEVE

1 Edmund Fawcett, *Conservatism: A Fight for a Tradition*, Princeton University Press, 2020, p. 329.

2 Richard Cockett, *Thinking the Unthinkable: Think-tanks and the Economic Counter-revolution 1931–1983*, HarperCollins, 1995, p. 92.

3 Andrew Gamble, *The Free Economy and the Strong State: The Politics of Thatcherism*, Palgrave, 1988.

4 Quoted in Gamble, *Conservative Nation*, p. 116.

5 Michael White, 'Fight for the right: who is the Tories' greatest hero?', *Guardian*, 25 September 2008.

6 See Emily Jones' excellent *Edmund Burke and the Invention of Modern Conservatism, 1830–1914: An Intellectual History*, Oxford University Press, 2017, for a full account of Burke's Conservative conversion.

7 R. R. Palmer, *Age of the Democratic Revolution: A Political History of Europe and America, 1760–1800*, vol. 1, *The Challenge*, Princeton University Press, 1959, p. 5.

8 Richard Bourke, *Empire and Revolution: The Political Life of Edmund Burke*, Princeton University Press, 2015, pp. 595-7; Gregory M. Collins, 'Edmund

Burke on slavery and the slave trade', *Slavery &Abolition*, 2019, 40 (3), 494–521.

9   See Mary Wollstonecraft, *A Vindication of the Rights of Men*, J. Johnson, 1790, which takes the form of an open letter to Edmund Burke.

10 Stuart Ball, *Portrait of a Party: The Conservative Party in Britain 1918–1945*, Oxford University Press, 2013, p. 63.

11 Ted Honderich, *Conservatism: Burke to Nozick to Blair?*, Pluto Press, 2005, p. 39. For the reactionary side of Conservatism, see also Corey Robin, *The Reactionary Mind: From Edmund Burke to Donald Trump*, Oxford University Press, 2017.

12 Karl Mannheim, *Ideology and Utopia: An Introduction to the Sociology of Knowledge*, Martino Fine Books, 2015 [1929], pp. 107–8.

13 François Bédarida, *A Social History of England 1851–1990*, Routledge, 2013, p. 63.

14 *Sunday Telegraph*, 12 April 1992. 'Thatcher has told friends that the poll tax won the election for the Conservative Party,' the article reports. 'She believes that it prevented many Labour supporters from registering on the electoral roll (in the hope of avoiding payment).'

15 Charles Moore, *Margaret Thatcher: The Authorized Biography*, vol. 2, *Everything She Wants*, Penguin, 2015, chapter 4.

16 *The Times*, 15 September 1973. See Ralph Miliband, *Class War Conservatism: And Other Essays*, Verso, 2015.

17 Janek Wasserman, *The Marginal Revolutionaries: How Austrian Economists Fought the War of Ideas*, Yale University Press, 2019, p. 261. See also Kojo Koram, *Uncommon Wealth: Britain and the Aftermath of Empire*, John Murray, 2022.

18 Daniel Anthony Cowdrill, 'The Conservative Party and Thatcherism, 1970– 1979: A grass-roots perspective', 2010, University of Birmingham, M. Phil.

19 The report in the *NYT* continues: 'Labor strategists believe that Mrs. Thatcher's speech has given them an important opening, which they can exploit with more of Mr. Callaghan's "steady-as-she-goes" brand of politics'. R. W. Apple Jr., 'Thatcher Speech Warms Up the British Campaign', *New York Times*, 19 April 1979.

20 Wollstonecraft, *A Vindication of the Rights of Men*, p. 109.

21 First quote: Robert Garner and Richard Kelly, *British Political Parties Today*, Manchester University Press, 1998, p. 57; second quote: Gamble, *Conservative Nation*, p. 34.

22 '"You Tories hate poor people!" Yup: we want to turn them all into rich people'. Daniel Hannan, Twitter post, 26 October 2020.

23 Edmund Burke, *Thoughts and Details of Scarcity: Originally Presented to the Right Hon. William Pitt, in the Month of November, 1795*, F. and C. Rivington, 1800.

24 The Trussell Trust, 'Number of people receiving three days' worth of emergency food by Trussell Trust foodbanks in the United Kingdom from 2008/09 to 2021/22', Statista, 30 April 2022.

25 Gamble, *Conservative Nation*, p. 103

26 Boris Johnson, 'A deal is oven-ready. Let's get Brexit done and take this country forward,' *Daily Telegraph,* 5 November, 2019.

3 RULING BRITANNIA:
AN ENDURING, EVOLVING ELITE

1 A. J. Davies, *We, the Nation: The Conservative Party and the Pursuit of Power*, Little, Brown, 1995. Also Adrian Wooldridge, 'We chopped its head off but nepotism slithers back, calling itself talent', *Sunday Times*, 27 July 2014.

2 'Family Feeling', *Time*, 14 November 1960. See also W. L. Guttsman, *The British Political Elite, 1955–1972*, MacGibbon & Kee, 1963.

3 Stewart, *The Foundation of the Conservative Party*, p. xiii.

4 Geoffrey Wheatcroft, *The Strange Death of Tory England*, Gardners Books, 2005, p. 190.

5 Geoffrey Wheatcroft, 'The End of the Etonians', *Spectator,* 17 January 2004, p. 22.

6 Perry Anderson, *English Questions*, Verso, 1992, p. 19.

7 Linda Colley, 'The Apotheosis of George III: Loyalty, Royalty and the British Nation 1760–1820', *Past & Present*, 1984, no. 102, pp. 94–129.

8 Bédarida, *A Social History of England*, p. 292.

9 Burke, *Reflections on the Revolution in France*, p. 63.

10 Catherine Marshall, *Political Deference in a Democratic Age British Politics and the Constitution from the Eighteenth Century to Brexit*, Springer International Publishing, 2021, p. 115.

11 Bédarida, *A Social History of England*, p. 140.

12 Iain McLean, in *What's Wrong with the British Constitution?*, Oxford University Press, 2009, p. 146. One letter from the King's secretary gave the Tory leader Bonar Law detailed instructions on how he should resist the Liberal PM's plans to grant Ireland independence.

13 Ruth Dudley Edwards, *Newspapermen: Hugh Cudlipp, Cecil Harmsworth King and the Glory Days of Fleet Street*, Random House, 2013. See also Andrew Lownie, *The Mountbattens: Their Lives and Loves*, Blink Publishing, 2019. 'Important people, leaders of industry and others, approach me increasingly saying something must be done,' he said. 'Perhaps there should be something like the Emergency Committee I ran in India.'

14 Jonathan Freedland, 'Enough of this cover-up: the Wilson plot was our Watergate', *Guardian*, 14 March 2006.

15 Brian Wheeler, 'The David Cameron story', BBC, 12 September 2016.

16 Rowena Mason, 'David Cameron says Queen 'purred down line' after Scotland no vote', *Guardian*, 23 September 2014.

17 Robert Saunders, 'Should we abolish the House of Lords, or reform it?', *New Statesman*, 12 August 2020.

18 Ian Aitken, 'They Like it There', *London Review of Books*, vol. 15, no. 15, 5 August 1993.

19 George Parker, 'Arcane, hereditary, all-male – and at the heart of British democracy', 11 November 2021, *Financial Times*.

20 Gabriel Pogrund and Tom Calver, 'Revealed: the truth about the peers who are born to rule', *Sunday Times*, 20 March 2021.

21 David Edgerton, *The Rise and Fall of the British Nation: A Twentieth-Century History*, Allen Lane, 2018, p. 118.

22 An analysis of Harrow's intake between 1885 and 1910, for example, recorded 'a significant and growing shift towards money rather than land as the basis of Harrovian wealth', with it 'ceasing to be an aristocratic school; and instead becoming "a cradle of plutocracy"', Francis Green and David Kynaston, *Engines of Privilege*, Bloomsbury, 2019, p. 77.

23 Simon Kuper, *Chums: How a Tiny Caste of Oxford Tories Took Over the UK*, Profile Books, 2022, p. 86.

24 Christopher de Bellaigue, 'Eton and the making of a modern elite', *1843*, 16 August 2016.

25 Harriet Blomefield, 'Does Alma Still Matter? A Report by Keystone Tutors on The Schools Educating The Nation's Elite', Keystone Tutors, 18 November 2020.

26 Rob Evans, 'Half of England is owned by less than 1% of the population', *Guardian*, 17 April 2019.

27 Charles Moore, *Margaret Thatcher: The Authorized Biography*, vol. 1, *Not For Turning*, Allen Lane, 2016, p. 81.

28 Malcolm Dean, 'Margaret Thatcher's policies hit the poor hardest – and it's happening again', *Guardian*, 9 April 2013.

29 Ian Gilmour, *Dancing with Dogma: Britain Under Thatcherism*, Simon & Schuster, 1992, p. 276.

30 Robert Watts, 30 years of the Sunday Times Rich List: how Britain has changed, *Sunday Times*, 6 May 2018. See also Edgerton, *The Rise and Fall of the British Nation*, chapter 19.

31 These figures, it should be noted, are underestimations: they are based on official records and so do not include all the wealth that is held in trusts and safe from scrutiny. The aristocracy have always excelled at minimising tax. In the words of the eighteenth-century satirist Charles Churchill: 'What is't to us, if taxes rise or fall, / Thanks to our fortune, we pay none at all.' See Chris Bryant, 'How the aristocracy preserved their power', *Guardian*, 7 September 2017.

32 Moore, *Margaret Thatcher: The Authorized Biography*, vol. 1, p. 389.

33 In 2003, upon Denis's death, their son Mark inherited the family title. He

was soon embroiled in scandal. A year later, in 2004, he was arrested and fined for financing – some allege helping to plot – a failed coup d'état in oil-rich Equatorial Guinea, allegedly to secure oil supplies. Thatcher maintained he thought he was financing an air ambulance service. There were calls to strip him of his title. But it could also be cast as the behaviour of an authentic aristocrat: an Old Harrovian seeking to plunder foreign lands for personal gain – what is more quintessentially English than that?

34 Nigel Harris, *Competition and the Corporate Society British Conservatives, the State and Industry 1945–1964*, Taylor & Francis, 2013, p. 276.

4 A CONSERVATIVE COUNTRY?

1 Veronica Lee, 'Countdown to Downton: Your essential guide to the TV event of the year', *Independent*, 4 September 2011.

2 Kate McCann, "'Outdated' peerage rules turn women into 'non-persons' says Downton creator', *Daily Telegraph*, 11 September 2015.

3 '33 new British TV period drama series to watch in 2019', British Period Dramas.

4 Jane Mattisson, 'Downton Abbey: a Cultural Phenomenon. History for the Many', *SIC,* no. 1, year 5, December 2014.

5 Mark Easton, 'Why does the UK love the monarchy?', BBC, 29 May 2012.

6 Tom Nairn, *The Enchanted Glass: Britain and Its Monarchy*, Verso, 2011, p. 204.

7 Bédarida, *A Social History of England*, p. 203.

8 Susan Pedersen, 'Triumph of the Poshocracy', *London Review of Books*, vol. 35, no. 15, 8 August 2013.

9 Reece Garcia, *Taking Back Control: Putting Work, Money, Politics and the Media in the Hands of the People*, chapter 1, The Book Guild Ltd, 2022.

10 Moore, *Margaret Thatcher: The Authorized Biography*, vol. 1, p. 387.

11 George Orwell, 'Boy's Weeklies', 1940.

12 Kate Fox, *Watching the English: The Hidden Rules of English Behaviour*, Hodder & Stoughton, 2014, p. 205.

13 Bédarida, *A Social History of England*, p. 76.

14 Jeremy Paxman, *The English: A Portrait of a People*, Abrams Press, 2001, pp. 188-90.

15 Nairn, *The Enchanted Glass*.

16 Ian St John, *Disraeli and the Art of Victorian Politics*, Anthem Press, 2010, p. 113.

17 Gamble, *Conservative Nation*, p. 62.

18 David Cannadine, 'The Context, Performance and Meaning of Ritual: The British Monarchy and the "Invention of Tradition", c. 1820–1977', in *The Invention of Tradition*, Eric Hobsbawm and Terence Ranger (eds), Cambridge University Press, 1992.

19   *Ibid.*

20   Bédarida, *A Social History of England*, p. 147.

21   Amy Walker, 'Do mention the war: the politicians comparing Brexit to WWII', *Guardian*, 4 February 2019.

22   Tony Blair, 'Let us Face the Future' – the 1945 anniversary lecture, Fabian Pamphlet 571, Fabian Society, London, 1995, p. 10. See also Mark Abrams, Richard Rose and Rita Hinden, *Must Labour Lose?*, Penguin Books, 1960.

23   Callum G. Brown and Hamish Fraser, *Britain Since 1707*, Routledge, 2010, p. 397. See also Michael Pinto-Duschinsky, *The Political Thought of Lord Salisbury*, Constable, 1967.

24   George Eaton, 'How Tory dominance is built on home ownership', *New Statesman*, 12 May 2021.

25   'A lack of invasions since 1066 – and of civil wars for over 350 years – has led to a confidence that property rights will last forever, and so to the high percentage of home ownership in England,' Harry Mount writes in *How England Made the English*, Viking, 2013.

26   A. S. Algarhi and A. Tziamalis, 'Does the UK economy grow faster under a Conservative or Labour government?', *Economics and Business Letters*, 2021, 10(2), pp.95–101.

27   Silver and McKenzie, *Angels in Marble*, p .218.

28   Philip Williamson, *Stanley Baldwin. Conservative Leadership and National Values*, Cambridge University Press, 1999.

29   Mark Fisher, 'Suffering with a smile', *Occupied Times,* 22 June 2013. See also Mark Fisher, *K-punk: The Collected and Unpublished Writings of Mark Fisher*, Repeater Books, 2018.

30   Stuart Hall, 'Gramsci and Us', in *The Hard Road to Renewal: Thatcherism and the Crisis of the Left*, Verso, 1988, p. 166.

31   'It goes almost without saying that this is a political culture in which Conservatism swims like a fish in the sea, and in which a Labour vote has always been a deviant one,' the historian R. W. Johnson once observed. R. W. Johnson, 'The national culture is a Tory culture', in *The Politics of Recession*, Palgrave, 1985, p. 234.

32   Silver and McKenzie, *Angels in Marble*.

5 THE NASTY PARTY: FLIRTING WITH THE FAR RIGHT

1   See Camilla Schofield, *Enoch Powell and the Making of Postcolonial Britain*, Cambridge University Press, 2013, p. 113.

2   Bow Group, *The Conservative Opportunity: Fifteen Bow Group Essays on Tomorrow's Toryism*, B. T. Batsford, 1965, p. 186.

3　Karl Marx and Friedrich Engels, *Selected Correspondence*, Progress Publishers, 1975, p. 220–24.

4　Daniel Renshaw, *Socialism and the Diasporic 'Other': A Comparative Study of Irish Catholic and Jewish Radical and Communal Politics in East London, 1889–1912*, Liverpool University Press, 2018, p. 90.

5　Martin Pugh, *Hurrah for the Blackshirts! Fascists and Fascism in Britain Between the Wars*, Pimlico, 2005, p. 89.

6　Harry Defries, *Conservative Party Attitudes to Jews 1900–1950*, Routledge, 2014, p. 90.

7　Maya Goodfellow, *Hostile Environment: How Immigrants Became Scapegoats*, Verso, 2020, p. 50.

8　*Ibid*, p. 67.

9　Moore, *Margaret Thatcher: The Authorized Biography*, vol. 1, p. 382.

10　First quote: *ibid*. Second quote: Charles Moore, *Margaret Thatcher: The Authorized Biography*, vol. 3, *Herself Alone*, Allen Lane, 2019, p. 514.

11　Benjamin Disraeli, *Lord George Bentinck: A Political Biography*, Colburn and Co., 1852, p. 356.

12　Priya Satia, 'A Man of His Time, and Ours', *Noēma*, 22 June 2021.

13　*Ibid*.

14　Michael J. Cohen, *Churchill and the Jews, 1900–1948*, Taylor & Francis, 2013, p. 51.

15　Sayeeda Warsi, *The Enemy Within: A Tale of Muslim Britain*, Penguin Books, 2017.

16　Harry Defries, *Conservative Party Attitudes to Jews 1900–1950*, p. 5.

17　Pugh, *Hurrah for the Blackshirts!*, p. 151.

18　*Ibid*.

19　*Ibid.*, p. 151.

20　See R. B. Cockett, Ball, Chamberlain and Truth, *The Historical Journal*, vol. 33, no. 1, March 1990, p. 131-142, p. 141.

21　Defries, *Conservative Party Attitudes to Jews*, p. 5.

22　Louise London, *Whitehall and the Jews, 1933–1948. British Immigration Policy, Jewish Refugees and the Holocaust*, Cambridge University Press, 2003, p. 13.

23　This quote is from Tim Tate, 'Treason, Treachery and Pro-Nazi Activities by the British Ruling Classes During World War Two', presented at the Inaugural Conference on Right-Wing Studies, 25–27 April 2019.

24　Andrew Denham and Mark Garnett, *Keith Joseph*, Routledge, 2002, p. 57.

25　Rule, S., 'Tories in Uproar Over Black Candidate', *New York Times*, 6 December 1990.

26　'The Conservative Crisis Over Islamophobia', Hope Not Hate, 12 June 2019.

27　See Brian Reed and Hamza Syed, *The Trojan Horse Affair*, podcast by the *New York Times*, published 3 February 2022.

28 See also Nesrine Malik, 'There are Tories of diverse origins and skin tones. What they need now is real difference', *Guardian*, 15 July 2022.

29 Mark Joseph Pitchford, 'The Conservative Party and the Extreme Right, 1945–1975', PhD, Cardiff University, 2009.

30 Boris Johnson, 'Keep calm, everyone – now is not the time to do a Nicolas Cage', *Daily Telegraph*, 28 April 2013.

6 THE TORY PRESS

1   Moore, *Margaret Thatcher: The Authorized Biography*, vol. 3, p. 3.

2   Matthew Engel, *Tickle the Public: One Hundred Years of the Popular Press*, Orion, 1997.

3   Steven McKevitt, *The Persuasion Industries: The Making of Modern Britain*, Oxford University Press, 2018, p. 115.

4   Fawcett, *Conservatism: A Fight for a Tradition*, p. 83.

5   Engel, *Tickle the Public*.

6   See for example: Mike Berry, 'No Alternative to Austerity: How BBC Broadcast News Reported the Deficit Debate', *Media, Culture & Society*, 38 (6), 2016; Stephen Cushion, Allaina Kilby, Richard Thomas, Marina Morani & Richard Sambrook, 'Newspapers, Impartiality and Television News', *Journalism Studies*, 19(2), 2018, pp. 162-181; Tom Mills, *The BBC: Myth of a Public Service*, Verso, 2020.

7   Gary Younge, 'The Tories can't win without the press. This isn't how democracy works', *Guardian*, 15 November 2019.

8   This section draws on the excellent history provided in Curran and Seaton, *Power Without Responsibility*, chapter 1-3.

9   *Ibid*, p. 21.

10 Alan J. Lee, *The Origins of the Popular Press in England, 1855–1914*, Croom Helm, 1976, p. 146–68.

11 Engel, *Tickle the Public*.

12 Charles Wintour, *The Rise and Fall of Fleet Street*, Hutchinson, 1989, p. 11.

13 A. J. P. Taylor, *Beaverbrook: A Biography*, Hamilton, 1972, p. 135. See also David Cannadine, *The Decline and Fall of the Aristocracy*, Yale University Press, 1990, p. 328.

14 Curran and Seaton, *Power Without Responsibility*, p. 85.

15 *Ibid*., p. 123.

16 James Thomas, *Popular Newspapers, the Labour Party and British Politics*, Routledge, 2004, p. 14.

17 Lynn Barber, *Demon Barber: Interviews by Lynn Barber*, Penguin Books, 1998, p. 178.

18 Lara Prendergast, 'Inside the court of Carrie Symonds, princess of whales', *Spectator*, 21 November 2020.

19   Quoted in Alan Rusbridger, 'Down among the Press Lords', *London Review of Books*, vol. 5, no. 4, 3 March 1983.

20   Andrew Sparrow, 'Revealed: the deal between Murdoch and Blair', *Guardian*, 24 February 2010.

21   Peter Oborne, 'Too close for comfort: Daniel Finkelstein embodies the collapse of boundaries between the media and politics', *Spectator*, 28 September 2013; Graham Ruddick, 'Ken Clarke: Tories had deal with Rupert Murdoch for 2010 election', *Guardian*, 23 November 2017.

22   Gill Bennett, *The Zinoviev Letter: The Conspiracy that Never Dies*, Oxford University Press, 2018, p. 132.

23   Thomas, *Popular Newspapers, the Labour Party and British Politics*, p. 15, 83, 103, 111.

24   'The Sun and MailOnline both take down stories claiming Jeremy Corbyn was 'dancing a jig' on way to Cenotaph', *Press Gazette*, 14 November 2016.

25   Daniel Trilling, 'Why did the Sun publish a far-right conspiracy theory?', *Guardian*, 9 December 2019.

26   Steven Woodbridge, 'Reaction or Revolution? Early Interwar Assessments of the Nature of British Fascism in the 1920s', *Storia e Futuro*, 50, 2019.

27   'Support for benefit cuts dependent on ignorance, TUC-commissioned poll finds', Trades Union Congress, 4 January 2013.

28   Oliver Wright, 'Suella Braverman criticises 'benefit-street culture' as Liz Truss faces warring ministers', *The Times*, 4 October 2022.

29   Richard Partington, 'Tax lost in UK amounts to £35bn – almost half, say campaigners, due to fraud', *Guardian*, 16 September 2021. (The amount of over-expenditure on benefits peaked during the pandemic, at £8.4 billion, offset by £2.5 billion of underpayments. This is more likely to be an exception than a trend.)

30   See Curran and Seaton, *Power Without Responsibility*, pp. 134–5.

31   Dan Hodges, Twitter post, 7 April 2022.

32   Will Woodward, 'Murdoch's Newscorp 'has paid no UK tax since 1988', *Guardian*, 19 March 1999.

33   'News UK and the Murdoch empire have more than 192 shell companies in tax havens', according to Mark Donne, director of the award-winning documentary *UK Gold*. TeleSur, 6 April 2016.

34   'Barclay twins' Ritz hotel pays no corporation tax', BBC, 17 December 2012. Jane Martinson, Barclay v Barclay, Tortoise, 2 March.

35   Paul Farrelly, 'Row over Express chief's tax avoidance', *Guardian*, 24 December 2000.

36   Arlie Russell Hochschild, *Strangers in Their Own Land. Anger and Mourning on the American Right*, New Press, 2016, p. 14.

37   Dominic Ponsford, 'Survey finds that UK written press is (by some way) the least trusted in Europe', *Press Gazette*, 2017.

38   Nick Davies, *Flat Earth News: An Award-winning Reporter Exposes Falsehood, Distortion and Propaganda in the Global Media*, Random House, 2011, p. 257.

7 'PERMANENT OPPOSITION':
THE BRITISH LABOUR PARTY

1   Tony Blair, *A Journey: My Political Life*, Arrow, 2011, p. 98.

2   Alex Callinicos, 'Betrayal and Discontent: Labour Under Blair', *International Socialism*, 72, September 1996.

3   'Labour "under-10s curfew" plan ignites row', *Guardian*, 3 June 1996.

4   Austin Chamberlain, who led the party between 1919 and 1921.

5   *Observer*, 2 June 1996.

6   Perry Anderson, 'Ukania Perpetua?', *New Left Review*, 125, Sept/Oct 2020. See also Curran and Seaton, *Power Without Responsibility*, p. 145-6.

7   Julia Day, 'Murdoch backs "courageous" Blair over Iraq', *Guardian*, 11 February 2003.

8   Curran and Seaton, *Power Without Responsibility*, p. 123.

9   John Lanchester, 'What is Labour for?', *London Review of Books*, vol. 27, no. 7, 31 March 2005.

10 Letter to the Labour Parliament, by Karl Marx, 9 March 1854.

11 Perry Anderson, *English Questions*, Verso, 1992, p. 23.

12 Mark Bevir, *The Making of British Socialism*, Princeton University Press, 2016, p. 307.

13 G. Foote, *The Labour Party's Political Thought: A History*, Palgrave Macmillan UK, 1997.

14 Edgerton, *The Rise and Fall of the British Nation*, p. 198.

15 Guttsman, *The British Political Elite*, p. 247.

16 Foote, *The Labour Party's Political Thought*, p. 32.

17 Maurice Cowling, *The Impact of Labour, 1920–1924: The Beginning of Modern British Politics*, Cambridge University Press, 2005, p. 362.

18 *Ibid.*, p. 350.

19 *Ibid.*, p. 359.

20 Bennett, *The Zinoviev Letter*, p. 68.

21 Charles L. Mowat, 'The Fall of the Labour Government in Great Britain, 1931', *Huntington Library Quarterly*, vol. 7, no. 4, August 1944, pp. 353–86, p. 385.

22 See Brian Abel-Smith, 'The Beveridge Report: Its Origins and Outcomes', *International Social Security Review*, 1992, 45(1–2), pp. 5–16.

23 Curran and Seaton, *Power Without Responsibility*, p. 76–7.

24 Thomas, *Popular Newspapers, the Labour Party and British Politics*, p. 14, Table 1.1.

25 Gamble, *Conservative Nation*, p. 34.

26 Bédarida, *A Social History of England*, p. 191.

27 *The Times*, 29 June 1946. See Green and Kynaston, *Engines of Privilege*, chapter 2.

28 Roland Quinault, *British Prime Ministers and Democracy: From Disraeli to Blair*, Bloomsbury, 2011, p. 167.

29 George Orwell, *The Lion and the Unicorn: Socialism and the English Genius*, 1941.

30 Anderson, *English Questions*, p. 42.

31 Edgerton, *The Rise and Fall of the British Nation*, p. 197.

32 James Donald and Stuart Hall, *Politics and Ideology: A Reader*, Open University Press, 1986, p. 150.

33 Gamble, *Conservative Nation*, p. 55.

34 Virou Srilangarajah, 'We Are Here Because You Were With Us: Remembering A. Sivanandan (1923–2018)', Verso blog, 7 February 2018.

35 Andrew August, *The British Working Class, 1832–1940*, Routledge, 2014, p. 249.

36 Cockett, *Thinking the Unthinkable: Think-tanks and the Economic Counter-revolution, 1931–1983*.

37 Edgerton, *Rise and Fall,* p. 499.

38 Jonathan Freedland, 'Better Labour lose power in 2010 than end up exiled for a generation', *Guardian*, 14 May 2008.

39 Tim Shipman, *All Out War: The Full Story of How Brexit Sank Britain's Political Class*, HarperCollins, 2016, p. 3. Craig Oliver, *Unleashing Demons: The Inside Story of Brexit*, Hodder & Stoughton, 2017.

8 A LEAP INTO THE DARK: TORY NATION IN CRISIS (2016–PRESENT)

1 Joe Murphy, 'Jeremy Corbyn will hang on as leader but the battle is far from over', *Evening Standard*, 21 September 2016.

2 Sebastian Payne, 'Labour's left and right wings want Jeremy Corbyn on the ballot paper', *Spectator*, 12 June 2015.

3 Rob Ford, Twitter post, 7 February 2019.

4 'SUN SAYS We urge our readers to beLEAVE in Britain and vote to quit the EU on June 23', *Sun*, 13 June 2016.

5 Rowena Mason, 'Daily Express owner Richard Desmond hands Ukip £1m', *Guardian*, 16 April 2015.

6 Curran and Seaton, *Power Without Responsibility*, p. 142.

7 Oliver, *Unleashing Demons*, p. 74. Thank you to Robert Saunders for bringing this quote to my attention.

8 Shipman, *All Out War*, chapter 26. See also George Parker, 'How David Cameron lost his battle for Britain', *Financial Times,* 18 December 2016.

9 Alex Morales, 'U.K.'s Osborne to Reap $790,000 From 48 Days' Work for BlackRock', Bloomberg, 8 March 2017.

10 'British Army "could stage mutiny under Corbyn", says senior serving general', *Independent*, 20 September 2015.

11 'Corbyn hits back at Blair after former PM's call to put party allegiances aside', *Guardian*, 23 April 2017.

12 Aaron Bastani, '"It's going to be a long night" – How Members of Labour's Senior Management Team Campaigned to Lose', Novara Media, 12 April 2020.

13   Charles Graves, *Leather Armchairs: The Book of London Clubs*, Coward-McCann, 1963, p. 64. See also Davies, *We, the Nation*.

14   'Johnson denies lying to Queen over Parliament suspension', BBC, 12 September 2019.

15   Rory Stewart, 'I hope I got out of the Tory party before it was too late', *Observer*, 6 October 2019.

16   Oliver Heath and Matthew Goodwin, 'For the first time, more people on low incomes voted for the Conservative Party than for Labour', Joseph Rowntree Foundation, 24 June 2020.

17   Daniel Finn, 'How Brexit Broke the British Left', *Catalyst Journal*, vol. 5, no. 3, 2021.

18   See Samuel Earle, 'Can Jeremy Corbyn Save Britain from Brexit?', *New Republic*, 2019.

19   David Graeber, 'The Center Blows Itself Up: Care and Spite in the 'Brexit Election', *New York Review of Books*, 13 January 2020.

20   Tony Blair, 'Let us Face the Future' – the 1945 anniversary lecture, p. 11; 'Gordon Brown on liberty and the role of the state', *Guardian*, 13 December 2005.

21   Michael White, 'The seeds of Jeremy Corbyn's victory were visible in 2008', *Guardian*, 14 September 2015.

22   Daniel Finkelstein, 'Corbyn's praise for deeply antisemitic book', *The Times*, 30 April 2019; Henry Zeffman, 'Corbyn saw antisemitism in history book but did not mention it in foreword', *The Times*, 2 May 2019.

23   Rachel Schulkins, 'Burke, His Liberal Rivals and the Jewish Question', *Otherness: Essays and Studies*, 2013, 3.2.

24   Bart Cammaerts et al, *Journalistic Representations of Jeremy Corbyn in the British Press*, LSE Report, July 2016.

25   Sarah Cox, 'Twice as much airtime given to Corbyn critics, new report shows', Media Reform Coalition, Goldsmiths, July 2016.

26   Paul Myerscough, 'Corbyn in the Media', *London Review of Books*, vol. 37, no. 20, 22 October 2015.

27   'Press hostility to Labour reaches new levels in 2019 election campaign', Loughborough University Centre for Research in Communication and Culture, 19 December 2019.

28   'U.K.'s Farage, Accused of anti-Semitic Rhetoric, Wins Big in EU Elections', *Haaretz*, 27 May 2019; 'Farage accused of perpetuating conspiracy theories linked to antisemitism', *Jewish Chronicle*, 22 November 2019.

29   Rafael Behr, 'I thrived on the tension and drama of British politics. Then I had a heart attack', *Guardian*, 16 January 2021.

30   Rowena Mason and Heather Stewart, 'Mike Pompeo tells Jewish leaders he would 'push back' against Corbyn', *Guardian*, 9 June 2019.

31   Matt Kennard, 'How the UK Military and Intelligence Establishment Is

Working to Stop Jeremy Corbyn Becoming Prime Minister', Declassified UK, 4 December 2019.

32 Tim Adams, 'A year on, did Change UK change anything?', *Observer*, 19 April 2020.

33 Ian Sample and Peter Walker, 'Covid response 'one of UK's worst ever public health failures'', *Guardian*, 11 October 2021.

34 Danny Dorling, 'Why has the UK's COVID death toll been so high? Inequality may have played a role', *The Conversation*, 4 March 2021.

35 Phillip Inman, 'UK economy likely to suffer worst Covid-19 damage, says OECD', *Guardian*, 10 June 2020; Izzy lyons, Daniel Capurro and Alex Clark, 'Britain's Covid response ranked one of toughest in the world', *Daily Telegraph*, 22 February 2021.

36 Tim Shipman, 'Will 'Red Tory' Johnsonism win the next election or collapse under its own contradictions?', *Sunday Times*, 9 October 2021.

37 Rachel Wearmouth, 'Rishi Sunak boasted of taking money from 'deprived urban areas' to help wealthy towns', *New Statesman*, 5 August 2022.

38 Joseph Schumpeter, *Capitalism, Socialism and Democracy*, Routledge, 1994 [1943], fn22 p. 281.

39 'Truss turns on the media', *Spectator*, 10 August 2022.

40 Jeremy Cliffe, 'The Truss Delusion: Liz Truss and the rise of the libertarian right', *New Statesman*, 28 September 2022.

41 Oliver Browning, 'Queen Elizabeth II's funeral 'most important event world will ever see', Lindsay Hoyle says', *Independent*, 18 September 2022.

42 John Burn-Murdoch, 'The Tories have become unmoored from the British people', *Financial Times*, 29 September 2022.

43 Littlewood knew Truss at Oxford, where she was an enthusiastic member of the Hayek Society.

44 George Parker et al, 'Pound tumbles below $1.09 after Kwarteng's £45bn tax cut package', *Financial Times*, 23 September 2022.

45 Harry Cole and James Heale, *Out of the Blue: The Inside Story of the Unexpected Rise and Rapid Fall of Liz Truss*, HarperCollins, 2022.

46 The *Daily Telegraph* published a piece by Conservative MP Nadhim Zahawi backing Boris Johnson moments before he withdrew. Headlined 'Get ready for Boris 2.0, the man who will make the Tories and Britain great again', the article was quickly deleted.

47 In 2017, the 7th Marquess of Salisbury was still worth £330 million, but this paled next to the family fortune of Sunak, a former Goldman Sachs banker who is married to the daughter of an Indian property tycoon, with a combined net worth of about £730 million.

48 Oliver Shah, 'George Osborne reborn: he's back in Downing Street for his second act', *Sunday Times*, 5 November 2022.

CONCLUSION

1 Anna Fleck, 'The UK'S Rich Are Getting Richer', Statista, 23 May 2022. 'Record year and quarter for political party donations and loans in Great Britain', Electoral Commission, 27 February 2020.

2 Geoffrey Wheatcroft, *The Strange Death of Tory England*, p. 25.

3 John Burn-Murdoch, 'Britons now have the worst access to healthcare in Europe, and it shows', *Financial Times*, 3 November 2022.

4 Kayleena Makortoff, 'City donations worth £15m raise concerns over influence on UK politics', *Guardian*, 6 June 2022.

5 George Parker et al, 'Inside Boris Johnson's money network', *FT Magazine*, 30 July 2021.

6 Sam Bright and Max Colbert, 'Who Are Johnson's 22 Big Money Backers? And Did They Influence the No Confidence Vote?', *Byline Times*, 9 June 2022.

7 Sumeet Desai, 'Conservatives put economy at centre of campaign', Reuters, 24 February 2010.

8 David Hare, 'Labour's criminal record – 3,600 new offences, and 86,637 inmates', *Guardian*, 8 April 2010.

9 Rowena Mason, 'One in 10 Tory peers have given more than £100,000 to party', *Guardian*, 29 December 2022.

10 Anthony Barnett, *The Lure of Greatness: England's Brexit and America's Trump*, Unbound, 2017, chapter 12.

11 Henry Mance, 'Is Britain tiring of the culture wars?', *Financial Times*, 14 July 2022; Patrick English, 'Is the stereotypical image of 'Red Wall' residents actually accurate?', YouGov, 17 May 2021; Kenan Malik, 'Culture wars risk blinding us to just how liberal we've become in the past decades', *Observer*, 21 June 2020.

12 John Burn-Murdoch, 'Britain is now a high-immigration country and most are fine with that', *Financial Times*, 12 May 2022.

13 Trinh Tu, 'Britons support paying more tax to fund public services – most popular being a new net wealth tax', Ipsos, 6 October 2020.

14 Nancy L. Rosenblum, *On the Side of the Angels: An Appreciation of Parties and Partisanship*, Princeton University Press, 2010, p. 457.

15 Stuart Hall, 'Blue Election, Election Blues', in *The Hard Road to Renewal: Thatcherism and the Crisis of the Left*.

16 'How Boris Johnson undid the Tory Party's mythology', *Economist*, 11 June 2022.

INDEX